Preventing Unemployment in Europe

This volume was supported by financial means of the Northrhine Westphalian government and the EU Joint Initiative ADAPT.

Preventing Unemployment in Europe

A New Framework for Labour Market Policy

Edited by

Paul Klemmer and Rüdiger Wink

Ruhr Research Institute for Regional and Innovation Policy, Germany

Edward Elgar
Cheltenham, UK • Northampton, MA, USA

Published by
Edward Elgar Publishing Limited
Glensanda House
Montpellier Parade
Cheltenham
Glos GL50 1UA
UK

Edward Elgar Publishing, Inc.
136 West Street
Suite 202
Northampton
Massachusetts 01060
USA

A catalogue record for this book
is available from the British Library

Library of Congress Cataloguing in Publication Data

Preventing unemployment in Europe: a new framework for labour market policy / edited by Paul Klemmer and Rüdiger Wink.
     p. cm.
  Papers presented at workshop on developing labour market policies.
  Includes index.
  ISBN 1-84064-513-X
    1. Labor market--Europe--Congresses. 2. Manpower policy--Europe--Congresses. 3. Unemployment--Europe--Congresses. I. Klemmer, Paul. II. Wink, Rüdiger.

  HD5764.A6 P74 2000
  331.12'042'094--dc21

ISBN 1 84064 513 X

Printed in the United Kingdom at the University Press, Cambridge

Contents

List of contributors

Kerstin Baumgart
RUFIS - Ruhr Research Institute for Innovation and Regional Policy, Ruhr University at Bochum

Dr. Dorothee Becker-Soest
RUFIS - Ruhr Research Institute for Innovation and Regional Policy, Ruhr University at Bochum

Prof. Riccardo Cappellin
Universita Tor Vergata, Rome

Henrik Halkier
Department for language and intercultural studies at Aalborg University

Prof. Henning Jørgensen
CARMA – Centre for Labour Market Research at Aalborg University

Prof. Dr. Paul Klemmer
RUFIS - Ruhr Research Institute for Innovation and Regional Policy, Ruhr University at Bochum

Dr. Matthias Knuth
Institute for Work and Technology, Gelsenkirchen

Prof. Luigi Orsenigo
Luigi Bocconi University, Milan

Dr. Reinhard Penz
Department of Labour, Women, Health and Social Affairs in Saxony-Anhalt

Philip Raines
European Policy Research Centre; University of Strathclyde, Glasgow

Christian Roth
Institute for Political Sciences, University of Tübingen

Dr. Markus Scheuer
Rhine-Westphalia Institute for Economic Research, Essen

Prof. Dr. Josef Schmid
Institute for Political Sciences, University of Tübingen

Prof. Dr. Thomas Straubhaar
HWWA Institute for Economic Research, Hamburg

Dr. Rüdiger Wink
RUFIS – Ruhr Research Institute for Innovation and Regional Policy, Ruhr University at Bochum

1. Preventing unemployment in Europe – an introductory overview

Paul Klemmer und Rüdiger Wink

1. PREVENTION AS THE KEY FOR OVERCOMING STRUCTURAL ADJUSTMENT PROBLEMS ON EUROPEAN LABOUR MARKETS

Over the last decade, labour markets in all member states of the European Union have been affected by major structural change. The internationalisation of markets, transformation of industrial production and the growing importance of the services sector are representative of the challenges levelled at the adaptive capacity of actors on the labour markets. The high, consolidated level of unemployment in the EU compared to the rest of the world is an indication that this transformation process has not yet run its course (cf. OECD 1997; Auer 1998). At the same time, the dynamics of the global economy are intensifying a need for adjustment from which national and continental markets are not immune (cf. Weidig et al. 1999; Borghans et al. 1996; Klemmer 1997; Lageman et al. 1999).

An analysis of the various strategies deployed in the EU member states for combating unemployment reveals a wide diversity of objectives, concepts and instruments (cf. EU 1998; Auer 1998; Walwei 1998; OECD 1994). If the reduction of unemployment rates and/or the proportion of long-term unemployed people in the total numbers of those unemployed as well as the increase in the employed population are taken as indicators of successful employment policy, the greatest impression is made by those national strategies which focus on enhancing the attractiveness of job-seekers for the respective labour markets. Buzzwords like 'employability' symbolise the transition from passive methods for averting or cushioning the risk of unemployment to active improvement of employment opportunities for those concerned (cf. Cox 1998; Suntum and Kröger 1999).

In this connection, the notion of preventive labour market policy acquires decisive importance. The term 'preventive labour market policy' refers collectively to various measures for

- initial and continuing training of workers,
- adapting the organisation of work within enterprises to changing market situations,
- fostering new forms of the division of labour between enterprises,
- supporting the establishment of new enterprises, and
- developing new forms of job placement and entry to employment.

The common feature of such measures is to influence in a targeted way the employment opportunities of those (still) in work or who have recently lost their jobs. They are meant to take effect *before* unemployment actually arises and to operate as a kind of 'early warning system' that fosters structural adaptation in the labour markets. Early deployment of this form of labour market policy is aimed at achieving three objectives:

- to maintain or expand the number of jobs available,
- to prevent human capital depreciating in value the longer unemployment continues, to prevent opportunities for re-entering employment from declining as a consequence, and
- to improve competitiveness by modernising corporate organisation and by making best use of human capital.

In those cases where European countries have successfully combated unemployment, the strategies deployed generally exhibit a high proportion of such preventive strategies (cf. OECD 1997; Auer 1998). Successes in the employment policy field are mostly linked to declining unemployment levels. Where such reductions are achieved, one can usually witness improvements in the basic economic framework, the world market position of domestic companies and a reduction in additions to the unemployment statistics. In contrast, fewer benefits are derived for the long-term unemployed or for regions with a high percentage of companies facing structural adjustment problems, or these benefits fail to materialise until labour market trends have markedly improved. Successful preventive strategies cannot overcome such structural configurations, or require time before they have real impacts (cf. Jørgensen, Chapter 7).

This volume and its separate articles are the output of a workshop centred on the perspectives for developing preventive labour market policies in Europe, against the background of existing experience with national strategies and the increasing influence that is exerted on labour market programmes by the European Union. Debate focused on three issues in particular:

(1)   To what extent is the conditional framework for preventive labour market policy undergoing change, and does this mean that programmes and instruments have to be adjusted to new challenges, addressees and factors?

(2)   What response mechanisms characterise national strategies in the field of preventive labour market policy, and what differences exist between the different countries in terms of their experience in this respect?

(3)   What learning processes can be triggered by exchanging national experience in the field of preventive labour market policy within the EU, and what role can the EU organs play in this connection?

This introductory overview outlines the core theses in each chapter in respect of these fundamental issues, and tries to situate these ideas in the overall context of the volume.

2. PREVENTIVE LABOUR MARKET POLICY IN A CHANGING ENVIRONMENT

In most European countries, preventive approaches to employment policy-making played a minor role for many decades. Labour market policy was dominated by passive protection of workers. This tendency continues to influence the basic setting for preventive labour market policy. Although the relevant actors – companies, contracting bodies in the policymaking and public administration domains, and the various organisations that implement employment policy measures – do perceive the pressures to achieve structural adjustments by modifying the conditional framework of markets, the search for appropriate response mechanisms is still influenced by the traditional perspective of passive labour market policies (cf. Klemmer et al. 2000 and Knuth, Chapter 5). Companies, for example, are aware of growing pressure to modify their production processes and products. However, the benefits of collaborating with preventive approaches to labour market policy, in the form of greater flexibility on the part of human capital, are rarely recognised. Organisations which implement standardised public-sector schemes for further training and retraining are acquiring greater incentives to adapt their programmes to new support criteria under preventive labour market policy and/or to the needs of companies. Yet the requisite organisational structures and competencies have yet to be developed.

A need for such adaptation is also visible in decision-making bodies in the policymaking and public administration domains. Whereas the successes of preventive labour market policy have been concentrated hitherto on worker groups that are relatively easy to integrate, it is imperative that the traditional target groups of labour market policy - older workers, immigrants, people with health disorders and women - be integrated in strategies for improving competitiveness. There is a risk that preventive labour market policy be accused of 'cream skimming' unless consistent, long-term improvements are achieved in a structural sense for the long-term unemployed as well. The overall issues pertain, therefore, to the adaptive capacity of those on both the giving and receiving ends of preventive labour market policy.

The chapters in the first part of the volume focus on the growing challenges to which these groups of actors are exposed. In Chapter 2, *Markus Scheuer* sheds light on the interplay between institutional conditions in the labour markets and the international competitiveness of national and regional economies. Preventive labour market policy is increasingly a locational factor that cannot operate properly if it is isolated from the needs and demands of international investors. This thesis is corroborated by *Thomas Straubhaar* in Chapter 3. Another element of preventive labour market policy is to generate attractive locational conditions in order to encourage an influx of skilled manpower, whose skills and qualifications can stimulate internal corporate reorganisation, new goals for initial and further training, and, last but not least, the creation of new jobs. On the other hand, if training and employment are concentrated within purely national confines, there is a risk of promoting training schemes that have nothing but structural weaknesses and 'missing the boat' as far as international markets are concerned. The specific content and design elements of preventive labour market policy are thus shaped to an increasing degree by international competition and the requirements of mobile investors and manpower.

In Chapter 4, *Dorothee Becker-Soest* and *Rüdiger Wink* provide an overview of existing structures in this sector and of structural changes that are taking shape. These are characterised by two trends. First, one can observe a growth in the complexity and diversity of the functions and schemes in the field of initial and continuing vocational training. In place of specialised vocational qualifications, there is now a plurality of modularised training schemes that are used by enterprises and workers according to their specific situational requirements. In many cases, competitive relations become established in the market in very particular segments only. Secondly, skilling and advisory schemes become meshed to an ever-greater degree, leading to systematic supply chains and transnational cooperations. Preventive labour market policy, focused as it is in most cases on the national or regional context only, is thus confronted with new players who threaten the competitiveness of established providers – who are mostly subsidised with public funds. In view of these two trends, there is now a need to redefine the object of preventive labour market policy and its relationship to market-induced changes to the way that initial and continuing vocational training are managed.

In most countries, preventive labour market policy action is limited to certain groups of people, threatened by or experiencing unemployment, who have relatively good opportunities of being reintegrated into labour markets. Problematic groups in the labour market are frequently eliminated from the official unemployment statistics by early retirement and public-sector job creation schemes. In Chapter 5, *Matthias Knuth* explains the dimensions as well as the financial and social impact of such procedures in many west European nations. In future, the success of preventive labour market policy will depend on whether or not perspectives are created for supporting specific target groups when major efforts are being made to adapt labour markets to structural change. Knuth highlights the need for a fundamental debate on labour market issues in the space that has opened up between social security, on the one hand, and improving the 'employability' of those in work, on the other, whereby the latter aspect will gain dramatically in importance in the context of demographic change and the crisis of social redistribution systems.

3. NATIONAL EXPERIENCE WITH PREVENTIVE LABOUR MARKET POLICY STRATEGIES

There are many overviews of the various schemes and instruments deployed by employment policymakers, and of the statistical trends evidenced by the labour markets in the member states of the European Union, and these provide a considerable body of material for analysing the specific features and success factors at national level (cf. Bertelsmann Stiftung 1998; OECD 1997; EU 1998; Dicke 1999; Münch 1999; Ozaki 1999; Tronti 1998). Given the challenges faced by preventive labour market policy, one can identify a variety of strategies. For the specific context of national experience and opportunities for transnational learning that is focused on in this volume, the aspects of greatest relevance are not so much the potential successes achievable with specific instruments, skilling or advisory schemes, but rather the systemic understanding of labour market management in countries with different institutional experience and traditions. Any such systemic understanding must include the perception and interpretation of action imperatives in the field of labour market policy, coordinating the competing interests of groups in society, and the implementation of preventive labour market programmes. The importance of these factors for the specific shaping of preventive labour market policies and their impacts on employment are the basis on which the preconditions and options for transferring employment strategies between different countries can be discussed. The countries chosen for closer study represent different institutional frameworks and objectives for national strategies in the field of preventive labour market policy.

Due to its narrow focus on the self-organising potential of markets, Great Britain is a country with a particularly liberal understanding of policy imperatives in the employment field. In Chapter 6, *Philip Raines* analyses the influence of foreign direct investment on the emphasis now placed on corporatist and market-induced coordination processes for surmounting structural adjustment problems in the labour markets. The attractiveness of Great Britain as a location for foreign direct investments is closely linked to the country's low wage levels and the greater freedom from trade union influence compared to other European countries. However, increasing demands in respect of human capital and modern production methods are inducing heightened interest among the social partners in concerted action to improve the 'employability' of British workers. If one looks at the growing market focus of labour market policy in Continental Europe, one can see a certain amount of convergence between European countries.

The market-based approach in Great Britain contrasts with experience in Denmark, as described by *Henning Jørgensen* in Chapter 7. The Danish response to the structural challenges on the labour markets was based, owing to the country's corporatist traditions, on bolstering the political importance of the social partners, combined with a devolving of responsibilities for the labour market to regional Round Tables in a more consensual approach. As a result, new employment policy strategies have been generated that demand a high level of flexibility and independent responsibility from each individual. In this way, industrial and service sectors, as well as the available range of advisory and skilling programmes, are to acquire structures that make them competitive at international level. For all the initial successes already achieved in terms of employment, this model raises a number of issues regarding the treatment of problematic groups on the labour market and the opening of preventive labour market policy strategies for other responses beyond the consensus approach at Round Tables.

Unlike the conditional framework in a relatively small country that is significantly dependent on global market trends, as in Denmark, institutional structures in the Federal Republic of Germany are under less direct pressure to adapt. The scale of structural unemployment was feathered for some considerable time by social security measures and public-sector job creation schemes. Faced with dramatic growth in unemployment to consistently high levels, especially in the eastern German states, established decision-making networks in the employment policy fields were exposed to increasing pressure to take action. Seemingly successful employment policies in other countries, based on collaboration between policymakers and the social partners, formed the starting point for 'Jobs Alliances' at regional and national level. In Chapter 8, *Reinhard Penz* provides examples for the action potential and difficulties that arose. Although the prerequisites currently exist for successful cooperation and for overcoming mental barriers to the creation and adaptation of advisory and skilling systems in response to a modified environment, the extent to which the necessary steps are implemented will not become apparent until later in the future.

In a context of favourable structural conditions, the labour markets of northern Italy are characterised by the dominant role played by in-company and inter-company processes for skilling and restructuring, whereby less influence is exerted by government schemes. This means that regional employment and industrial policy are closely intertwined. *Riccardo Cappellin's* and *Luigi Orsenigo's* contribution in Chapter 9 illustrates in a series of examples the interdependencies between support for networks between companies at regional level, in which autonomous pathways for adapting for global markets have been developed, and the enhanced competitiveness of jobs in the region. Such networks are based on institutional adaptations to market processes between micro-enterprises along a value-creation chain. However, these institutional trends are fostered by local and regional infrastructural schemes, e.g. for linking initial and further training in companies, technological research on innovations, and in-company or inter-company application not only in 'industrial districts', but increasingly in 'learning regions' and 'innovative milieux'. Unlike corporatist and collaborative systems, what is happening here is a stronger formation of informal and virtual networks between different actors at regional level. This adds to purely market-based relations.

The examples from different countries show clearly that different institutional solutions were chosen in response to similar challenges for preventive labour market policy. Nowhere can a pure form of coordination system – market-based, government or corporatist control – be identified. On the contrary, specific responses are made to specific challenges, and the appropriateness of such adaptive responses needs time to materialise. Preventive labour market policy in Europe can thus be described as a 'patchwork'.

4. PERSPECTIVES WITH REGARD TO EUROPEAN LEARNING PROCESSES

Given the plethora of overviews of national employment strategies and their comparative success, international 'benchmarking' approaches are in their heyday. With examples of 'good practice' in the field of preventive labour market policy, ideas are to be brought together in pools, against which national programmes can be measured and from which national politicians and authorities can learn (cf. Streeck 1998; Tronti 1998; Blancke and Schmid 1999; Walwei 1998). Moves towards a detailed 'Joint Employment Policy' in the European Union are being given an extra boost by this benchmarking process (cf. EU 1998; Höcker 1998). However, what the various chapters on preventive labour market policy in different countries show is the multi-layered nature of the specific problems encountered when adapting labour markets at national and regional level, and of the institutional solutions designed in response. This means that European learning processes cannot be reduced to schematic copying of successful programmes and instruments, but that complex pathways for exploring and adapting new ideas in specific settings are what is needed. The three contributions on this topic within this volume illuminate the opportunities of and the limit to such processes, from different perspectives.

In a first approach, the interactions between national policy frameworks is seen as the result of coordination between central government and the region, and the growing control exercised at European level by supranational programmes and competencies. In Chapter 10, *Henrik Halkier* analyses the impacts of interaction between these three levels on the concerns, resources and trajectory of preventive labour market policy at local level. This analysis indicates the risk that European cooperation may result less in a further dimension of experience and ideas for preventive labour market policy than in national support programmes being substituted by European funding. At the same time, coordination between different levels of market control is an opportunity for boosting regional development and for promoting institutional diversity if adequate incentives are provided. Multilevel governance thus requires new forms of control in order to unleash incentives for genuine integration and processing of experience gained in other countries and regions.

The second approach opens this sample study of interaction within a system of multilevel governance to a more generalised analysis of the prerequisites for steering the national implementation of preventive labour market policy by the European Union. *Josef Schmid* and *Christian Roth* present in Chapter 11 the 'soft and indirect' approach of the joint employment policy in the EU, on the one hand, and the specific response mechanisms in the various implementation bodies of the single member states, on the other. A special focus is directed here at the impacts wrought by differences in national implementation regimes – general political and administrative frameworks, industrial relations and labour administrations – for the success of control efforts and the associated transnational transfer of institutional experience. By comparing unitarian and federal, corporatist, pluralistic as well as centralised and decentralised systems of organisation in the member states, hypotheses are generated regarding the potential for learning and feedback effects at the level of preventive labour market policy.

The third approach adds to the analysis of supranational induced European learning processes, by analysing national prerequisites for transnational transfer of institutional experience. In Chapter 12, *Paul Klemmer et al.* extend the study to include not only the incentive effects of supranational control but also the potential for institutional learning processes generated by inter-locational competition between the countries and regions of Europe. Based on a comparative analysis of learning processes in political and corporate organisations, the conditions for extending, diffusing and processing the international ideas pool for preventive labour market policy is reviewed. The effect of these learning processes is not so much a harmonisation of national and regional strategies, but rather an increase in the diversity of European 'patchworks' of preventive labour market policy, the separate elements of which can be adapted to the specific geographic and temporal conditions in which action is taken.

Taken together, the collection of chapters in this volume provides an overview of the variety of challenges and response mechanisms in the field of preventive labour market policy. The debate about the content and methods of European comparisons of employment strategies highlights the importance of a European perspective when analysing adaptation strategies on the various labour markets. However, the chapters that relate to perspectives for European learning processes also indicate the difficulties involved in addressing the complex and differentiated conditions for action at the level of single regions and economies. Preventive labour market policy will thus continue to be a focus of institutional innovations at different levels of co-ordination, and of diversified interdisciplinary debate on the content and methods for analysing European learning processes.

REFERENCES

Auer, P. (1998), 'Monitoring of Labour Market Policy in EU Member States', in P. Auer (ed.), *Employment Policies in Focus. Labour Markets and Labour Market Policy in Europe and Beyond – International Experiences*, Berlin: Edition Sigma, 11-35.

Bertelsmann Stiftung (1998), *Internationales Beschäftigungs-Ranking*, Gütersloh: Bertelsmann.

Blancke, S. and J. Schmid (1999), 'Innovation, Variation, Diffusion: Lernende Politik im Bundesstaat', in S. Blancke and J. Schmid (eds), *Vom Vergleich zum Lernen. Zwei Beiträge zur materiellen Föderalismusanalyse*, Tübingen: WIP Occasional Paper, 5-12.

Borghans, L., A. de Grip and H. Heijke (1996), *Concepts and Methodology for La-bour Market Forecasts by Occupation in the Context of a Flexible Labour Market*, Luxemburg: European Communities.

Cox, R.H. (1998), *From Safety Net to Trampoline. Labor Market Activation in the Netherlands and Denmark*, Tübingen: WIP Occasional Paper.

Dicke, H. (1999), *Fortbildung in Europa. Systeme, Strukturen, Ergebnisse*, Tübingen: Mohr.

European Commission (ed; 1998): *Labour Market Policies in the EU and Member States. Joint Report on Employment*, Luxemburg: European Communities.

Höcker, H. (1998), 'The Organisation of Labour Market Policy Delivery in the Euro-pean Union', in P. Auer (ed.), *Employment Policies in Focus. Labour Markets and Labour Market Policy in Europe and Beyond – International Experiences*, Berlin: Edition Sigma, 191-214.

Klemmer, P. (1997), 'Divergenz oder Konvergenz in Europa? Implikationen neuer Rahmenbedingungen der Wirtschaft', in Akademie für Raumforschung und Lan-desplanung (ed.), *Räumliche Disparitäten und Bevölkerungswanderungen in Eu-ropa. Regionale Antworten auf Herausforderungen der europäischen Rau-mentwicklung*, Hannover: ARL, 57-75.

Klemmer, P., K. Baumgart, D. Becker-Soest and R. Wink (2000), *Innovative Beschäftigungsinstrumente in Europa. Analyse der institutionellen Voraussetzun-gen ihrer transnationalen Implementation*, Bochum, mimeo.

Kröger, M. and U. v. Suntum (1999), *Mit aktiver Arbeitsmarktpolitik aus der Beschäftigungsmisere? Ansätze und Erfahrungen in Großbritannien, Dänemark, Schweden und Deutschland*, Gütersloh: Bertelsmann.

Lageman, B. and K. Löbbe (1999), *Kleine und mittlere Unternehmen im sektoralen Strukturwandel*, Essen: RWI.

Münch, J. (1999), 'Berufliche Weiterbildung in der Europäischen Union – aus-gewählte Aspekte und Problemfelder', in D. Timmermann (ed.), *Berufliche Weiterbildung in europäischer Perspektive*, Berlin: Duncker & Humblot, 11-30.

Organisation of Economic Co-operation and Development - OECD (ed.) (1994): *Jobs Study. Evidence and Explanations, Part II: The Adjustment Potential of the Labour Market*, Paris: OECD.

Organisation of Economic Co-operation and Development - OECD (ed.) (1997), *Employment Outlook*, Paris: OECD.

Ozaki, M. (ed; 1999), *Negotiating Flexibility. The Role of the Social Partners and the State*, Geneva: International Labour Office.

Streeck, W. (1998), *The Internationalization of Industrial Relations in Europe. Pros-pects and Problems*, Cologne: MPI for the Study of Societies.

Tronti, L. (ed; 1998), *Benchmarking Employment Performance and Labour Market Policies. Final Report of the Employment Observatory Network*, Berlin: WZB.

Walwei, U. (1998), 'Beschäftigungspolitisch erfolgreiche Länder: Konsequenzen für Deutschland', *Mitteilungen aus der Arbeitsmarkt- und Berufsforschung*, **31**, 334-347.

Weidig, I., P. Hofer and H. Wolff (1999), *Arbeitslandschaft 2010 nach Tätigkeiten und Tätigkeitsniveau*, Nürnberg: IAB.

PART ONE

Preventive labour market policy in a changing environment

2. The importance of labour market flexibility in the location decisions of international corporations

Markus Scheuer

INTRODUCTION

In recent years, economic debates in Germany have focused to a major extent on the recurrent issue of Germany's locational strengths and weaknesses and its attractiveness for domestic and foreign investors. The opening of the Central and Eastern European countries and the increasing globalisation of markets has intensified that debate anew. In addition to the taxes and levies imposed on companies and the inflationary labour costs resulting from high wages and, above all, high secondary labour costs, one factor that has also played a key role in the debate has been the regulatory management of labour markets and the extent to which flexibility on those markets has been fostered or obstructed by such moves.

Despite this fact, economic researchers have given little attention so far to the differences in labour market regulation and the effects these have on investment decisions and employment activities on the part of multinational corporations. This lack of research interest contrasts starkly with the popular view that, in the wake of Thatcherism, the extensive liberalisation of the British labour market was a major incentive for direct investments and that the inflexible labour markets of Continental Europe were causing companies to relocate in other countries, or deterred Asian and US American investors from investing and creating jobs. Great Britain and Germany, in particular, are considered to be prime examples among the larger European nations of how labour market flexibility can be enabled, or prevented, respectively. This chapter presents the results of a German–British study that investigated the importance of different motives behind investment decision-making by the persons responsible in internationally operating companies in the automobile and chemicals industry.[1] In the following, the most important results are merely outlined as they pertain to the labour market. It has to be emphasised, however, that even a more detailed statistical analysis of inward investment flows qualifies a number of prejudicial opinions in this respect.

First, we provide an overview of the various forms of labour market flexibility as well as the hypotheses regarding their specific arrangements and their impact on the two countries being compared, Germany and Great Britain, before we focus in the second part on the empirical results of the study. The chapter ends with some conclusions for economic policy.

1. FORMS OF LABOUR MARKET FLEXIBILITY

As is common in economic science, there is no generally accepted delineation or definition of the term 'labour market flexibility'. This concept, too, has several dimensions, whereby macroeconomic aspects did not play a role in the study. The main focus of the latter was rather on the microeconomic dimension of flexibility, in other words on the capacity of particular companies and their employees to adapt their production systems to existing and anticipated changes in markets, products and production processes.

Perhaps the most controversially debated form of flexibility is that of pay agreements, i.e. the direct costs of labour manifested as wage levels and non-wage labour costs. These play no role in the following description, which concentrates on the specific conditions under which companies are compelled to set up their production and employment systems. A distinction is made in this connection between three forms of flexibility:

Numerical flexibility refers to the capacity of employers to modify the size and composition of their workforce. This capacity is limited by costs which are generated when the internal human capital is adapted to changing needs and conditions. Limitations ensue above all from legal or collective bargaining restrictions on the recruitment or dismissal of employees. This can relate to the core workforce of companies, or to the freedom to have a marginal workforce for feathering the impact of capacity fluctuations. Another aspect concerns the option to employ part-timers and temporary employees, especially for marginal activities. In some countries, most notably Great Britain, this type of employment, often described as 'atypical', is viewed by employers as being less cost-intensive, in that the social insurance burden is less than for those in 'standard employment'.

Temporal flexibility relates to working hours and the options available to employers to design working hours to suit their requirements. This includes, besides the definition of 'standard' working hours or, conversely, the definition of when extra costs arise in the form of overtime bonuses, the option of specifying what constitutes overtime in the first place, and/or when working hours are to be adjusted to fit changing demand. These adjustments can be necessitated, on the one hand, by more or less severe fluctuations in production due to seasonal effects that are then handled by the workforce in the form of working hours accounts, without bonuses being payable, or, secondly, by efforts on the part of corporate management to maximise the use of production capacity by extending machine operation times, in the form of shift or weekend work.

Functional flexibility, in contrast, refers to the ability of employees to cope with specified and/or changing demands by skills level, task definition and overall productivity performance. The capacity of individual employees to adapt to rapidly changing demands and/or to assume a wider range of responsibilities determines the flexibility available to companies in this respect. This applies in cases, for example, when temporary bottlenecks in production occur, or in companies that would like to increase their productivity by organising their employees into groups charged with responsibility for performing particular tasks without management interference. The success of such approaches depends on how flexible employees can be deployed as a result of their skills and commitment.

2. HYPOTHESES

It goes without saying that companies will try to exploit any opportunity to improve their profitability by increasing the degree of flexibility provided by labour as a factor. However, it should be realised that parallel use of these various forms is not possible in many cases, and that they tend to mutually exclude each other. If a company pursues a strategy to enhance numerical flexibility by introducing atypical employment relationships, or attempts to manage fluctuations in capacity utilisation by lay-offs and new recruitment, as the situation demands, a high level of functional flexibility will be difficult to achieve. As already indicated, the latter requires a well-trained workforce, which is then unlikely to accept a very discontinuous form of employment in return. One particular problem in this context concerns those skill elements that are company-specific, i.e. which are acquired in the company itself and can only be used there. These skills could only be generated through the investment of time and effort by both employer and employee, and may be lost for good when capacity fluctuations are cushioned using the external labour market, since there is no assurance that companies can avail of employees they had previously made redundant as soon as the need arises. Put another way, when a company possesses functional flexibility, the transaction costs involved in changing jobs are relatively high, which then makes it unprofitable to pursue a strategy of numerical flexibility.

There is another reason explaining why the various forms of flexible labour deployment cannot be substituted for each other at will. Problems caused by a lack of functional flexibility, e.g. by a workforce being unable to adapt to new and perhaps more complex technologies, cannot normally be surmounted by numerical or temporal flexibility, i.e. by recruiting new workers or introducing overtime. However, a certain amount of complementarity is conceivable in some cases, for example when more flexible working hours regimes in combination with higher or improved skilling of employees leads to a situation in which new machinery can be optimally exploited.

Depending on the type of production system that is typically associated with the particular industry, one can therefore expect that companies' needs for certain forms of labour market flexibility will vary accordingly. In all likelihood, the capacity for functional flexibility will be closely linked to the level of skills required. Conversely, companies whose production is based more on the use of low-skill workers are more likely to focus their efforts on exploiting numerical and temporal flexibility.

Another factor that must not be underestimated is the willingness and commitment on the part of employees to participate in the various strategies for improving profitability by increasing productivity. The individual or collective openness to change on the part of employees is crucially important, not only for everyday involvement at the workplace, but also and in particular in cases where the aim is to acquire new skills and qualifications through further training in the company or on a private basis.

This is closely linked to the kind of representation that workers have. Numerical flexibility can be achieved most easily where labour is weakly represented. On the other hand, a powerful worker representation body may be helpful for companies when the aim, for example, is to increase temporal flexibility by concluding in-house agreements. This can be even more relevant with regard to functional flexibility, when worker representatives are actively involved in designing and implementing further training schemes, and generally contributes towards a climate of acceptance within the company for additional efforts of this kind. In contrast, companies will have difficulty achieving any form of flexibility if there are permanent conflicts between management and workforce.

In addition to these more internally specific factors, the ability of companies to deploy the labour factor in a flexible way is also shaped by the regulatory framework. Regulation can be understood in this connection as the conditional framework within which the various players on the labour market can operate. These conditions include regulations in both law and collective bargaining agreements, addressing issues such as health and safety at work, unfair dismissal, or regulations covering non-standard employment, working hours, holiday entitlement, night and weekend working, or shop opening hours. However, individual companies generally have a more or less substantial range of scope for specifying, within the legal constraints, the actual conditions for its own productive operations and flexibility of work.

The comments made so far have suggested more or less explicitly that the basic economic attitudes prevailing in a country, and especially those between labour and capital – sometimes referred to as consensual versus conflict-laden – are also of major importance for achieving certain forms of flexibility. Whereas Germany is traditionally rather more corporatist, and endeavours to achieve consensus between conflicting parties, Great Britain was long considered a perfect example of industrial relations characterised by conflict, even outright animosity. This was one of the main reasons for the powerful offensive launched by the Thatcher government to emasculate the trade unions. Nevertheless, industrial relations in Germany are still much less conflict-ridden than in Britain (Table 2.1).

Table 2.1: Selected indicators for 'industrial relations'

	Germany	UK
Percentage of workforce covered by pay agreements (1990)	90	47
Number of working days lost through strikes (annual average per 1000 employees)		
- *1984-88*	50	400
- *1989-93*	20	70

Source: Adnett (1996); Hegewisch and Brewster (1993).

Within Europe, Germany and Great Britain are prime examples for different types of labour market flexibility, whereby Germany is not only heavily regulated, but also boasts an excellently trained workforce; functional flexibility can therefore be expected to play a major role in this respect, and be especially interesting for investors for whom this aspect is uppermost. On the other hand, Great Britain is generally considered to have a very deregulated labour market, and prides itself on placing few obstacles in the way of corporate flexibility. However, there are frequent complaints about the country's low productivity,[2] which is partially due to the lack of manpower skilling. One can therefore expect that Great Britain will be attractive above all for companies that are primarily interested in numerical and temporal flexibility.[3]

The conclusions to be drawn from the foregoing can be expressed in the following hypotheses that need to be examined:

(1) The ability of companies to make progress in certain domains of labour market flexibility is a key factor in the selection, redistribution or maintenance of locations for mobile, international investment capital.

(2) Great Britain has a reputation among international investors as providing a relatively high degree of numerical and temporal flexibility, whereas Germany has greater benefits when it comes to functional flexibility.

(3) Compared to Germany, this strong reputation for labour market flexibility in Britain has a positive impact in attracting and keeping large-scale investments in manufacturing industry; in contrast,

(4) Germany's good reputation for functional flexibility has boosted its capacity to attract manufacturing investments of higher quality than the United Kingdom is capable of.

However, it is necessary first of all to examine the basic question as to which role labour market factors play at all in the investment decisions of multinational companies.

3. THE RELATIONSHIP BETWEEN FLEXIBILITY AND INVESTMENT DECISIONS

3.1 Methodology of the study

In order to test the above hypotheses, a series of case studies were conducted in Germany and Great Britain. Structured personal interviews were held with managers of multinational corporations that have made direct investments in one of the two countries. The interviews focused on the motives behind the respective investment decision. Special attention was given to the influence of labour market factors and to differences in flexibility, labour costs, labour market regulation and collective bargaining systems.

A total of 46 interviews were conducted, 22 in Germany and 24 in Great Britain. Companies were selected that operated production centres in both countries; factories operating under different regulatory regimes could thus be compared. The survey covered British companies with investments in Germany, German companies with investments in Great Britain, and investors from other countries with production sites in both countries. By applying this approach, we could not only identify the particular experience that investors had with the labour market in the respective countries, but could also obtain information about whether different types of investments were made at different locations. The random sample contains 15 pairs, i.e. cases in which both the parent company and the national subsidiary in one of the two countries were questioned (eight in the chemicals industry and seven in the car industry). This enabled a comparison to be made of factories within the same corporation, and also provided an impression of the different perspectives from which investment decisions are seen – an aspect that is dealt with in greater detail in the following.

For the purposes of the project, investors were selected from two sectors of industry – car manufacturing and the chemicals industry – in order to identify sectorally specific influences. Both are highly internationalised industries in which a substantial volume of direct investments are made in both Great Britain and Germany. For both industries, it is important to achieve the highest level of employment flexibility possible and to make further improvements on that level. Each of the two industries must increase the utilisation time for the respective stock of capital, requires highly skilled personnel, and is faced with seasonal fluctuations in demand, which means that the need for flexible forms of employment is considerable. Furthermore, these are sectors of industry with different degrees of labour intensity.

Twenty-nine of the companies surveyed have their head office in Germany, seven in Great Britain and ten in a third country, whereby the sample also reflects the greater number of German investors with factories in Great Britain. Companies that considered investing in one of the two countries, but did not do so in the end, comprise the weakness, or 'blind spot' of this selection procedure. The motives and rationale for their behaviour could not be included in our analysis.

3.2. Results of the case studies

In order to identify the motives that moved companies to make first investments in a particular country, the interviewees were given a list of ten possible determinants. They were asked to state whether the various motives were 'very important', 'important' or 'unimportant' for their decision. Their responses were weighted by a factor of 2, 1 or 0 in order to calculate the average importance of the motives. To avoid duplicates, the responses of the parent company only were taken in those cases where two interviews were carried out in the same multinational company.

It was sometimes difficult for interviewees to answer questions about the reasons for initial investments, especially when these were made some time ago. In other cases, investments were made within the wider context of company takeovers that overshadowed any specific reasons for investing in Germany or Great Britain. Hence, the responses we obtained did not always relate to specific investment decisions, but tended to reflect general considerations about the determinants for investment in the respective country.

Furthermore, describing the importance of the various factors on a scale of only three may be rather inadequate for decisions shaped by a large number of factors, and where a particular combination of factors may be more important than a very clear benefit provided by a single factor.

Table 2.2: Importance of investment factors in relation to location of investment (weighted averages)[a]

	Companies investing in Germany	Companies investing in the UK	All companies
Access to key markets or customers	1.63	1.52	1.55
Access to raw materials and/or inputs	0.13	0.35	0.29
Quality of physical or economic infrastructure	0.38	0.48	0.45
Labour market factors	0.63	0.69	0.68
Access to R&D or technologies	0.50	0.44	0.45
Government incentives/subsidies	0.13	0.75	0.57
Taxes	0.38	0.66	0.58
Regulation by government	0.25	0.50	0.42
Trade barriers	0.13	0.22	0.19
Language and cultural factors	0.13	0.48	0.38

Sample: 31 case studies.

a Weighting: 2 = very important, 1 = important, 0 = unimportant.

However, the outcome of the survey on investment motives was so clear-cut that these methodological objections have little import. In both countries, access to a market or to key customers was by far the most important reason for making direct investments in the specific country (Table 2.2). This may mean that the investor was either a 'market-seeking' company aiming to further its own globalisation, or a company pursuing a 'follow-the-customer' strategy, i.e. was seeking access to the respective market because a customer so wanted. Labour market factors ranked second, but were significantly less important. Differentiating between Germany and Great Britain, and taking the different number of cases into consideration, we find no fundamental variation in the ranking of investment motives. The only exception is 'government incentives/subsidies', which are much more important for investments in Great Britain than for those in Germany. This accords with the different policies pursued by the two countries in order to attract foreign investors. In this respect, Great Britain offers much greater incentives and lower taxes on companies than is the case in Germany. Some of the interviewees specified other important motives that were not on the predefined list. The most frequently mentioned was the strength of sterling in recent years, which severely weakened the attractiveness of the country for foreign investors.

Table 2.3: Importance of investment factors according to industrial sector (weighted averages)[a]

	Automotive industry	Chemicals industry	All companies
Access to key markets or customers	1.54	1.55	1.55
Access to raw materials and/or inputs	0.08	0.44	0.29
Quality of physical or economic infrastructure	0.31	0.56	0.45
Labour market factors	0.92	0.50	0.68
Access to R&D or technologies	0.38	0.44	0.45
Government incentives/subsidies	0.76	0.45	0.57
Taxes	0.69	0.50	0.58
Regulation by government	0.54	0.39	0.42
Trade barriers	0.30	0.11	0.19
Language and cultural factors	0.54	0.28	0.38

Sample: 31 case studies.

a Weighting: 2 = very important, 1 = important, 0 = unimportant.

The respective weight attached to the various investment motives is rendered more visible if one distinguishes between the two industries focused on in the study (Table 2.3). Although market access remained by far the most important reason for investing, it is apparent that labour market factors and government incentives play a much greater role in the labour-intensive automotive industry than in the chemicals industry. The greater importance of labour as a factor for the car industry is also shown by the greater significance it attaches to language and cultural factors.

One interesting outcome of the study that should also heighten awareness for how hastily conclusions can be drawn from isolated statements or experience about the behaviour of companies with international operations is shown by comparing the survey results for the head offices and the national subsidiaries of the same companies (Table 2.4). Although market access was the predominant motive for both, much greater importance is attached to the other determinants for investments by the decision-making parent company than the national subsidiaries perceive. This is understandable, in that the responsible persons at head offices are able to compare different potential locations, and are compelled to take all relevant factors into consideration when making their decision. This is a perspective that interviewees in the local subsidiaries quite obviously did not have. It may be that the specific circumstances in which they work, e.g. taxation, language and culture, are taken for granted to such an extent that they are not aware of how important these factors can be when viewed externally.

Table 2.4: Importance of investment factors as assessed by head offices and national subsidiaries (weighted averages)[a]

	Head offices	National subsidiary
Access to key markets or customers	1.66	1.53
Access to raw materials and/or inputs	0.27	0.07
Quality of physical or economic infrastructure	0.60	0.39
Labour market factors	0.67	0.53
Access to R&D or technologies	0.46	1.07
Government incentives/subsidies	0.74	0.27
Taxes	0.60	0.07
Regulation by government	0.60	0.07
Trade barriers	0.20	0.00
Language and cultural factors	0.53	0.07

Sample: 15 case studies.

a Weighting: 2 = very important, 1 = important, 0 = unimportant.

In contrast, subsidiaries believe that access to research facilities and technologies is of much greater importance than head offices assess it to be. This is probably due to a certain exaggeration of one's own importance within the corporation as a whole, and the awareness that R&D will play an increasingly important role in the future. In one case study, for example, the fact that the research department was left in Great Britain after the production plant was closed down was ascribed to its performance, whereas the parent company specified government subsidies as the reason.

Table 2.5: Factors having increasing importance for future investment decisions (number of cases)

	Total	Automobile companies	Chemicals companies	Head offices	Subsidiaries
Access to markets and/or customers	6	2	4	3	4
Access to raw materials and/or inputs	2	0	2	1	1
Physical or economic infrastructure	4	1	3	1	1
Labour market factors	12	7	5	5	11
Access to R&D or technologies	0	0	0	0	1
Government incentives/subsidies	1	0	1	1	0
Taxes	4	3	1	2	0
Regulation by government	5	2	3	3	0
Trade barriers	1	0	1	0	0
Language and cultural factors	1	1	0	0	0
No. of case studies in sample	31	13	18	15	15

As already mentioned, the case studies were not confined to identifying the motives for the first investment move in the respective country. The more detailed study of follow-up investments and re-investment is also of special importance, since in these cases the most important motive no longer applies, or is at least much less relevant, once market access has actually been gained. The interviewees were therefore asked to specify the factors that determine follow-up investments, or which have a greater influence on future investments. Not all interviewees gave detailed answers to these questions, while many said that motives did not undergo any fundamental change. For this reason, the following list can only provide some rough indications, and must be interpreted with due caution. However, the basic tendency is clear: the labour market is the most important – or at least the most frequently mentioned – factor when companies must decide where to confine or increase their production, where to manufacture new products, or where production must be concentrated in order to achieve economies of scale. In other words, once a company has established a presence in a particular market, market-related factors lose importance as parameters for decision-making. Here, too, the influence of the labour market appears to be greater in the automotive industry than in the chemicals industry, and subsidiaries consider it to be more important than head offices do (Table 2.5).

Further questioning of companies about the importance of specific labour market factors generated results that largely confirmed our expectations (Table 2.6). Factors assessed as important or very important included direct labour costs, manpower flexibility and access to skilled labour. The latter pertains to the availability of high-quality human capital both on the external labour market and within the companies themselves.

Further confirmation of our advance hypotheses is obtained when the findings are regionally differentiated according to investment location. Companies investing in Germany value the skills of employees more than any other factor, whereas investors in Great Britain attach greatest importance to wages and non-wage labour costs. To a certain extent, this corroborates the conventional notion that Germany attracts investors who need skilled personnel, whereas the attractiveness of Great Britain consists on the whole of lower labour costs, even though the above results prompt the question as to how significant such cost differentials actually are in the last analysis. Interestingly enough, investors in both countries emphasised the immense importance of flexibility in the deployment of manpower, thus indicating that this factor is crucial in both countries.

Table 2.6: Significance of labour market factors (weighted averages)[a]

	Companies investing in Germany	Companies investing in the UK	All companies
Availability of skilled labour	1.78	1.09	1.29
Direct labour costs	1.11	1.50	1.39
Non-wage labour costs	1.00	1.23	1.16
Flexibility of employees	1.45	1.50	1.49
Level of labour market regulation	1.00	0.87	0.91
Industrial relations	0.89	0.87	0.88

Sample: 31 case studies.

a Weighting: 2 = very important, 1 = important, 0 = unimportant.

Those responsible in the companies were also asked where they considered the benefits in one of the countries to lie in respect of these various labour market aspects. However, only a minority felt able to comment, and to specify clear advantages on the part of Germany or Great Britain (Table 2.7). Yet again, our findings provided confirmation for expectations and biases regarding the two labour markets: in Germany, higher skill levels and productivity are valued, whereas the benefits in Great Britain are seen on the costs side and in the low level of labour market regulation. Given that Great Britain scores markedly higher on flexibility, it can be assumed that the interviewees were not thinking first and foremost of functional flexibility.

Table 2.7: Importance of various labour market factors in Germany and the United Kingdom (no. of companies)

	Benefits in Germany	*Benefits in the UK*
Availability of skilled labour	18	0
Direct labour costs	0	17
Non-wage labour costs	0	16
Flexibility of employees	2	7
Level of labour market regulation	0	10
Industrial relations	2	1

Sample: 31 case studies.

As already emphasised on several occasions, it is imperative to differentiate between the various forms of flexibility, since they are based on different frameworks, meet different needs and are barely substitutable for each other. This is the case, at least, for numerical and temporal flexibility, on the one hand, and functional flexibility, on the other. A separate block of questions was therefore put to the interviewees regarding the specific expectations that their companies levelled in respect of these two most important forms of flexibility.

Table 2.8: Importance of various aspects of numerical and temporal flexibility according to sector (weighted averages)[a]

	Automobiles	Chemicals
Ease with which workforce can be expanded or reduced	0.71	0.38
Handling of unfair dismissal rules	0.79	0.38
Ease with which temporary employees can be hired	1.21	0.93
Ease with which part-time employees can be hired	0.07	0.26
Options for varying the working week	1.50	0.97
Options in respect of night and weekend shifts	1.65	1.12

Sample: 31 case studies.

a Weighting: 2 = very important, 1 = important, 0 = unimportant.

In the case of numerical and temporal flexibility, the factor to which most importance was attached was the option to alter working hours (either by varying the number of hours per working week or by introducing special shifts) and opportunities to conclude temporary employment contracts without incurring any major incremental costs (Table 2.8). Only a few companies placed great value on the ability to conclude contracts for part-time employment, and only a few more considered it important to adjust the workforce size at short notice and without major problems to the intensity of capacity utilisation. In the chemicals industry, especially, temporal flexibility is considered important for maximising the use of capital stock by running shift systems that enable continuous production. In contrast, the necessity of having this kind of flexibility was explained primarily in terms of 'lean production' systems that involve 'just-in-time' delivery, enable companies to set up 24-hour shift systems and to respond at short notice to variations in demand.

There were no differences between Germany and Great Britain as far as the considerable value attached to these aspects of flexibility was concerned. What was interesting, however, was that only few companies could establish any noticeable differences in the ability of the two countries to meet their needs in this respect, although the majority of those companies that were able to do so stated that Great Britain was more flexible (Table 2.9). This confirms both the hypotheses set forth in this chapter as well as common assumptions, but it became apparent from the intensive discussions with corporate decision-makers that Germany's seemingly obvious drawbacks as regards numerical and temporal labour market flexibility often existed in theory only, rather than imposing any genuinely serious constraints on companies operating there, particularly since recent efforts to liberalise the labour market have had a noticeable impact. In some cases, the rigid German system ultimately proved to be more flexible than the British one, due to the exceptions provided in regulations, e.g. for weekend work in the chemicals industry, and the willingness of works councils and workforces to play a responsible and cooperative role.

Table 2.9: Comparison of numerical and temporal flexibility in Germany and the United Kingdom (no. of companies)

	Germany	UK
Restrictions on flexibility	6	2
Benefits from flexibility	3	9

Sample: 31 case studies.

As expected, even greater importance was attached in both countries to functional flexibility than to numerical and temporal flexibility (Table 2.10). The unanimous verdict was that Germany provides benefits in respect of the most important factor for functional flexibility, the level of training. However, this pertains first and foremost to vocational training, in which the traditional merits of the dual system compared to Anglo-Saxon forms of relatively informal 'learning by doing' and/or 'training on the job' obviously continue to operate. In the opinion of the companies surveyed, better training was also the most important reason for the higher productivity levels in Germany. One British company that had invested in Germany discovered that similar results can be achieved in both countries, as a basic principle, but that British workers with lower skill levels impose much higher demands on management. Some companies said that there were no major differences between the two countries as regards the skills of their employees, but these were usually companies whose production did not necessitate a particularly high proportion of well-trained workers.

Table 2.10: Importance of various aspects of functional flexibility (weighted averages)[a]

Possibility of assigning different activities to employees	1.37
Ability of workers to take on additional responsibilities	1.45
Ability of workers to work in groups	1.42

Sample: 31 case studies.

a Weighting: 2 = very important, 1 = important, 0 = unimportant.

Nevertheless, one can say that functional flexibility in German factories is generally greater, within one and the same company, than in the British factories. Flexibility ultimately ensues from the level of training, on the one hand, and the manner in which production processes are organised, on the other. The interviews uncovered numerous examples of German and British companies currently undergoing reorganisation as 'learning companies'. British subsidiaries can thus be pioneers of new work methods within the corporate network. This reflects the minimal resistance waged in Great Britain against the introduction of such systems, especially where the trade unions are weak, where a company has been recently taken over, and where the workforce was less focused on a particular production system. In this context, one German investor from the automobile industry described the British factory he had acquired as 'a brownfield site with a greenfield mentality' that provided his company with the first opportunity to introduce commitments for minimal production waste, stricter monitoring of quality standards, cellular production and other work methods. Of course, this highlights the greater necessity of introducing new methods in Great Britain – since many companies are still geared to the production systems of the old proprietors –, in order to achieve productivity gains and approach the German level. In some cases, however, it was pointed out in this connection that much more had to be invested in the British workforce than would have been necessary in similar German cases to achieve the same level of productivity.

Attention was drawn at the same time to the poor 'performance' that many British factories continue to generate. Two investors in our survey said they had to close down British factories due to persistent productivity problems; no such comments were made in the course of our study about similar cases in Germany. It also became clear that, wherever they are introduced, new forms of work organisation spread relatively fast throughout multinational corporations, since all factories are faced with a similar pressure to maintain high productivity levels. Here, again, benefits are generated by the higher levels of skilling in Germany, since new technologies are accepted with much greater ease. Interviewees were agreed that this also applies to new forms of work organisation, that in those cases in which such changes were implemented in several factories concurrently, German workforces accepted them faster and with fewer problems than their British counterparts.

4. SUMMARY AND CONCLUSIONS

As indicated by this presentation and discussion of the empirical study on the influence of labour market factors on the investment decisions of automobile and chemicals companies with international operations, the most important results are:

- The extent to which labour market flexibility in Germany and the United Kingdom is thought to differ is usually exaggerated. In general, both countries exhibit all types of flexibility, especially temporal and functional flexibility. Which particular kind of flexibility prevails depends on the specific corporate culture, industrial relations, production conditions in the particular companies, and skill levels among the workforce.
- Consequently, enhanced flexibility can be achieved by companies at locations in both countries. On the other hand, the study did not reveal any significant differences or barriers on account of national differences in labour market regulation. In many cases, however, the higher skill levels of German workers enabled productivity increases to be achieved more rapidly.
- Decisions regarding direct investments in Germany or in the United Kingdom were not influenced (in the case of initial investments) or little influenced (in the case of follow-up investments) by labour mar-

ket differences. This applies to the factors of both wage costs and the regulation of flexibility.

*   Although the United Kingdom enjoys a good reputation among foreign investors on account of its low wages and non-wage labour costs, our study revealed that other motives are ultimately decisive for investments in the United Kingdom. Access to new markets and/or certain customers was by far the most important factor.

What do these findings mean in relation to the persistent complaints about Germany's locational drawbacks, especially as regards its allegedly so inflexible labour market? On the one hand, one might be inclined to send out an 'all clear' message – even given the lack of reliable data on the actual volume of direct investments in the various countries. All the more so, in that the differences between Germany and Great Britain are often negligible compared to much greater differences vis-à-vis other potential locations, especially in eastern Europe and Asia. To that extent, conditions in the German labour market and their importance for investment decisions must be evaluated in the context of the respective national circumstances, an aspect that the present study cannot cover. Consideration must also be given to the fact that only those investors were interviewed in the study who have actually acquired some practical experience with the German labour market. One cannot conclude from this the number of locational decisions by international companies that have excluded Germany on account of its poor reputation. However, one may assume that the number is substantial.

The results of the study make one thing quite clear, however. They should sharpen awareness among all those bearing responsibility in this field that the traditional German system of vocational training is a valuable asset. Not only does it enhance functional flexibility and thus the competitive strength of companies; the numerical and temporal flexibility required by companies cannot be had in many cases without the appropriate training and skills. There are grounds for concern that the reduced willingness, especially among major corporations, to participate to an appropriate extent in training the next generation (due to the costs involved) may have considerable and long-term repercussions for the economy. British companies, in any case, who have neglected vocational training all too often in the past, frequently refer to problems in this area that may even prevent them from using the legal opportunities for making production more flexible.

NOTES

1. See Raines et al. (1999).
2. The former Secretary of State for Trade and Industry, PeterMandelson, once commented that, 'Across the whole economy, productivity in the United States leads the UK by some 40 per

cent while France and Germany are 25-30 per cent ahead, although of course with much higher levels of unemployment and of course non-wage costs and regulations much higher than in the United Kingdom'. Speech by the Rt. Hon. Peter Mandelson MP to the British American Chamber of Commerce, New York, 13 October 1998 (http://www.dti.gov.uk/Minspeech/mandel2.htm). See also the figures based on OECD data which confirm these ratios in Table 9, p. 25 of Raines et al. (1999).
3. See the comparison of selected indicators of temporal flexibility inRaines et al. (1999), Table 8, p. 24.

REFERENCES

Adnett, N. (1996), *European Labour Markets: Analysis and Policy*, London: Addison-Wesley.
Hegewisch, A. and C. Brewster (1993), *European Developments in Human Resource Management*, London: Kogan Page.
http://www.dti.gov.uk/Minspeech/mandel2.htm.
Raines, P.; R. Döhrn; R. Brown and M. Scheuer (1999), *Labor Market Flexibility and Inward Investment in Germany and the UK. An Anglo-German Foundation Report*, London: Anglo-German Foundation (forthcoming in Germany under the title *Arbeitsmarktflexibilität und Direktinvestitionen in Deutschland und Großbritannien*, one in a series, published by the Rhine-Westphalian Institute for Economic Research.

3. International mobility of the highly skilled: 'Brain Gain', 'Brain Drain' or 'Brain Exchange'?

Thomas Straubhaar[1]

1. INTRODUCTION

The Green Card initiative by the German chancellor Gerhard Schröder has brought back migration issues into the focus of the political debate – not only in Germany. Remarkably enough, a rather fast growing part of the public opinion has slowly changed its mind. More and more natives and citizens realise that the consequences of immigration are very complex and ambiguous. Economic effects depend on the magnitude, the speed, the intensity and the structure of immigration flows with regard to age and qualification. Furthermore, they depend on the economic business cycle of the receiving economy (especially the magnitude of unemployment) and the ability to cope with a rapid structural change.

Economic theory has stressed the ambivalence of migration issues (for a very recent evaluation see Fischer 1999). In a nutshell, it has been indicated that migration is an arbitrage phenomenon in a short run and consequently supports positively the adjustment process of an economy. The long term effects of migration are not so clear cut. In many cases, migration will not matter that much, at least not for long-run growth and development processes. And *if migration matters, it is emigration and not immigration that might become a macroeconomic 'growth problem'!* The basic reasoning behind this statement is that *economically* induced inflows of workers increase or at least do not decrease per capita income in the *immigration* area. This positive evaluation of immigration in a neoclassical framework is confirmed by the so-called New Growth Theory. It evaluates very positively the additional availability of 'imported' human capital. An inflow of human capital might produce positive externalities that spill over to other sectors and regions of the host economy. Thus, regions should *a priori* be interested in becoming the targeted destination of mobile qualified labour force.

In light of the positive evaluation of immigration of qualified labour force, it is the intention of this chapter to discuss more precisely the question, of how societies could attract and keep highly skilled people. While historically, the United States have been extremely pragmatic and have rolled out red carpets to immigrants with specific skills (see Carrington and Detragiache 1999 for details), Europe has been reluctant to open its borders. It is only nowadays that minds start to change after qualified workers in the information and communication sectors have become scarce. The German chancellor's idea to offer about 20 000 green cards to computer and software specialists from outside the European Union (EU) is a clear signal that new ideas gain attention. Why should the EU leave the playing field to other areas of the world?

In what follows, I discuss in section 2 of the chapter three case studies which represent (i) a 'Brain Gain', where there is an increasing level of human capital, (ii) a 'Brain Exchange', where there is no net loss or gain of human capital but movement between areas and (iii) a 'Brain Drain', where there is a net loss of human capital. In section 3, some theoretical considerations of the New Growth theory are discussed shortly with reference to positive externalities. In section 4, the discussion turns to how best to accumulate human capital, whether it is creation or use that is important, and how the European Union could develop a successful 'Brain Gain' strategy (i.e. 'how can Europe be Americanised?'). The final section summarises the main issues of the chapter.

2. SOME STYLISED FACTS

Once again the USA seems to be best prepared for the needs and trends of the 21st century. Due to its long immigration tradition the US economy is open enough (and labour markets are flexible!) to welcome the global citizens that are looking around for the most promising places to live, to work, to earn money and to spend it. The USA has, for a long time already, been well aware of the benefits to the US population that could be collected by capturing mobile skilled foreign professionals. Thus, a real business has been established that starts with education, goes on with attractive local complementarities (like sand, sun and fun) and ends with easy access to the local labour market for foreign specialists.

The 'export' of education services (by an 'import' of foreign students) has become a money machine for the US. Every year foreign students contribute over $7bn to the US economy (see List 1998). They draw about 1/2m foreign students. The growth rate of foreign students in the USA is 5% p.a. (see Brinck 1999). This not only qualifies education as one of the best selling US exports, but also means that, in effect, the US is experiencing a net 'Brain Gain'. 'Almost half of all the PhD recipients in the USA in any year are now foreigners' (Mahroum 1999: 19). This 'Brain Gain' has consequences, not just for the 'education business', but also for the future of the economy.

This raises the question as to why American education is so popular and what are the consequences? Apart from the promise of 'excellent lesson quality and excellent professors' (for which the students are willing to pay on average $5000 per year) they also, more than often, offer a seducing study environment. And this goes far beyond attractive 'sun, sea and sand' dimensions for leisure! There are close links between universities and industry, thus the students themselves can make valuable contacts and thereby improving future career possibilities. It is also a good opportunity for them to improve their English language abilities (intensive English courses are offered), English will be the language of the 'globalised' world. American study time is short, with masters courses and the like lasting only 1 or 2 years. And probably most important is that successful foreign students have a very good chance to get an allowance to stay on in the US. In early 2000, the US congress has discussed a 'Brain Act' (Bringing Resources from Academia to the Industry of our Nation Act) that offers foreign students the opportunity to get a work permit in the US. If a US employer is willing to pay a fee of about US$ 1000 they can hire students directly after their graduation (see *Neue Zürcher Zeitung* 2000 for more details).

As a result of this openness towards foreign students a large number of jobs for US-Americans are created, directly and indirectly. Merely to provide for the service demands of the foreign students, about 100 000 jobs are created (see Brinck 1999). For example, jobs are created directly through the need for lectures, tutorials and student administration. Also, jobs are created indirectly through the extra demand for consumer goods and local services that the extra students generate.

What is even more important than the immediate benefits in terms of student fees and the direct or indirect employment effects are the longer term (growth) impacts on the economy. First, during their time of study, foreign students become used to the American way of life. They consume American products and study with the aid of apparatus, hardware and software produced by American firms like IBM and Microsoft. Then, in their careers and future, they become promoters of American lifestyle. Thus even after they leave the US they will keep their 'American way of life'. They will buy a Ford and not a Volkswagen, they are familiar with Compaq and not with Siemens, they are trained with Windows and not with a European software.

Secondly, and of greater direct consequence to the US economy, many of the successful students, and especially the very successful, stay in the USA after their studies have ended. They stay and work for American companies or apply for jobs with American firms that send them to work in their former country of origin. About 50% of all (European) doctoral graduates stay in the USA when they have finished their studies, and many do not return at all (see Mahroum 1999:20).

Compared to the US, Europe is increasingly unsuccessful at attracting the highly skilled. This is especially troublesome because many (if not most!) European universities offer almost tuition-free higher education! 'It is only with Japan that the EU enjoys a surplus. ... The number of Europeans going to North America is double those arriving from there' (Mahroum 1999: 21). Of course the main reason is that the immigration options for people from outside the EU into the EU are extremely restrictive. And even for students or PhD candidates the hurdles to surmount are time-consuming, troublesome and even sometimes rather arbitrary. In the field of education, foreign diplomas and certificates are not fast and easily treated as equivalent to domestic ones – which again generates waiting, information and application costs. Consequently, and not really surprisingly, it can be seen that fewer and fewer foreign students are choosing European universities. For example a study by the 'Deutsche Studentenwerk' has shown that a large number of foreign students were accidentally there or because of an exchange programme. Also, that if they had been able to choose, most of them would have gone to another country (see *Das Parlament* 1999)

This low tendency for the highly skilled to come from the outside to the EU to study and to stay here corresponds to the inner-EU experience. Despite all the efforts to stimulate the mobility of the higher qualified labour force within the EU, the amount of migration of the highly skilled is low and it increases only slowly (see Wolter and Straubhaar 1997). Contrary to the 'Brain Gain' strategy of the US the EU migration can be evaluated in terms of a 'Brain Exchange'. This 'Brain Exchange' experience of Europe is also being fuelled by the Europeanisation of production, which has occurred over the past decade or so. The Europeanisation of production has come about through a wide variety of causes including developments in microelectronics, competition from abroad, and the process of European integration. In many cases short term (business or project oriented) trips and cross-border commuting or the statistically non-relevant intra-firm mobility of technical and managerial experts (internal labour market movements) are far reaching substitutes for 'traditional' migration flows. In some (smaller) EU countries (in particular Sweden, Holland and Ireland) graduates are trained to become suitable for work abroad and to be able to cope with the growing internationalisation of the business activities of their domestic companies (see Mahroum 1999).

Table 3.1: Brain Drain from Eastern Europe according to the literature

Country of emigration	Volume and occupation of emigrants	Country of destination
Russia		
1990	250 scientists of the academy of science (20%)	Not specified; permanent contracts
1991-93	18 000 scientists and Intellectuals	Among others Germany
1992	7000-70 000 Scientists	Israel (44 000 engineers, 8500 Ph.Ds)
1991	600 members of the academy of science; the most productive 4% of the emigrants are students, 80-90% want to leave permanently	Contracts , primarily Israel, Germany & the US
Bulgaria		
1990-92	40 000 scientists	Work in the West
from 1989	20 000 scientists per year	Primarily Germany, Ireland, France, UK; intend to emigrate permanently
Ex CSSR		
1989	34.4% of the emigrants are intellectuals	Germany
Hungary		
?	Many want to emigrate permanently	US
Rumania		
1980-84	12.1% of the emigrants were highly qualified	Germany, Hungary & Israel
Poland		
1980-87	76 300 academics	Germany, US, France and others
1983-87	59 700 with university degree	Germany
1980s	19 800 Engineers, 8800 Scientists & academics, 5500 doctors, 6000 nurses	From 81-88 approx. 50-55% migrated to Germany, a great part being ethnic German emigrants (*Aussiedler*)

Source: Wolburg (2000)

A third stylised fact can be seen in eastern Europe. Here, a 'Brain Drain' is one of the most severe economic problem for the near future and especially for the negotiation process of becoming new EU members. According to the microeconomics of migration (see Fischer et al. 1997) it would be most probably the skilled, relatively young and dynamic men who will leave central and eastern Europe to look for their luck in other countries of the EU – most likely Germany. But then, an old story gains new interest. It is the negative effect of the emigration of skilled people on those left behind which has been called 'Brain Drain' in the development literature. By definition 'brain drain' is the permanent emigration of qualified persons. Table 3.1 provides a short survey of some recent studies on the brain drain in eastern Europe.

To stress further the loss of brains in eastern Europe, the example of the migration flows towards Germany is self-evident. The *skill ratio* (i.e. the share of highly qualified immigrants out of all immigrants) might serve as a measure for the instantaneous human capital content of migration. By summing up the qualificational specific migration pattern over time we can then construct an index that displays the average qualificational structure of migration within the period considered. This is done in the following Table 3.2 where the qualificational structure of migration within the period of 1992-94 is analysed.

Table 3.2: East European cumulated immigration flows into Germany according to qualification, 1992-94, in 1000 Persons

Sending Country	Aggregated immigrants according to qualification		
	highly qualified (1)	Total (2)	skill ratio (flows) (3) = (1):(2)
Poland	9.02	48.41	0.19
Ex CSSR	1.76	10.6	0.17
Hungary	3.78	10.87	0.35
Romania	6.11	63.47	0.10
Bulgaria	3.74	9.65	0.39
Ex Yugoslavia	18.58	236.16	0.08
Albania	1.11	14.72	0.08
Ex USSR	37.79	370.63	0.10
Total	*81.89*	*764.51*	*0.11*

Source: Straubhaar and Wolburg (1999).

Table 3.2 demonstrates that the cumulated share of highly qualified immigrants varies across countries. Whereas it is highest for Bulgaria, immigrants from the former Yugoslavia exhibited the lowest skill ratio. This is not very surprising since the civil war in the former Yugoslavia induced asylum migration which cannot be compared to voluntary economically induced migration taking place in the other countries. From Table 3.3 we see that the share of highly qualified people in the German population is 0.13 for the period considered. Compared to the average qualification of people residing in Germany, the human capital content of immigration from Poland, the former Czechoslovakia, Hungary and Bulgaria is significantly higher. Consequently, we can indeed observe a definite 'Brain Drain' for those eastern European countries.

Table 3.3: Aggregate cumulated skill ratios of migrants in Germany, 1992-94

Aggregate cumulated skill ratio (stock)	*Average (1992-94)*
German population	0.13
Poland	0.19
Ex CSSR	0.21
Hungary	0.22
Romania	0.21
Bulgaria	0.17
Ex Yugoslavia	0.04
Albania	0.07
EX USSR	0.27

Source: Straubhaar and Wolburg (1999).

To summarise this section, the stylised facts make it obvious that we have a brain gain for the US, a brain drain for Eastern Europe and a brain exchange with no clear strategy in the European Union. Why does the EU not change gear and play an active strategy to attract brains from all over the world? In particular, the (skilled) migrants from the Eastern European candidates should be seen as a positive economic stimulus to the EU economy and not a danger that has to kept out.

3. SOME THEORETICAL CONSIDERATIONS

Why is it so important to attract brains and to accumulate human capital? In this section I will provide some arguments to show the macroeconomic reasoning behind a brain drain strategy. The key factor lies in the positive externalities that are related to the immigration of skilled people. While *pecuniary* externalities of migration stem from an alternation of relative factor rewards in response to migration and are of no direct importance to the impacts of factor allocation, the so-called *technical* externalities of the mobility of highly qualified people are much more important. Characteristic of the latter is that the aggregate welfare for the society as a whole can be affected. To keep a long story extremely short, I only refer to the main results of the extensive brain drain literature that starts with the seminal work by Grubel and Scott (1966), Berry and Soligo (1969) and reaches a first climax with the work by Bhagwati and his scholars (see Bhagwati, 1976, 1976a, 1979, 1985, 1985a; Bhagwati and Dellalfar, 1973; Bhagwati and Hamada, 1974; Bhagwati and Rodriguez, 1975).

First, *positive technological externalities of immigration* arise by the additional human capital that is available to the host economy. The theoretical arguments go back to the development literature of the 1950's (the famous *Hirschman, Myrdal, Perroux, Wallerstein* divergence or vicious circle or core-periphery view). They have seen a revival in the mid-1980's with the birth of the so-called New Growth Theory. Starting with the seminal papers by *Paul Romer* (1986, 1987, 1990) or *Robert Lucas* (1988) the immigration of skilled migrants has been evaluated as stimulating the dynamics of economic growth (see Walz 1996 for a specific treatment of migration effects in a new growth world). According to the New Growth models, a distinction should be made between skills, that are tied to people, and knowledge, which is not tied to individuals (see Figure 3.1).

a) *Human capital*, or skills, can be thought of as inseparable from people, they are achieved through investment during the course of a person's life, and they have a finite lifetime (i.e. the life span of the individual). As a result, the use of human capital is rival and ownership rights make it possible to exclude those who are not willing to pay for its employment (e.g. through contracts). Thus, skills can be labelled as private goods. As such, the carrier of these skills is also able to internalise the benefits by demanding a better income and working conditions.

b) *Knowledge*, however, is not tied to individuals and is, thus, non-rival. Insider knowledge can be fully internalised, but other knowledge is generally available and is, therefore, not firm specific. However, property rights can be used to protect knowledge from competitors, for example through patents. This ability, to partially internalise knowledge, creates the incentive for private firms to invest in research and development. The remaining knowledge that can not be fully internalised creates positive externalities that spill over the entire economy, and can be, more or less, costlessly used. The costs invested in the production of new knowledge are high; however, the marginal costs of using it are very low. So general knowledge can be relatively cheaply used in terms of imitation and reproduction. The technological externalities created by knowledge, in the form of increasing returns to scale, therefore, produce a long term positive effect on the growth of an economy, in opposition to the Neo-classical Theory. Also noteworthy is that, because the results from investment in knowledge can not be fully internalised, it is likely that in the markets a sub-optimal level of knowledge is produced. This provides the reasoning for state subsidy of basic research.

Figure 3.1: Knowledge and Skills in a new growth framework

TECHNICAL FEASIBILITY $\rightarrow$ LEGAL FEASIBILITY $\downarrow$	SKILLS • Rival • Factor-bounded • Embodied in persons	KNOWLEDGE • Non-rival • Non-factor-bounded • Non-embodied in persons
FULL EXCLUDABILITY	*Human Capital*	*Specific Knowledge* (Insider knowledge)
PARTIAL EXCLUDABILITY	*Mobile skilled people* (Job jumpers)	*Specific Technologies* (Patents)
NO EXCLUDABILITY		*Basic Knowledge*

Source: Own presentation following Romer (1990).

Secondly, a further source for positive externalities of the mobility of highly skilled people are *locally limited spillovers*. They stem from the fact that in reality, skills and knowledge can not be totally separated. The use of skills is a prerequisite for the creation of new knowledge. As a result, knowledge is also bound to individuals. Also, employees can change their jobs and, even when there are restrictions on the transferring of knowledge, they will transfer a part of their knowledge and, therefore, produce a positive externality for the new employer. Thus, there is an absolute symbiosis of skills (that can be internalised) and knowledge spillovers. This leads to the point that positive externalities of general knowledge are in fact locally limited, because, firstly, the use of skills makes possible a transformation of knowledge into products and services. Studies have shown that this interaction does not happen evenly, but is locally clumped around catalyst crystallisation points, i.e. areas with a concentration of researchers and firms, who convert their knowledge into goods and services (the 'Silicon Valley' effect described by Zucker, Darby and Armstrong 1998 or Zucker, Darby and Brewer 1998).

Thus, the stimulating growth effects of knowledge externalities, and the fact that knowledge spillovers are locally limited are the key issues for the positive macroeconomic impact of the stock and flow of highly skilled people. The evidence that knowledge is unevenly dispersed in clusters means that a 'core-periphery' divide occurs, with underdeveloped 'periphery' countries or regions losing the highly skilled, and thus income potential, to the higher developed 'core' regions, who gain from an over-proportional income increase. Thus, disparity is enlarged. So the 'Brain Drain' restricts growth in the less developed 'peripheral' regions and encourages it in the 'core'.

The effects of the 'Brain Gain - Brain Drain' are the same as those encapsulated by Lucas (1990) in his article entitled 'Why doesn't capital flow from rich to poor countries?' Less developed regions have a lack of skilled people, who allow higher capital profitability to be achieved. This means that capital stays away. Therefore, average productivity is low. This provides a bigger incentive for the highly skilled to leave, and the 'Brain Drain' is intensified. Thus, a 'vicious circle' develops. Southern Italy provides a vivid example of this (the so-called 'Mezzogiorno' effect).

To summarise, from a domestic macroeconomic point of view it is definitely more positive to follow a brain gain strategy than to become a brain drain area. Of course, this provokes the question concerning what determines the starting point of the vicious circle and whether by policy actions areas have a choice to become core or periphery.

4. ACCUMULATION OF HUMAN CAPITAL: MAKE OR IMPORT?

As far as human capital accumulation generates some positive spillover effects for an economy, a strategic decision has to be taken by the policy makers: Should they produce their brain gains by themselves and invest in the accumulation of human capital by publicly subsidising schooling and research activities? Or should an economy 'free ride' and 'import' human capital that has been produced outside the country (and that has been financed by others!)? This is a fundamental strategic decision. Historically the solution had a strong tendency towards a home-based accumulation of human capital. Schooling and the education of students have been seen as typical national tasks. However, the national dimension of human capital has changed dramatically in recent years. Advances in microelectronics, further progress in computer technology, new telecommunications developments and modern transportation systems have reduced transaction costs and the costs for long distance movements of human capital. Human capital has become internationally mobile. People can move around the world within hours, their human capital goes even faster and is available world-wide within seconds. Highly skilled people have the opportunity to communicate and sell their knowledge around the globe. As such, they can choose their place of residence by maximising the expected return on their human capital investments. For this, they do not even have to move in person. Cyberspace and internet allow them to become functionally mobile while staying at their home base. All this means that the place of generation or production and the place of use of human capital might differ substantially.

If, for the moment, we lay aside information, selection and efficiency problems of the human capital production and assume that positive externalities are indeed achieved, this still raises the question of the use of human capital and the location where its spillovers can really be captured. Even when subsidy of the production of human capital is successful, this does not necessarily mean that the benefits will increase the welfare of that economy where they are produced. In reference to the previous discussion on the effects of the mobility of the highly skilled, it can be seen that subsidy of the production of human capital may actually lead to the subsidy of other countries if the highly skilled then migrate. Thus, investing in human capital creates even larger negative effects in a 'Brain Drain' situation i.e. when the country of production is 'losing its minds' to other nations.

The success of the Americans in the accumulation of human capital, in terms of 'Gaining Brains', begs the question: How can the European Union implement a successful 'Brain Gain' strategy? With this in mind, it is important to stress that a successful 'Brain Gain' strategy requires that Europe creates the environment to which the highly skilled are attracted. This statement shifts the focus from the production of skills and knowledge towards the use of it. The main issue is how to capture the geographically localised positive (knowledge) externalities of skilled people. If we look at the US we see immediately how successful the US plays this strategy. America is good at attracting the highly skilled because of a number of natural and unnatural benefits. Quality of life is very important to the highly skilled. They want to live where the weather is nice and the environment is clean. Safety, freedom of choice, flexibility to do and to move, secured property rights and a friendly surroundings in which they can raise healthy children are additional factors that influence the decision. Therefore, in addition to natural attributes, such as clean air and water, man-made political and social factors play a role in attracting the highly skilled.

Sadly enough, the EU ignores the fundamental economic relevance of highly skilled immigration. This is especially true with regard to Eastern

Europe. In the nearby back yard (or front garden?) of the EU, highly skilled people with a strong affinity to Western Europe, with specific European language skills and with a familiarity to Western European culture and habits could and should be motivated to come to the EU instead of leaving Europe for the US. But in the EU and especially in Germany there is still a fear of being invaded by a trek of people from the East.

However, for long term macroeconomic growth, the openness of the system is important, such as openness to innovation and knowledge, and the openness to foreigners. The ability to enter and leave without significant barriers such as residence registration and other 'red tape' could make the difference. Also, prospects for family members and tax levels are mobility influencing factors which are important in attracting highly skilled foreigners into the EU. In the case of America, there are close connections between research centres (such as universities) and industrial development (see Jaffe 1989). These clusters attract the highly skilled. Firstly, they attract students who think about future career prospects and secondly, they attract the highly qualified from other areas because of high wages, an innovative environment and career prospects. In turn, the supply of the highly skilled attracts other companies to locate in these 'core' areas.

Evidence can be seen of this in Europe too. For example, in economics and business administration students choose Frankfurt because of a close connection to the banking places. Many work for the banks during their studies to earn money but also to try to secure a future job. The banks themselves also have a cheap way of vetting future employees and enjoy the advantage of having a good supply of highly educated people from the universities and the other banks.

In addition, an attempt to replicate the attractive university structure of the US is under way in Europe, slowly but this is progressing on an increasing scale. Many American universities establish branches in Europe. 'The International University in Germany' has opened its doors recently. This is a private, fee paying, university that offers an American university structure. All courses are in English and three quarters of the students are foreign. The foreign students are required to learn German during their two year study of Information Technology or Business Administration and the German students learn another language, in addition to English. Also, there is a very close connection with industry. Students work during their time of study for DaimlerChrysler, SAP, Alcatel, Deutsche Telecom, Siemens, IBM, Microsoft and others, who, in addition, contribute largely to the funding of the university. Industry is showing a lot of interest and if successful, this could represent the way forward to a successful 'Brain Gain' strategy in Europe.

5. SUMMARY AND CONCLUSIONS

The aim of this chapter was to shift the focus from a negative prejudice about immigration towards a much more positive evaluation. More and more the migration pattern changes from a blue-collar migration of low qualified workers towards a white-collar mobility of highly skilled professionals. It has to be stressed strongly that strikingly enough most migrants are relatively well qualified. Just to mention a new IMF study (Carrington and Detragiache 1999:47), the US data show that immigration flows of individuals with no more than a primary education are quite small, and reach only about 500 000 individuals out of a total of 7 million immigrants! 'For most countries, people with a tertiary education have the highest migration rate ... Thus, migrants to the Unites States tend to be better educated than the average person in their home (that is the sending) country, and the proportion of very highly educated people who migrate is particularly high' (Carrington and Detragiache 1999:48). So, these data clearly indicate that there is a substantial brain drain. Another question of quite similar importance is, why should only the US get a brain gain. Why not the EU?

The immigration of the highly skilled is crucial and decisive for the growth and wealth of nations in the 21st century. Once again this is clearly seen and strategically developed in the US. The USA attracts highly skilled people from all over the world because of a number of natural as well as artificial benefits ('sun, sea, and sand', close relations between industry and universities etc.) and, therefore, experiences a 'Brain Gain' that stimulates growth. In the case of Europe, mobility is mainly intra-European, representing a 'Brain Exchange'. This is being fuelled by the Europeanisation of production and the creation of an internal labour market. However, the EU lacks the magnetic power to attract highly skilled foreign scientists and to become a leading centre of research intensive (service) production. For Eastern Europe there is a fear of a 'Brain Drain' that will not be directed towards the EU but rather towards the US.

As opposed to the traditional Neoclassical Growth Theory, the New Growth Theory argues that human capital produces positive knowledge externalities that spill over the economy in which they occur. Therefore, countries which have high levels of human capital, grow more quickly. Due to the fact that spillovers are locally limited, there is a strategic interest in creating clusters by concentrating human capital intensive research and production activities around catalyst crystallisation points like Silicon Valley.

As a result, a 'core-periphery' divide develops, such that there are dynamic highly developed 'core' regions and underdeveloped 'periphery' regions. Thus, the highly skilled gravitate towards the 'core', which gains from a more than proportional increase in income. A 'vicious cycle' develops; the poor regions become poorer and the rich regions become richer and the 'Brain Gain/Brain Drain' effect is intensified.

The creation of human capital faces a number of problems, not least of which is the fact that subsidy of human capital production can lead to subsidy of other countries if the highly skilled emigrate. Thus, the result arises that, in order to keep and accumulate human capital, countries have to make themselves attractive to the highly skilled in terms of openness to innovation, strong links between research and industry, openness to foreigners, a flexible system, low taxes and so on. These man-made political factors of relative attractiveness complement natural elements, like clean air and water, that are considered attractive by the highly skilled, who can choose their place of residence by maximising the return on their human capital investments.

Therefore, attractiveness plays a large role in the accumulation of human capital. It does start with a high-standard, ambitious education system. But this first step is not enough. Education needs to be supported by the existence of factors that will hold the highly educated and attract the highly skilled from other areas and countries. So it remains to be seen if projects such as 'The International University in Germany' will be successful in producing and attracting the highly skilled. Industry is being actively enthusiastic, implementing a large amount of investment and supplying students with work experience. However, this brain gain strategy will be successful only if these new highly educated, highly skilled, multilingual students stay. This will be the case if the EU policy makers, opinion leaders and vested interest groups realise that skilled immigrants do not hinder but support economic prosperity. Global citizens of the 21st century have many options. Closed doors here and red carpets there could mean that the brains of the future will be lured by the Americans.

NOTES

1. This article is part of the HWWA's research programme 'Internationalisation of Labour Markets'.

REFERENCES

Berry, R.A. and R. Soligo (1969), 'Some Welfare Aspects of International Migration', *Journal of Political Economy*, 77, 778-794.

Bhagwati, J. N. (1976), 'The brain drain', *International Social Science Journal*, 28, 691-729.

Bhagwati, J. N. (1976a), *The Brain Drain and Taxation: Theory and Empirical Analysis*; Amsterdam: North-Holland, Vol. 2.

Bhagwati, J. N. (1979), 'International Migration of the Highly Skilled: Economics, Ethics and Taxes', *Third World Quarterly*, **1**, 17-30.

Bhagwati, J. N. (1985), *Dependence and Interdependence: Essays in Development Economics*; Vol. 2, Oxford: Basil Blackwell.

Bhagwati, J. N. (1985a), 'The Brain Drain: International Resource Flow Accounting, Compensation, Taxation and Related Policy Proposals', in J.N. Bhagwati (ed.), *Dependence and Interdependence: Essays in Development Economics*; Vol. 2, Oxford: Basil Blackwell, 303-346.

Bhagwati, J. N. and W. Dellalfar (1973), 'The Brain Drain and Income Taxation', *World Development*, **1**, 94-101.

Bhagwati, J. and K. Hamada (1974), 'The Brain-Drain, International Integration of Markets for Professionals and Unemployment', *Journal of Development Economics*, **1**, 19-42.

Bhagwati, J. and C. Rodriguez (1975), 'Welfare-theoretical analysis of the Brain-Drain', *Journal of Development Economics*, **2**, 195-221.

Bhagwati, J. N. and J.D. Wilson (1989), *Income Taxation and International Mobility*, Cambridge: MIT Press.

Brinck, C. (1999), 'Deutsche Provinzialität. Warum unsere Universitäten für ausländische Studenten nicht attraktiv sind', *Die Welt*, 17 July 1999.

Carrington, W.J. and E. Detragiache, E. (1999), 'How Extensive is the Brain Drain? ', *Finance & Development*, **36**, June 1999, 46-49.

Das Parlament (1999), 'Ausländische Studierende – Willkommene Gäste – Eine Fachtagung. Lernen in Deutschland – Noch Attraktiv? ', 12/19 November 1999.

Fischer, P. (1999), *On the Economics of Immobility*, Bern: Paul Haupt.

Fischer, P., R. Martin and Th. Straubhaar (1997): 'Should I Stay or Should I Go? ', in T. Hammar et al. (eds.): *International Migration, Immobility and Development*, Oxford/New York: Berg, 49-90.

Grubel, H.G. and A. Scott (1966), 'The International Flow of Human Capital', *American Economic Review*, **56**, 268-274.

Jaffe, A.B. (1989), 'Real Effects of Academic Research', *American Economic Review*, **79**, 957-970.

List, J. (1998), *Lehr- und Forschungsstandort Deutschland*, Köln: Deutscher Instituts Verlag.

Lucas, R. E. (1988), 'On the mechanics of economic development, *Journal of Monetary Economics*, **22**, 3-42.

Lucas, R. E. (1990), 'Why Doesn't Capital Flow from Rich to Poor Countries?', *American Economic Review*, **80**, 92-96.

Mahroum, S. (1999), 'Skilled Labour (Competing for the Highly Skilled: Europe in Perspective)', *Science and Public Policy*, **26**, 17-25.

Mahroum, S. (2000): *The International Mobility of Highly Skilled Professionals: The Case of Academics*. PhD dissertation Hamburg: HWWA (forthcoming).

Neue Zürcher Zeitung (2000): 'Förderung des 'Brain Drain' nach Amerika (Visa-Erleichterungen für Wissenschafter und Spezialisten)', No. 61, 13 March 2000.

Romer, Paul M. (1986), 'Increasing Return and Long-Run Growth', *Journal of Political Economy*, **94**, 1002-1037 (original: Working Paper 27, University of Rochester, October 1985).

Romer, Paul M. (1987), 'Growth Based on Increasing Returns Due to Specialization', *American Economic Review*, **77**, 56-62.

Romer, Paul M. (1990), 'Endogenous Technological Change', *Journal of Political Economy*, **98**, 71-102.

Straubhaar, Th. and M. Wolburg (1999): 'Brain Drain and Brain Gain in Europe',

Jahrbücher für Nationalökonomie und Statistik, **218**, 574-604.

Walz, U. (1996), 'Growth (Rate) Effects of Migration', *Zeitschrift für Wirtschafts- und Sozialwissenschaften*, **116**, 199-221.

Wolburg, M. (2000), *On Brain Drain, Brain Gain and Brain Exchange within Europe*, PhD-thesis, Hamburg: HWWA.

Wolter, A. and Th. Straubhaar (1997): *Europeanisation of Production and the Migration of the Highly Skilled*, Hamburg: HWWA.

Zucker, L.G., M.R. Darby and J. Armstrong (1998), 'Geographically Localized Knowledge', *Economic Inquiry*, **36**, 65-86.

Zucker, L.G., M.R. Darby and M.B.Brewer (1998), 'Intellectual Human Capital and the Birth of U.S. Biotechnology Enterprises', *American Economic Review*, **88**, 290-306.

4. Further education in Europe – welcome to the market economy?

Dorothee Becker-Soest and Rüdiger Wink

1. FURTHER EDUCATION – FROM AN UNSALEABLE PRODUCT TO THE GREAT NEW HOPE OF THE KNOWLEDGE SOCIETY

No modern manual of company management, no forward-looking political speech and no reference to the work society of the future is conceivable, at the beginning of the 21st century, without a reference to the overarching importance of education and training, which will certainly increase in the years to come. New interpretations in economic theory for explaining endogenous growth, and models for explaining regional differences in economic development point to the fundamental influence of training schemes on offer, to the quality of labour skills and the ability to generate and above all implement innovations within the economic process (cf. Lucas 1988; Finegold and Soskice 1988; Bode 1998; Klemmer 1998; Keane and Allison 1999). These findings emphasise not only the importance of high-quality primary training and the special opportunities open to highly skilled persons on the international labour markets. But also, buzzwords like 'lifelong learning', 'computer integrated training' and 'new social skills' are evidence for a new understanding of what training implies (cf. Tuijnman and Schömann 1996; Gries et al. 1998). It is no longer viewed as a basis for one's employment future, established primarily in the youth phase and enabling interest to be earned on this investment in training over subsequent decades. A society in which specialised knowledge and skills are progressively devalued by ever-shorter innovation cycles can no longer afford such an interpretation, because the consequence is that a burgeoning group of workers is systematically and permanently excluded from the labour markets on account of their obsolete skills, and that human capital becomes an increasingly scarce resource. Further education, as a process of ongoing skill acquisition during one's career, is therefore becoming an increasingly essential requirement for the following:

- preventing a devaluation of available human capital,
- broadening the basis for innovations and their application in production processes,
- preventing the creation or growth of structural unemployment, and
- maintaining the competitiveness of European locations for inward investment relative to low-wage countries in other parts of the world.

This new assessment of further education relates to a sector that is organised throughout Europe in two largely autonomous segments (cf. Bodenhofer and Ofner 1999). On the one hand, there are many private-sector providers of *further education for managers*; these providers populate a higher price segment. The demand for such services generally comes from companies who want to invest in the personnel development of their management echelons. On the other hand, there are *standardised programmes of further education* on the market that focus on specific areas of expertise and specific occupational domains. Demand arises here either from the personal initiative of employees or as contracts with the labour administration or local government bodies, who expect the chances of integrating unemployed people to improve if further training and retraining are provided. In most European countries, these existing systems of further education do not meet the requirements generated by structural developments (cf. Nuissl 1999; O'Connell 1999). New content and forms of placement are just as much in demand as a new focus on target groups and integration in in-company processes. Further education, as an in-house development tool and a strategy of preventive labour market policy, is therefore on the threshold of incisive changes. The following analysis centres on the manifestations and consequences of this transformation. Specifically, it seeks to answer three questions:

- To what extent have the requirements in respect of continuing vocational training changed, and what instruments are basically available to companies and employees for satisfying these requirements?
- What shortcomings in respect of coordination exist in meeting these needs, and what task must be fulfilled as a result by economic and employment policymakers?
- Against this background, how can selected strategies for reforming further education in European states, and the initiatives of the European Union best be assessed?

After answering these three questions, the chapter concludes with an outlook for the future distribution of responsibilities between the market and the political sphere in managing the supply of and demand for further education.

2. FURTHER EDUCATION AS AN INTEGRAL COMPONENT OF PERSONAL AND IN-COMPANY KNOWLEDGE MANAGEMENT

2.1 Further education and new demands on employees

The member states of the EU differ substantially in the way they organise and utilise initial and further education (cf. Münch 1999; Dicke 1999); these differences will be examined in greater detail in the course of this chapter. Whatever these differences, all systems of further education are subject to similar pressures to adapt, in that global structural trends are imposing new demands on employees. These demands include

- ongoing, short-term adaptation to new fields of activity and new jobs,
- integration within new organisational forms of production, combined with 'social skills' such as team-spirit, sense of responsibility and flexibility,
- customer-focus, even at workplaces in industrial production that are far removed from sales activities,
- willingness and capability of working on a self-employed basis, rather than in doomed industries, and
- ability to integrate oneself into companies with international operations, with all the language and cultural demands this involves.

Responding to these demands is a matter of economic life and death for both companies and their employees. The key starting point for this response is the realisation that the skills and competences of workers are not static entities, defined by the training an employee received at some stage before joining a company and available thenceforth in immutable form. It is rather the case that skills and competences develop continuously, and that they can be influenced both externally, through extra courses and training schemes by professional providers, or internally through integration within business processes. The changing demands levelled at vocational skills also show that such continuous development and improvement is urgently needed if the devaluation of human capital and the loss of competitiveness on the part of employees is to be stopped. From the viewpoint of the company and the employee, the objective must therefore be to deploy the available instruments for modifying skill profiles in such a way that the existing skill profile approaches the required standards in the best possible way. This requires extensive coordination of the various instruments for influencing this process.

This view of how companies and employees organise skilling is a clear indication that the classical form of further education, namely participation in courses and the external communication of vocational expertise, is merely one element in a broad assortment of strategic approaches. Contrary to much academic and political input, further education must be understood in a comprehensive way as the outcome of diverse mechanisms for conveying and adapting new knowledge and experience to employees and unemployed people. Within companies, these mechanisms include the acquisition of skills and routines on-the-job in day-to-day cooperation with others, and through targeted training efforts by co-workers and superiors (cf. Hujer et al. 1999; Wiskemann 2000). At the industry-wide level, they are supplemented by knowledge gained through working with suppliers and customers, examples being training on new equipment, or the definition of new quality standards (cf. Lundvall 1992; Lowey 2000; Cappellin and Orsenigo, Chapter 9 in this volume). Within international competition, it is crucially important for companies that, by optimising internal organisational procedures, they learn to manage knowledge available in the company in such a way that employees are given incentives to activate their knowledge, while at the same time providing the conditions for the dissemination of knowledge within the company and the value-creation chain (cf. Burgel et al. 2000; Mytelka and Delapierre 1999; Senker and Sharp 1996). On the one hand, this enhances the productivity and innovative capacity of a company. On the other, the dissemination of knowledge and know-how puts employees in a stronger position and extends their implicit knowledge.

In this context, further education by professional providers of such services are an integral element in a system of corporate organisation. Such external input is one way of procuring vocational expertise and the general prerequisites for corporate reorganisation. Unlike the traditional demand for further education, the use of externally provided training pertains in rare cases only to standardised content. What is increasingly important is coordination not only with internal organisational procedures and the requirements these impose on employees, but also with existing incentives to enhance skills so that the competences acquired are translated directly into practical activity and expanded upon. This involves three additional dimensions to the relationship between companies, employees and the providers of further education: a performance-related, an organisational and a content-based dimension.

2.2 The performance-related dimension: further education as an element in the personnel development programme

As already touched upon, the communication of vocational skills are one element in a comprehensive, inner-company system of organisation for activating and disseminating knowledge. In selecting and designing further education services, this necessitates close coordination of training measures with internal organisational developments. In each specific case, an answer must be given to the question as to which competences already exist in the company, how these competences are to be activated, what developmental needs exist, which competences must therefore be fostered through further education and how these competences are to be put into effect within the company. Inner-company reorganisation processes, personnel development programmes and further education are closely geared to each other in this process (cf. Klemmer et al. 2000; Wiskemann 2000; O'Dell and Jackson Grayson 1998). Standardised courses cannot meet such needs. What are needed, in contrast, are *customised further education modules* that enable internal demand to be covered on the basis of reorganisation and needs analyses in respect of skill profiles. Providers of further education programmes are therefore increasingly compelled to become *systems providers*, e.g. through internal growth or collaboration with business consultants and other further education providers. Conversely, the organisation and sourcing of further education programmes becomes an integral part of the service range provided by business consultants.

This extended function of further education also leads to changes in the time dimension. In place of one-off training schemes centred on specific dates and times and with a specific syllabus, there is now a development process in which single skilling modules can be coordinated to match the ever-changing job requirements that employees must meet. The function of training is redefined as a consequence. Rather than conveying a distinct body of pertinent skills and knowledge for a specific occupation, training in the future must be focused from the outset on supplementary learning, because new skilling requirements and job changes mean that specific knowledge is inevitably devalued in the course of vocational training (cf. Tuijnman and Schömann 1996; Backes-Gellner 1999). The focal points of training therefore relate to relatively general core qualifications and basic knowledge that then strengthen the worker's abilities to extend his or her skills in a modularised fashion. For each individual employee, this means launching into lifelong learning that protects against the pitfalls of 'missing the boat' as far as structural trends are concerned. For the providers of further education this development involves, besides a focus on systemised programmes, the necessity for greater orientation to long-term customer relations with companies and their employees, in order to provide tailor-made programmes.

2.3 The organisational dimension: further education as the result of participative developments

Changes in the range of training services provided are accompanied by a redefinition of how further education programmes are devised in the first place. In ideal-typical terms, further education programmes are designed in response to existing skill profiles and the specific in-company needs for external knowledge input. The classical form of predefined courses is unable to meet this need for greater flexibility. The precondition is therefore intensive *collaboration* between the company and the provider of further education before any programme is carried out. Given the virtually unforeseeable developments brought about by technological progress and the high specificity of situative needs, it is necessary in many cases that the company and further education provider agree upon content or even work together.

This involvement of the company in further education schemes also continues throughout the actual execution phase and subsequent translation into practice. By coordinating curricula with in-company reorganisation, it is possible to ensure that the skills and knowledge conveyed are genuinely put into practice, thus preventing demotivation on the part of employees who see no meaning or purpose in further education unless it can be applied. 'Distant and computer-based training' provide employees with additional opportunities to adjust the sequence and application of further education as they see fit, and to adapt it to the conditions under which they operate.

This implies additional requirements of a technical, specialist and organisational nature that providers of further education schemes must meet. In technical terms, it is necessary to include and flexibly deploy *modern IT infrastructures and programs*. In terms of professional skills, what are needed are skills in cooperating with companies and employees in order to develop training schemes that match the specific situation. Since the companies themselves do not usually have any conclusive overview of existing skills and development potential, the provider must have a strong customer focus in addition to diversified experience across many different sectors. The effort involved is much greater, given the need to include flexible, specially adapted modules and participative elements – cooperation with companies and employees – in the design of training provision.

2.4 The content dimension: further education as all-round development of competences

The overview of changing requirements in respect of employees' skills and how they are deployed in a company has already shown that skilling in a knowledge society can not be reduced to skilling in the narrow sense of specialised, occupational skills. The increasing trend towards tertiarisation in all areas of the economy, combined with the necessity of greater customer and service focus, as well as changes in the organisation of production that lead to team-spiritedness and a sense of individual responsibility being called for, are among the best-known reasons why 'social skills' are demanded more and more (cf. Klodt et al. 1997; Welfens et al. 1999). Thus, even below the management level, further education is usually more than the conveyance of computer skills, instruction in using new machinery, or language courses, as many prejudices would otherwise suggest.

For the providers of further education schemes, these changes necessitate new types of training and new forms of teaching. Attention is centred less on communicating technical knowledge that is partly learned on the job or during the instruction provided by plant suppliers, but rather the querying and developing of *personal competences*. Such content also reinforces the need to synchronise training with internal organisation processes. Only when employees realise that modified competences are also called for and rewarded in company routines do they receive incentives to become actively involved in further education schemes. The outstanding importance of intensive collaboration between further education providers and companies, as well as integration with extensive in-company reorganisation processes is evidenced here again.

In summary form, there are three trends that shape the development of further education in a society in which knowledge has become a major production factor:

- The qualifications of employees will be based in future above all on the presence of social skills and the capacity of individuals for continuous ('lifelong') development of their knowledge and competences.
- Further education is a major corporate responsibility that involves not only hiring professional providers, but also the optimisation of in-company and inter-company knowledge generation and dissemination.
- The providers of further education services face the challenge of developing comprehensive and situatively adapted systems that enable participative involvement in the design of training by those on the demand side, as well as the fostering of personal social competences.

Until now, this chapter has concentrated on sectoral trends in an industry affected by the transition to a knowledge-based society. In the sections that follow, we examine the extent to which these changes are creating new challenges for economic and employment policymakers. A special emphasis is laid on the consequences for preventive labour market policy.

3. PROMOTING FURTHER EDUCATION – A TASK FOR PREVENTIVE LABOUR MARKET POLICY?

3.1 Reasons for government intervention into markets for further education

Further training and retraining are considered in most European countries to be a typical instrument for improving the labour market chances of unemployed people (cf. Schmid 1996). In addition, there are many initiatives that use further education activities as a means of overcoming structural adjustment problems. The objective in such cases is not so much to support further education management in multinational corporations. It can be assumed for such companies that they are financially and organisationally in a position, as typical consumers of strategic business consultancy services, to adapt their demand for further education to the challenges posed by a knowledge society, without external assistance. Furthermore, these companies are less significant for employment policy because they tend to cut more jobs than they create, whereas new jobs are mainly created in SMEs and newly-established businesses (cf. Fritsch 1997; Fendel and Frenkel 1998; Welfens 1999). With other types of company as well, however, the basic question must be raised from a market economy perspective as to why the state should intervene on its own initiative and in regulatory fashion, rather than allowing the market to ensure appropriate adjustment by companies, employees and further education providers. Three arguments are normally put forward in favour of government intervention: 1) market deficits in establishing and adjusting the further education infrastructure, 2) shortcomings among SMEs with regard to coordination and information, and 3) the neglect of disadvantaged groups on the labour market. These arguments will be scrutinised in the following.

3.2 Deficits in the further education infrastructure

At the beginning of this chapter we mentioned that the 'market' for further education is clearly segmented. On the one hand, there is a high-priced segment geared to multinationals, while on the other, providers have specialised on certain standardised training programmes and conducting government-funded further education measures. Due to the relatively unchanging demand for standard courses over a period of decades, and the granting of government contracts on the basis of personal connections and years of routine in many cases, providers that do not operate in the high-price segment are characterised by relatively low levels of flexibility and market focus (cf. Klemmer et al. 2000; O'Connell 1999; Bodenhofer and Ofner 1999). It was not until governments ran out of money and the number of participants in standardised further education courses dwindled that this group felt compelled to modify the services it provides. Since these are mostly small enterprises with little knowledge of the market, the pace of change is slow. In many cases, they lack the knowledge to design training systems that integrate with reorganisation and personnel development programmes. Furthermore, the image of further education providers among SMEs is too negative for partnerships to develop with the aim of developing new further education programmes.

Policymakers argue, in turn, that government demand and government subsidisation of demand by private-sector companies and employees are needed in order to maintain and reform the existing infrastructure of further education schemes. Without state support, no training programmes would be provided, and structural adjustment would be made more difficult for SMEs and employees below management level. State interventions are also seen as an opportunity for concentrating information about what is required of further education, and for generating targeted initiatives for collaboration between different providers of further education. Programmes such as those organised under Objective 4 of the European Social Fund and the EU Community Initiative ADAPT are therefore aimed at helping innovative further education schemes get off the ground so that they can penetrate the market and disseminate at transboundary level.

Problems arise, however, when start-up support turns into a long-term focus on government support programmes. The programmes referred to were used, for example by classical organisers of publicly funded retraining and employment programmes, to compensate for the disappearance and/or limitation of central government funding. For companies and their employees, as consumers of government funded further education, the question that is often asked concerns the quality and market focus of the provider. Given this uncertainty, there is a risk that SMEs are given incentives to use programmes that are viewed as less urgent, or that were planned anyway (support for the 'second best', or the risk of deadweight). For policymakers, this calls for stricter controls on the innovatory content and the infrastructural contribution of training schemes. From the viewpoint of competition policy, such political selection of individual providers is a dubious practice, since potential entrants to the market for further education services are disadvantaged or without political support when they have to charge higher prices than competitors who receive government funds. To what extent such assistance actually helps to create or expand a market cannot be discovered until government subsidies are removed and providers are put to the test. However, this would require a hard-line approach letting the market filter out less successful providers, thus placing the providers under a permanent existential threat. The intensification of competition for inward investment and the constraints on government budgets can favour such harshness and the termination of long-standing relations between government bodies and further education providers, especially at regional level.

3.3 Promoting further education in SMEs

SMEs face particular problems as consumers of further education services, for three reasons (cf. Heger 1999). First, demand from a single company is too small, from the viewpoint of training providers, to achieve sufficient participant numbers for profitable operations. Cooperation with other companies is often heavy on transaction costs, because corresponding needs are often only present in competitor companies, the will for independence on the part of the entrepreneur can be violated, and experience and capacities are absent. Secondly, the 'market' for further education and consultancy is particularly opaque for SMEs, in that they have little experience and few skilled personnel for such work. The lack of certifications and benchmarking studies make it difficult to access suitable providers, since providers in the high-price segment are not an option for financial reasons. Thirdly, further education in SMEs – especially in combination with major reorganisation – is considered relatively costly, because there are no substitutes for absent staff and knowledge is predominantly conveyed through training on the job and the inter-company division of labour.

At the same time, SMEs are increasingly viewed as the 'backbone' of national employment strategies, since start-ups and structural adjustments create new jobs, while the regional presence of head offices facilitates collaboration in employment programmes. In many European countries and EU programmes, support for further education in SMEs is an explicit goal. Such support primarily entails

- promoting further education cooperation between SMEs in regional and sectoral alliances,
- subsidising specific training schemes for SMEs, and
- measures to sensitise SMEs to the importance of further education and for providing them with information on providers and the quality they offer.

From the market economy perspective, these measures must be evaluated in a differentiated manner. As a basic principle, one must reject the notion that policymakers must educate SMEs about the importance of further education and that the latter must overcome 'entrepreneurial failures'. The pressure to adapt that markets exert is a clear signal to companies that certain development strategies are imperative. 'Failing' companies lose momentum in markets and are punished with exclusion. In many cases, however, companies' dispensing with further education programmes of their own is an indication that alternative in-company and inter-company strategies have their advantages (cf. Huggins 1998; Sforzi 1996). Further training through incompany routines and training within supply chains play a growing role in corporate development strategies. This trend is little perceived by the public due to the internal nature of such arrangements, which means that 'failing' companies can well number among the active personnel developers.

However, in those cases where policymakers act to reduce transaction costs, important stimulation is given to the adaptation of SMEs. Such action can include support for regional and sectoral networks, by providing initial coordination. However, such networks should not be understood as 'all-purpose tools', but must be examined with regard to the special situative features of the case at hand. What is missing quite often at regional level, is an appropriate sectoral mix or people who can breathe life into inter-company cooperation. In such cases, external boosts are unlikely to have much impact. What appears to be more important is a focus on cooperation set-ups already in existence (cf. Heinze et al. 1998; Sternberg 1998). Transaction costs can also be reduced by concentrating and certifying further education programmes. Measures such as the 'University for Industry' in Great Britain, which brings together and initiates further education programmes, or the presentation of exemplary reorganisation and further education schemes in North-Rhine Westphalia (in Germany) are cases in point (cf. Klemmer et al. 2000). On the other hand, there is a latent risk of these measures setting certain priorities (e.g. computer-based training in Great Britain) and targeting certain kinds of programme. Here, too, the evaluation of further education programmes and adjustment strategies of SMEs by the market is decisively important in the medium term, to avoid the risk of a 'pretension of knowledge' (Hayek 1996) through government-funding.

3.4 Further education of disadvantaged groups in the labour market

The term 'Disadvantaged groups in the labour market' refers to people with characteristics that lead to a greater likelihood of them becoming and remaining unemployed. These include age, formal qualifications, gender, nationality and state of health. This group finds it difficult to obtain employment, and is the first to be affected by redundancies (cf. ILO 1999; OECD 1997). Given their particular exposure to labour market risks, this group is disproportionately affected by structural marginalisation. The lack of any consistent integration in corporate processes makes it difficult for them to adapt to changing skill requirements. In order to prevent structural unemployment and permanent exclusion of this group from the labour markets, specific measures have been developed in all European countries to train and employ this target group. As a consequence of changing economic conditions for in-company further education, this training strategy, too, is being confronted with new challenges. Less formal qualifications and evidence of having taken part in government funded employment projects are welcome experience from the viewpoint of companies. Successful skilling and increased employability of unemployed people require a linkage between the conveying of competences and integration in in-company processes.

Since companies are prepared only in rare cases to seek further education for members of these problematic groups, their place is taken on the demand side of the further education markets by government bodies. The structural changes on the further education markets, already referred to, will also lead to repositioning on the part of those providing such services. Mergers to form systems providers, with integrated consultancy and training services, modularised programmes and transboundary market focus are pressurising even established organisers of government-funded training programmes to adapt. Labour administrations and policymaking bodies can only work on the basis of successful training schemes for disadvantaged groups in which competences are gained that are also in demand in the labour markets. When government authorities are the ordering party, this means expanding the group of potential providers to include business consultancies with integrated further education programmes and companies in which integration in in-company routines is assured. Starting points may be provided by the job rotation model in Denmark, which envisages support for in-company further education being combined with temporary vacancies being filled by unemployed people, with the option of gaining in-company experience, and by the organisation of temporary employment for unemployed people in the Netherlands (cf. Jørgensen, Chapter 7 in this volume; Weinkopf 1996). Problems arise here for two reasons. First, there is a risk of 'cream skimming', i.e. support not being used to integrate disadvantaged groups, but rather a situation in which those with greater attractiveness for companies obtain job experience due to their greater capacity for integration (Schmid 1996). Secondly, because of their lower attractiveness as 'stand-ins' or 'temps' and their lack of qualifications, members of disadvantaged groups risk being excluded permanently from the labour markets.

From the market economy perspective, there are two other, fundamental objections. On the one hand, the willingness to cooperate on the part of private-sector companies and large business consultancies is limited. Acceptance generally extends to measures for facilitating in-company reorganisation and training; the integration of disadvantaged groups, who mostly entail higher costs for integration and further training, is generally met with reservations. On the other hand, any government-sponsored demand for further education is open to the accusation of assuming knowledge about labour market demands that cannot be present unless tested by markets themselves. A focus on occupational profiles that are already heavily subscribed and will be filled to overflowing in the future, and support for skills that cannot prevail in the market are potential consequences. Proposals by market economy advocates point in the direction of low-wage sectors and the issuing of skilling and integration certificates to disadvantaged groups of the unemployed that can then be used by those concerned to further their own training or to enter directly into employment (Berthold and Fehn 1998; Snower 1994). Such an approach takes particular account of the different skilling potentials of those affected. Training is a not a promising strategy for all disadvantaged groups, because basic skills and motivation are sometimes absent. However, in many European countries these economically informed proposals run contrary to political practice. Precisely in countries like Germany, targeted state management of skill acquisition, and the maintenance of relatively high wage levels by international comparison, even for standardised and less training-intensive jobs, are viewed as essential components of a socially equitable system. The result for labour administrations and political decision-makers is a continuous challenge to adapt the competitiveness of those in disadvantaged groups to the rising and changing demands of the labour markets.

In summary, the need and the scope for action in connection with government intervention into the provision of further education are also changing, against a background of structural trends in a knowledge-based society. Three theses characterise this shift:

- The traditional segmentation of further education can no longer be upheld in view of the trend towards integrated, systems-based programmes in response to in-company reorganisation processes. Convergence leads not only to greater pressures to adapt on the part of former organisers of government-funded further education, but also to a broader range of further education providers for SMEs and employees below management level.
- This means that for state interventions to foster the provision of further education the support instruments must shift to measures aimed at reducing transaction costs, e.g. for defining and communicating quality standards, for promoting collaboration between SMEs to form buying collectives, and for obtaining information on new training and consulting products. In contrast, direct financial support for further education schemes runs the risk of creating products that would otherwise have no prospects of market acceptance, and in this way risks missing the opportunity to keep up with worldwide structural trends.

- On the other hand, markets are becoming a central focus in the selection of further education services. The decisive criterion for the sustained success of further education programmes is the compatibility with in-company and inter-company strategies for knowledge management. For providers of standardised further education services and publicly funded retraining measures, this makes it necessary to develop a customer focus in order to cope with new competitors and market relations.

4. FURTHER EDUCATION AND MARKET CO-ORDINATION – SOUGHT AND FOUND?

This chapter begins with a somewhat provocative title suggesting that further education in most European countries is not a service like others which are exclusively traded in private-sector markets. There are many state-funded schemes, certain further education clients are subsidised, or, as in the case of unemployed people, are compelled by the threat of financial sanctions to buy in further education services. The following overviews convey a brief impression of the diversity of further education systems, based on a description of institutional conditions and financial engagement in five countries.

Table 4.1: Basic concepts and objectives of further education

	Objective	*Target group*
Denmark	Basic and supplementary vocational training; further education for adjustment and advancement	Unskilled and semi-skilled workers; skilled workers
France	Preparation for work; further education for adjustment and advancement; retraining	Young workers with no training; employees, especially if threatened by unemployment
Germany	Further training and retraining; 'learning on the job'	Non-employed people and employees
Great Britain	Obtaining certain skill levels	Employees and job-seekers
Italy	Regional initial and further education, as well as specialisation; in-company training for adjustment and advancement	(Young) unemployed people; employees

Source: modified from Münch (1999), 14ff.

This institutional diversity shows that there are different experiences in the management of further education by government bodies. In those countries where the state plays a relatively important role in providing further education programmes, many problems have arisen in connection with incentives and quality. Denmark, for example, is a country with a particularly high level of acceptance and support in society for further education, and exemplifies an early transition from state-managed further education schemes to management through demand-side preferences, combined with increasing autonomy of further education providers. The result over the past decade has been the generation of manifold new schemes that facilitated, above all, the participation of those on the demand side as well as the development of social competencies. Conversely, Great Britain is an example of a further education system in which little importance is attached to formal qualifications, and where the state is attempting, by subsidising young workers and job-seekers and exerting direct influence on the further education provided by state-commissioned or state-supported bodies, to enhance the attractiveness of further education. Approaches involving control through government demand are shown to be less successful compared to the mobilisation of demand with 'learning accounts' and 'training credits'.

Table 4 2: Funding systems for continuing vocational training

	Funding volume (figures for single years between 1987 and 1992)	*Percentage of total employees* (in %)	*Funding rule*
France	18 787 MECU	33	Company contribution, depending on wages and salaries paid
Germany	34 250 MECU	approx. 25	Collective bargaining arrangements
Great Britain	23 224 MECU	48	None
Italy	5200 MECU	3	Company contribution, depending on wages and salaries paid

Source: modified from Münch (1999), 23ff.

A common feature of European approaches to promoting further education is the realisation that the selection and evaluation of further education programmes by market demand is increasingly important, in that a high and broad-based effectiveness of skilling strategies cannot be achieved until acceptance by private-sector markets has been gained. The focus on market allocation also brings us to the direction taken by preventive labour market policy, which is to keep pace with structural trends on internationalised markets by increasing the competitiveness of people threatened by unemployment.

The prerequisite for such a market-based strategy succeeding is the willingness to accept the control mechanisms of the market, also in the field of further education. Two aspects in particular deserve mention here that generally meet with little political acceptance. First, it is inevitable in markets that less successful providers must abandon the market if they are unable to adapt their products and services to demand-side preferences. Government-funded measures and sustained support to service providers to adapt to new further education requirements make it difficult to enhance the competitiveness of employees and reduce transparency for companies and workers. The quality of training schemes can become a secondary aspect in decisions on further education if state support means that prices are artificially lowered. Secondly, the integration of further education into strategies for in-company knowledge management and lifelong growth of competences leads to increasing diversity and complexity of occupational biographies and 'skilling careers'. Precisely in those countries with a highly-developed tradition of rigidly defined vocational training and occupations, the transition to modularised and case-related skilling processes is difficult to manage. In many cases, companies and employees are thought to invest too little in further education, whereby in-company and inter-company elements of knowledge transfer are overlooked. In future, skills and competences on the part of employees will increasingly resemble 'patchworks' and will be comprised of a large number of separate learning modules and in-company routines. The aim will not be to define in advance the content and processes of further education throughout an occupational career, but rather to ensure that the separate programmes on offer match real demands. To that extent, the changes occurring in the field of further education have feedback effects on the organisation and content on school-based education and vocational training. In conclusion, the arrival of further education in a market economy can only be the first step on the road to a market-based education and knowledge system.

REFERENCES

Backes-Gellner, U. (1999), 'Betriebliche Aus- und Weiterbildung im internationalen Vergleich', in: D. Timmermann (ed.), *Berufliche Weiterbildung in europäischer Perspektive*, Berlin: Duncker & Humblot, 65-92.

Berthold, N. and R. Fehn (1998), 'Die zehn Gebote für den Arbeitsmarkt', in P. Klemmer, D. Becker-Soest and R. Wink (eds), *Liberale Grundrisse einer zukunftsfähigen Gesellschaft*, Baden-Baden: Nomos, 353-372.

Bode, E. (1998), *Lokale Wissensdiffusion und regionale Divergenz in Deutschland*, Tübingen: Mohr.

Bodenhofer, H.-J. and F. Ofner (1999), 'Weiterbildung nach der Lehre', in D. Timmermann (ed.), *Berufliche Weiterbildung in europäischer Perspektive*, Berlin:
Duncker & Humblot, 31-63.

Burgel, O., G. Murray, A. Fier and G. Licht (2000), *The Rapid Internationalisation of
High-Tech Young Firms in Germany and United Kingdom*, London, Mannheim:
Forschungsbericht.

Dicke, H. (1999), *Fortbildung in Europa. Systeme, Strukturen, Ergebnisse*, Tübingen:
Mohr.

Fendel, R. and M. Frenkel (1998), 'Do Small and Medium-Sized Enterprises Stabilize
Employment? Theoretical Considerations and Evidence from Germany', *Zeitschrift für Wirtschafts- und Sozialwissenschaften*, **118**, 163-183.

Finegold, D. and D. Soskice (1988), 'The Failure of Training in Britain: Analysis and
Prescription', *Oxford Review of Economic Policy*, **4**, 1-13.

Fritsch, M. (1997), 'New Firms and Regional Employment Change', *Small Business
Economics*, **9**, 437-448.

Gries, T., S. Jungblut and H. Meyer (1998), 'Humankapitalabschreibung, Wachstum
und Arbeitslosigkeit', in R.K. v. Weizsäcker (ed.), *Bildung und
Wirtschaftswachstum*, Berlin: Duncker & Humblot, 105-124.

Hayek, F.A. v. (1996), 'Die Anmaßung von Wissen', in F.A. v. Hayek, *Die Anmaßung von Wissen. Neue Freiburger Studien*, Tübingen: Mohr, 3-15.

Heger, B. (1999), *Weiterbildungsinteressen und Weiterbildungsmöglichkeiten in
mittelständischen Unternehmen. Eine empirische Untersuchung in nordhessischen
Betrieben*, Frankfurt: Peter Lang.

Heinze, R.G. et al. (1998), 'Industrial Clusters and the Governance of Change: Lessons from Northrhine-Westphalia' in H.-J. Braczyk (ed.), *Regional Innovation
Systems. The Role of Governances in a Globalized World*, London: Macmillan,
263-283.

Huggins, R. (1998), 'Local Business Co-operation and Training and Enterprise Councils: The Development of Inter-Firm Networks', *Regional Studies*, **32**, 813-826.

Hujer, R., K.-O. Maurer and M. Wellner (1999): 'Analyzing the Effects of On-the-Job
vs. Off-the-Job Training on Unemployment Duration in West Germany', in L.
Bellmann; V. Steiner (eds.), *Panelanalysen zu Lohnstruktur, Qualifikation und
Beschäftigungsdynamik*, Nürnberg: IAB, 203-237.

ILO - International Labour Office (ed., 1999), *Key Indicators of the Labour Market*
(KILM), Geneva: ILO.

Keane, J. and J. Allison (1999), 'The Intersection of the Learning Region and Local
Regional Development: Analysing the Role of Higher Education', *Regional Studies*, **33**, 896-902.

Klemmer, P. (1998), 'Wandel in der Konvergenzforschung', in U. Heilemann et al.
(eds), *Entgrenzung als Erkenntnis- und Gestaltungsaufgabe*, Berlin: Duncker &
Humblot, 33-46

Klemmer, P., K. Baumgart, D. Becker-Soest and R. Wink (2000), *Innovative Beschäftigungsinstrumente in Bochum. Analyse der institutionellen Voraussetzungen
ihrer transnationalen Implementation*, Bochum: mimeo.

Klodt, H., R. Maurer and A. Schimmelpfennig (1997), *Tertiarisierung in der
deutschen Wirtschaft*, Tübingen: Mohr.

Lowey, S. (2000), 'Unternehmenskooperationen, Globalisierung und die Aufwertung
des Regionalen', *Jahrbuch für Regionalwissenschaft*, **20**, 55-77.

Lucas, R.E. jr. (1988), 'On the Mechanics of Economic Development', *Journal of
Monetary Economics*, **22**, 3-42.

Lundvall, B.-A. (1992), 'User-Producer Relationships, National Systems of Innovation and Internationalisation', in B.-A. Lundvall (ed.), *National Systems of Innovation: Towards a Theory of Innovation and Interactive Learning*, London: Macmillan, 45-67.

Münch, J. (1999), 'Berufliche Weiterbildung in der Europäischen Union – ausgewählte Aspekte und Problemfelder', in D. Timmermann (ed.), *Berufliche Weiterbildung in europäischer Perspektive*, Berlin: Duncker & Humblot, 11-30.

Mytelka, C.K. and M. Delapierre (1999), 'Strategic Partnerships, Knowledge-Based Networked Oligopolies, and the State', in A.C. Cutler, V. Haufler and T. Porter (eds.), *Private Authority and International Affairs*, Albany: State University of New York Press, 129-149.

Nuissl, E. (ed.; 1999), *Adult Education and Training in Europe. Evaluation of the Adult Education Action within the SOCRATES Programme*, Frankfurt: Deutsches Institut für Erwachsenenbildung.

O'Connell, P.J. (1999), *Adults in Training: An International Comparison of Continuing Education and Training*, Paris: OECD.

O'Dell, C. and C. Jackson Grayson (1998), *If Only We Knew What We Know. The Transfer of Internal Knowledge and Best Practise*, New York: Free Press.

OECD – Organisation for Economic Co-operation and Development (ed., 1997): *Employment Outlook*, Paris: OECD.

Schmid, G. (1996): 'New Public Management of Further Training', in G. Schmid, J. O'Reilly and K. Schömann (eds.), *International Handbook of Labour Market Policy and Evaluation*, Cheltenham, UK, and Brookfield, US: Edward Elgar, 462-488.

Senker, J. and M. Sharp (1996), 'Organizational Learning in Cooperative Alliances: Some Case Studies in Biotechnology', *Technology Analysis and Strategic Management*, 9, 35-51.

Sforzi, F. (1996), 'Local Systems of Small and Medium-Sized Firms and Industrial Changes', in: OECD (ed.), *Networks of Enterprises and Local Development. Competing and Cooperating in Local Productive Systems*, Paris: OECD, 99-119.

Snower, D. (1994), *Converting Unemployment Benefits into Employment Subsidies*, London: CEPR-Paper No. 930.

Sternberg, R. (1998), 'Innovierende Industrieunternehmen und ihre Einbindung in intraregionale versus interregionale Netzwerke', *Raumforschung und Raumordnung*, 56, 288-298.

Tuijnman, A.C. and K. Schömann (1996), 'Life-long Learning and Skill Formation', in G. Schmid, G., J. O'Reilly and K. Schömann (eds.), *International Handbook of Labour Market Policy and Evaluation*, Cheltenham, UK, and Brookfield, US: Edward Elgar, 462-488.

Weinkopf, C. (1996), *Arbeitskräftepools. Überbetriebliche Beschäftigung im Spannungsfeld von Flexibilität, Mobilität und sozialer Sicherheit*, München et al.: Rainer Hampp.

Welfens, P.J.J. (1999), *Globalization of the Economy, Unemployment and Innovation. Structural Change, Schumpetrian Adjustment, and New Policy Challenges*, Berlin et al.: Springer.

Welfens, P.J.J., J.T. Addison, D.B. Audretsch, T. Gries and H. Grupp (1999), *Globalization, Economic Growth and Innovation Dynamics*, Berlin: Springer.

Wiskemann, G. (2000), *Strategisches Human Resource Management und Arbeitsmarkt. Personalplanung als Grundlage eines systematischen Beschäftigungsmanagement*, Baden-Baden: Nomos.

5. 'How long does it take to turn around a tanker?' - Worker displacement and preventive labour market policy in Germany

Matthias Knuth

---

1. INTRODUCTION

In most EU member countries, it seems to be very popular to introduce new political strategies to prevent unemployment. But what are the actual characteristics of *preventive* labour market policy and can we identify a drift towards such strategies in countries which are affected by intensive problems of structural unemployment? This chapter aims to develop some initial answers to some of the questions belonging to the great confusion about preventive labour market policy and its possibilities. The analysis begins by defining the term 'preventive labour market policy' in greater detail so that the specifically German approach in this field can be characterised. The opposite of preventive labour market policy is then described at length, namely the largely unbroken acceptance in Germany of unemployment at the end of one's working life as a form of early retirement that even seems a worthy goal for many (Section 3). Scope for preventive labour market policy can only ensue to the extent that this pattern is overcome. Section 4 deals with attempts to turn the tanker in this direction. An assessment is made of the reforms of labour market policy introduced in 1998. A brief comparison with current practice in Austria and France is provided so that recent German experience can be framed in a broader perspective.

2. PREVENTIVE LABOUR MARKET POLICY

This chapter focuses on only one aspect of preventive labour market policy. In order to specify this particular aspect, we first outline the entire range of preventive labour market policy so that the current stage in the development of preventive labour market policy in the various fields of action can then be characterised.

2.1 Classification according to stages of intervention

Preventive labour market policy refers to early interventions in the unemployment process aimed either at preventing unemployment from arising in the first place, or, at least, at stopping it from being too firmly established. Preventive approaches can be classified according to the time of intervention relative to the time at which unemployment would be expected to arise were no intervention made. One can distinguish between three stages in the production of unemployment risks:

(1) *Exposure*: in this stage, the factors determining unemployment take shape and form. A distinction can be drawn between a) individual and b) company-based risk factors. These different types mutually interact and reinforce each other. For example, relying on obsolete production concepts threatens the competitiveness of a company and the employability of its workers, who may eventually be thrown onto the labour market with outdated skills and work habits if the company should collapse.

(2) *Overt threat:* The company plans to reduce the workforce size, to close a plant or a department. Specifically identified workers must expect to become redundant unless effective action is taken to ward off such unemployment. The concept 'threatened by unemployment' is defined by law in Germany and forms the starting point for interventions of active labour market policy.

(3) *Manifestation:* Unemployment has already arisen. In this stage, one can only speak of preventive intervention if it occurs within the first few weeks after a person signs on the dole. Everything thereafter is 'curative' policymaking for those workers who are already on their way out of the labour market.

Individual exposure to unemployment arises not only in the employment system, but is also rooted in primary socialisation, in the educational and vocational training system and in migration policies. In the same vein, macroeconomic policymaking and regional development policy can also be viewed in terms of unemployment prevention. However, the latter are autonomous policy fields that should not be subsumed under labour market policy.

Table 5.1: Stages of preventive intervention

Exposure		Threat	Manifestation
Individual factors	Company-based factors		
No vocational training, or only in outdated form; Many years of service in same company; Company-specific skills; Advanced age; Inadequate language skills	Lack of innovation; organisational shortcomings; Focus on price-based rather than quality-based competition	Foreseeable loss of employment; No new job prospects; Limited responsibility	Registration as unemployed; Identification of placement barriers

2.2 Preventive labour market policy in Germany

The plea for preventive labour market policy is an old one in Germany, but as far as practical implementation is concerned, it is still a recent and undeveloped area of political action. This development can be characterised as follows, structured according to the three stages of intervention distinguished above:

1. Training employees is seen as something for which companies bear responsibility. State intervention or regulation of continuing training is rejected above all by employers and their federations (Beer 1997). Modernisation of companies is thought to come under innovation and economic policy, and is carried out with no explicit focus on employment and the labour market. In Germany, there is no preventive labour market policy in the fullest sense of the term, i.e. early intervention in the very stage at which the employment level is exposed to risk.[1]
2. Interventions when there is a definite threat of unemployment, which operate before unemployment actually occurs but which are usually unable to prevent job losses, are a key element in the labour market policy reforms in place since 1998.[2] These reforms will be described in Section 4.2 below.
3. According to the literal wording of the law, every unemployed person in Germany must be available for placement by the employment office and must utilise every opportunity to find employment. However, specific planning of intervention is not envisaged until the person has been un-

employed for six months, and can also be postponed if measures 'are not yet necessary or possible'. Such intervention, if it occurs at all, comes too late and is too non-committal, so one cannot speak here of any preventive labour market policy in relation to manifest unemployment.

In Germany, the only existing form of generally applicable preventive labour market policy is found in the middle stage of intervention, where there is an overt threat of unemployment. This chapter therefore concentrates on that particular phase, when the person concerned is still employed, but the decision has already been taken to make him or her redundant. In addition to the workers affected, the partners involved in preventive intervention in this phase are necessarily the employers and the works councils. In order to understand the problems faced when implementing a specific form of preventive labour market policy in the 'overt threat' phase, it is necessary to describe how the social partners at company level typically and traditionally deal with job cuts.

3. PASSIVE ADAPTATION TO STRUCTURAL CHANGE: OLD-AGE UNEMPLOYMENT AND EARLY RETIRE-MENT

Any description of how job cuts are traditionally handled must begin by examining the traces that this procedure leaves on the labour market. We follow these traces back to the sectors and companies in which they begin, then describe the conditional framework in social security law before finally characterising the overall pattern of passive adaptation.

3.1 Unemployment and age

Combating youth unemployment is correctly a key topic on the political agenda, and one on which government and the social partners reach agreement most easily in their attempts to forge an 'Alliance for Jobs'. Germany has been relatively successful in this field up to now – in West Germany at least: the unemployment rate among young people under 25 has remained slightly under the general unemployment rate despite the fall in employment levels during the 1990s. In no other EU country is the ratio between the youth employment rate and the general unemployment rate as good. The percentage of young people among the unemployed has fallen considerably, although this is due in large measure to demographic factors.

Figure 5.1: Unemployment by age groups, West Germany, 1983-1998

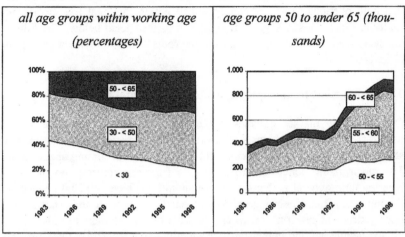

| all age groups within working age (percentages) | age groups 50 to under 65 (thousands) |

Source: Official information released by the Federal Labour Office, annual figures for 1998

Inversely to the declining proportion of young people among the unemployed, that of older people aged 50 and more has risen sharply, primarily because of the dramatic increase in the absolute numbers of unemployed people in the 55 to < 60 age group. This growth is only partially the result of demographic factors. This explains the divergent growth of unemployment rates according to age group (cf. Table 5.2).

Table 5.2: Age-group-specific and general unemployment rates in western Germany[4]

Age group	1992	1998
< 20 years of age	5.5	9.4
20 – < 25 years of age	6.2	10.8
50 – < 55 years of age	6.9	12.3
55 – < 60 years of age	15.2	22.4
60 – < 65 years of age	15.9	20.5
Total	7.3	10.9

Source: Arbeitsmarkt in Zahlen 1998, Bundesanstalt für Arbeit (Labour Market Figures, 1998, Federal Labour Office)

Whereas unemployment among young people is a constant issue, unemployment among the older population is mentioned, if at all, as a individual's problem, not a social problem. Early retirement is debated as a public issue in Germany, where there is little opposition to the notion that early retirement is an instrument by which the old make way so that young people can be employed. The rampant problem of long-term unemployment is the subject of a very different debate. However, there is no focus in public debate on the fact that both phenomena are intimately linked within the legal framework currently in force. This linkage is discussed in further detail below. The following section examines the question as to the roots of unemployment among the older generation.

3.2 Employment-to-unemployment flows by age and sector

Official labour market statistics in Germany are highly inadequate for the purposes of structural analysis of flows. The employment-to-unemployment statistics suggest that older workers are less at risk of becoming unemployed. The unsurprising conclusion to be drawn from the statistics on those re-entering employment is that the older unemployed have minimal chances of finding a new job. Their unemployment usually ends when they start receiving a retirement pension. Yet where do the growing numbers of older unemployed people we find in the statistics actually come from? Are they formerly young unemployed people who have stayed unemployed and are now old? Or does the relatively small number of older people moving from employment to unemployment gradually accumulate to the levels shown because unemployment is so insurmountable and tenacious when older people are affected?

Questions like these can only be answered using representative data on individual life-courses concerning employment and unemployment. We have just ventured into the very first steps towards investigations of this kind. The following analysis[5] is based on the IAB Employee Sample (cf. Bender and Hilzendegen 1995). As for employment, this set of data contains only employment relationships subject to social security contributions.[6] As far as unemployment is concerned, it contains only successful claimants of some sort of wage replacement. Displaced workers will be eligible for such a replacement as a rule since they will usually have been working and paying contributions for sufficient periods before entering unemployment.

Based on these data, employment-to-unemployment transitions by age, computed as percentages of employees of the respective age, for three different years (1980 – 1988 – 1994) have been analysed. In our context, the following results are worth mentioning:

- The incidence of entering unemployment from employment is highest for the young (presumably occurring, in many cases, on completion of their apprenticeships) and for older workers approaching their sixtieth birthday.

Table 5.3: Employment-to-unemployment flows by age and all sectors

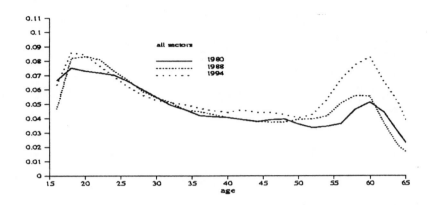

Table 5.4: Employment-to-unemployment flows in the commercial sector

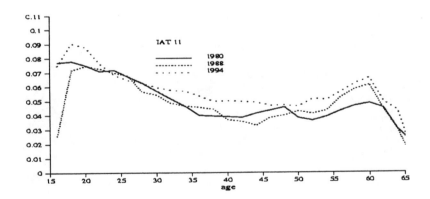

Table 5.5: Employment-to-unemployment flows in the business sector

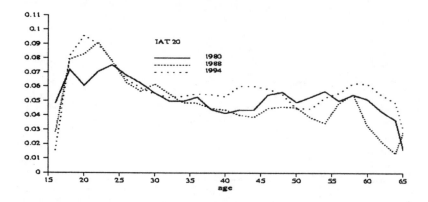

Table 5.6: Employment-to-unemployment flows in the engineering sector

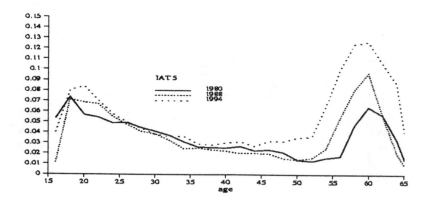

• Whereas there has been almost no change regarding the risk of unemployment for ages of 25 to 40, the peak for the young has risen slightly, mainly during the 1980s, and the peak for the older employees has risen dramatically, mainly in 1994 as compared to 1988. In 1994, exits from employment into unemployment exceeded 8% of the employees just below 60.

We may conclude from these results that there is a pervasive pattern of exit into unemployment among employees approaching the ends of their working lives. However, this pattern is by no means uniform, as the analysis for some sub-sectors shows. In the engineering industries[7], the trend towards rising rates of exit into unemployment for workers in their fifties is much more conspicuous than it is in the employment system as a whole. In commerce as a traditional service sector, the old age peak of exits into unemployment has just recently begun to form. In business services, as a newly emerging service sector, we do not yet find a clear exit pattern related to older age.

While in our analysis employment-to-unemployment transitions were broken down by sectors, using sectoral levels of employment as the category of reference, Wübbeke (1999) broke these data down by birth cohorts and gender in order to show how pervasive unemployment is as a link between employment and retirement in individual life-courses.[8] It was found that between 20% and 25% of men (but also between 17% and 21% of women) within each of the birth cohorts of 1920 to 1925 drew unemployment compensation immediately after the last job they held in their lives (Wübbeke 1999: 110). Disaggregation by age at the time of exit showed marked peaks at 59. There was also a strong and highly significant influence of establishment size: Male workers in establishments with 500 or more employees in their late fifties bear the highest risk of experiencing unemployment as the final stage of their working lives (Wübbeke 1999: 115).

Findings like these are somewhat surprising, considering the legal, institutional and cultural factors that operate in Germany: the family model based on the 'male breadwinner' continues to hold sway in West Germany to a much greater extent than in most European societies or in eastern Germany. Two of the three social selection criteria applied to layoffs – age and length of service[9] – place older people at an advantage compared to younger employees. The 'years of service' criterion favours those with a continuous employment history – men, in other words. Compliance with statutory rules is monitored by works councils and trade unions more effectively in larger than in smaller companies[10], yet older men in large industrial companies face the greatest risk of becoming unemployed – if one ignores the youngest age group up to 25.

This paradox can only be explained in terms of the linkage in Germany between unemployment and retirement.

3.3 Unemployment as a passage into retirement

Even though the statutory retirement age in Germany is 65 for men, the proportion of those belonging to the cohort born between 1920 and 1925 and whose last notification of employment to the social insurance bodies occurred when they were aged 65 or 66 was a mere 8% (Wübbeke 1999: 108). This means that very few indeed actually work until they are 65[11]; early retirement has formed a large percentage of all passages into retirement since as far back as the 1970s, and the figure increased still further during the 1990s (cf. Figure 5.2). Nevertheless, between the end of employment and official retirement there is a gap that is increasingly filled by unemployment. In 1996, 36% of men and 11% of women in western Germany were unemployed prior to receiving their retirement pension (Rehfeld 1998: 169f.)[12]. For men, unemployment is the most common status before retiring, i.e. more men proceed from unemployment to retirement than from employment or non-employment. The laws governing retirement and pensions are partly the reason for this pattern.

Unemployment lasting for at least 12 months gives entitlement to an old-age pension at the age of 60 – until recently to a full pension without deductions. In addition, women have the option of retirement at 60, irrespective of their employment situation, if they have paid social security contributions for more than ten years after their 40th birthday.[13] Both sexes may receive a pension at 63 if they have paid contributions for at least 35 years. Persons who cannot work because of chronic illness or disability receive a special category of pension until they are transferred to an old-age pension – prematurely at 60, if they have managed to pay contributions for a sufficient period before the disability stopped them from working, and otherwise at 65.

The relevant conclusion in our context is that for German males without an officially recognised physical handicap or disability, unemployment lasting for at least 12 months is the only pathway to an early pension at 60. Pensions by virtue of unemployment have steadily become more frequent since the mid-1970s and they have exploded in the last downswing since 1992 (cf. Figure 5.2).

If East Germany is included in our analysis (see the group of columns on the right of figure 5.2), the drama of the German pension system stands out even more clearly. East Germany accounts for about 25% of the population of West Germany, but in the peak year of 1995 its contribution to early retirement because of unemployment was of an order of magnitude approaching West German levels.[14] This shock to the pension financing system formed the background to the pension reforms enacted between 1995 and 1997, which are described below.

Figure 5.2: Entries into old-age pensions by category of entitlement, 1960 to 1997, West Germany (1995 to 1997 also for Germany as a whole), thousands

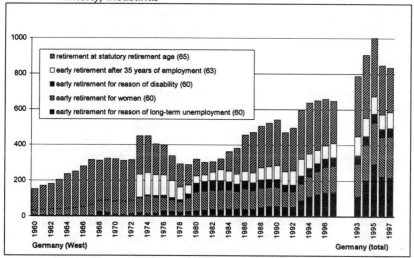

Source: VDR (Association of Public Pension Insurance Providers);
www.vdr.de/Internet/vdr/Statistik

Table 5.7: Exit paths from employment (examples; age in years/months)

	Without unemployment assistance		with unemployment assistance		with unemployment assistance
			Legal framework 1987-1997		since 1.4.1997
Age	Event/Status	Age	Event/Status	Age	Event/Status
		55/0	Exit to unemployment	55/0	Exit into unemployment
57/4	Exit to unemployment		32 months' unemployment benefit		26 months' unemployment benefit
	32 months' unemployment benefit	57/8	28 months' unemployment benefit	57/2	34 months' unemployment benefit
60	Early pension due to unemployment	60	Early pension due to unemployment	60	Early pension due to unemployment

A major factor contributing to the formation of this passage to early retirement via unemployment was the progressive, age-based graduation of unemployment benefit entitlement, in a series of stages between 1984 and 1987, from a general 12 months to as much as 32 months for older recipients. If this eligibility period is fully exploited, it is possible for an older worker to exit working life at the age of 57 years and four months. If unemployment assistance, the lower benefit level granted for an unlimited period after unemployment benefit expires, is also made use of, it is possible to stop working even earlier. However, the reforms enacted in 1997/98 reduced the eligibility period for unemployment benefit, in that entitlement to the maximum duration of unemployment benefit can no longer be reached by the age of 55.

3.4 The traditional pattern of passive manpower reductions

The paradoxical situation in which unemployment among older workers has grown dramatically and disproportionately despite the greater legal protection afforded this group, can be explained as follows. Unemployment is an acceptable fate for many older men because it enables them to receive a pension at 60 that they would not otherwise have received until the age of 63 at the earliest[15]. If the unemployment benefit received is improved by a compensatory settlement, this option is even more attractive. Particularly for those who experience working life as arduous and of little motivating interest, a net income of 75-80% without the burden of work can be a welcome alternative. Although concentrating workforce downsizing on older employees may be expensive for companies, given that these workers receive the highest compensation, this is offset to a certain extent by the fact that redundancies are thus achieved with little conflict, and that the average age of the workforce is reduced.[16] The trade unions are interested in middle-aged workers keeping their jobs as paying members, and staying within the trade union organisation. Their rationale for laying off older workers is that the latter would make room for younger people. The empirical evidence for such a generational swap is rather weak, however (see Knuth 1999a), because the early retirement option is mainly exercised in companies and sectors with declining employment levels and a low rate of new recruitment.

The upshot is that early retirement is the path that works councils and employers always find it easiest to agree upon in companies where the workforce is reduced. This has decisive consequences for preventive labour market policy in Germany. Preventive labour market policy makes little sense for people who are at the end of their working lives and to whom unemployment benefit plus compensation is offered as a bridge to a retirement pension. This form of unemployment, which occurs extensively in Germany, cannot be overcome either in the overt threat stage or after it is manifested, by preventive employment promotion measures aimed at searching for and finding a new job. The only source of help would be intervention during the earlier exposure stage (see Table 5.1) that either helps to prevent job cuts in the first place or leads to older workers remaining in employment until they have reached retiring age. The consequence in the case of unavoidable workforce reductions would be that the burden of adapting would have to be borne by younger and middle-aged employees. These would then be the addressees of preventive support.

The pension reforms in the 1995–1997 period and the reform of labour market policy in 1997/98 are aimed, on the one hand, at making early exit from working life unattractive, and, on the other, at providing employers and works councils with instruments for promoting re-employment and hence for laying off young and middle-aged workers at less social cost.

4. ATTEMPTS AT REORIENTATION: REFORMS OF THE PENSION SYSTEM AND LABOUR MARKET POLICY

Since 1990, the burden of economic restructuring in the wake of German unification has been financed in large measure by transfers within the social insurance systems, causing contribution levels to rise to unprecedented levels[17]. When the boom triggered by German unification began to wane, West Germany was hit by a wave of redundancies, especially in industry and the building sector. In the same period, from 1992 onwards, the populous age group comprising all those born between 1934 and 1941 reached early retirement age. Economic, structural and demographic trends converged and reinforced each other, confronting social policymakers with a choice between (1) increasing contributions to even higher levels, (2) reducing benefit levels or (3) limiting any further growth in the number of people dependent on such benefits. To prevent contributions from increasing still further, the decision was made for a combination of options (2) and (3). With regard to pensions, in particular, workers theoretically have the choice for a number of years of either accepting a lower pension or working longer. This means that the focus on shortening working life, raised in 1984 to government policy status by the ruling Christian–Liberal coalition, was officially reversed in 1995 by the very same government coalition. The new government coalition of Social Democrats and Greens that came to office in autumn 1998 has to date failed to elaborate a clear strategy on this issue.

The following analysis is concentrated on those measures aimed at preventing the premature exit of older workers and at promoting the re-employment of young and middle-aged workers when jobs are cut. A comparison with the strategic approaches adopted in two neighbouring European states serves to sharpen our view for the specific characteristics of preventive labour market policy in Germany.

4.1 Sanctions against the passive pattern of workforce adjustments

Between 1995 and 1997, changes were made to the pension laws with the aim of gradually making 65 the normal retiring age in actual practice as well. Early pension payments on the grounds mentioned above are still possible until 2011, but are subject to graduated deductions based on the month of birth. For all those born after 1942, this means that their pension is 18% lower than the full pension if they want to draw the latter at 60 years of age due to unemployment. Similar regulations apply to the other two types of early pension receipt, i.e. for women's pensions (*Frauenaltersrente*) and old-age pensions for those who have made insurance contributions for very many years. The aim here is to make the early retirement option less attractive for workers, or to compel companies to pay additional benefits that make early retirement considerably more expensive than previously.

As was shown in Overview 2, unemployment can last longer, as a transition from employment to retirement, than the maximum 32 months in which unemployment benefit can be drawn, if the lower unemployment assistance is also included[18]. In the past, regular payments made by former employers to boost net incomes to a level specified in the redundancy compensation plan or separation agreement were not taken into account in the means test for determining the amount of unemployment assistance. This exception has been discontinued since 1999, with the result that any payments by employers are offset by equal reductions in the payments made by the employment office, and that such payments no longer make any sense. Financial assets obtained as a one-off compensation payment are exempted from inclusion only to the extent that they do not exceed DM 10 000[19]. An early retirement passage lasting more than 32 months involves a phase of very low net income while receiving unemployment assistance, and for that reason is no longer acceptable to those concerned.

In Germany, no social insurance contributions are deducted from redundancy compensation payments, but the latter have to be declared as income and taxed if they exceed certain exempted levels. These were cut by a third as from 1.1.99. On reaching the age of 55 and after a minimum of 20 years' service, only DM 24 000 of settlement money is now tax-exempted, compared to DM 36 000 previously.

The reform introduced in 1997 by the Christian-Democrat/Liberal government had envisaged that redundancy compensation payments should partially offset unemployment benefit as well. Anyone receiving a payment that exceeded a graduated allowance, based on age and years of service, should receive only half the level of unemployment benefit, the other half being set off against the excess amount until the latter was reduced to zero. This regulation was not due to come into force until April 1999, after the general elections in autumn 1998. The Social-Democrat/Green government was therefore able to rescind what it viewed as an anti-constitutional[20] and socially inadequate measure before it came into effect.

However, of all the various sanctions against the 'passive' method of cutting workforce size by means of redundancies and compensation payments, followed by early retirement due to unemployment, it is precisely those with which workers would have been directly confronted at the start of unemployment that have now been done away with. The other sanctions – tax liability, possibly lower level of unemployment assistance, lower pension entitlement – do not impact until later and for that reason are not a direct deterrent. This explains why, in current case studies on job cuts in 1999, it is still common practice in many companies to exploit every option for laying off older workers, with early retirement the basic perspective[21]. It is only when this is not enough to achieve the job cuts considered necessary that other workers are laid off who are potential addressees for a preventive labour market policy. In the most favourable case, the various parties within a company deliberate on active employment promotion measures and utilise one of the two new instruments that are described in the next section.

4.2 The new instruments for promoting preventive programmes

As part of the 1998 labour market policy reforms, one entirely new type of instrument was introduced, while another was redesigned.

4.2.1 Grants for preventive measures as part of redundancy compensation schemes

In companies with more than 20 employees[22], works councils have had the right since 1972 to insist on a redundancy compensation plan if the employer plans restructuring measures involving significant disadvantages for a substantial proportion of the workforce. In any case, job cuts of certain dimensions depending on the size of the company are covered by the definition of restructuring[23]. The redundancy compensation plan is supposed to compensate for the financial disadvantages that arise for employees as a result of the planned restructuring. Such redundancy compensation plans are mainly focused on the payment of settlements[24] that help, in the case of older workers, to finance the transition to pension entitlement.

Since early 1998, on the basis of the reformed labour market policy, the social partners in companies have had a new instrument of preventive labour market policy at their disposal if they design the redundancy compensation plans in a different way than had normally been the case up to then. If, instead of or in addition to the usual settlements, the redundancy compensation plan envisages forms of support aimed at new employment for those laid off, for example skills, outplacement or employability training, then the costs of these measures, including wages, are eligible for grant aid for the duration of participation. The maximum level of grant support is calculated from the average annual expenditure on unemployment benefit per recipient (almost DM 17 000 in 1999). The support must be in reasonable proportion to the costs borne by the company itself. Cost elements that do not correspond to any additional expenditure are also recognised as self-borne costs, e.g. the provision of rooms and facilities, as well as the wages for participants, which the company would have had to bear anyway during the notice period.

In the two years since this instrument was introduced, more than 5,000 people in just under 100 different companies around Germany have received support. That is not a great deal in view of the fact that, each year, more than two and a half million people move from employment to unemployment[25]. On average, less than one third of the potential funding per person is used, and the schemes supported consist in the majority of cases of outplacement training of only a few days' duration.

One likely cause of this new instrument being used to such a minimal extent is the fact that it is still little known. From the viewpoint of companies, there is a need for support based on preventive labour market policies only in those cases where early retirement, expiry of temporary employment contracts and voluntary termination are not sufficient to achieve the required level of job cuts. Another probable factor, however, is that the incentives offered by the instrument are too weak. Companies do not derive any direct benefits from exploiting the instrument; there is no direct financial incentive for workers to participate besides the diffuse prospect of finding a job more easily as a result of the support scheme. The lack of incentives is probably responsible for the low extent to which the funding available is taken advantage of. For protracted and thus more costly schemes, companies would have to release employees from work for longer periods and bear a greater cost burden. This would lead to a reduction in the compensation settlements that companies would be prepared to pay to workers under a redundancy compensation plan, an aspect that workers and their works councils would not accept.

Despite these limitations, the instrument seems to have positive impacts on balance, if the very patchy data at hand are anything to go by: the rates of re-employment among 'graduates' of such schemes are more than 50%. That is more than would be expected if no support had been organised.[26]

4.2.2 Preventive employment promotion during short-time working caused by economic restructuring

Short-time working is a traditional instrument for maintaining employment during a serious economic downturn (see Mosley et al. 1995). For periods in which there is no work, the workers concerned receive substitute pay, 'short-time money' (*Kurzarbeitergeld*). The latter operates in effect as a pay subsidy aimed at giving companies a chance to waive redundancies that would otherwise be financially imperative. The percentage of normal pay levels received in this form is the same as that of unemployment benefit. Periods in which short-time money is received are not deducted if unemployment benefit is drawn at a later date.

Since the 1980s, and more intensively since German unification, short-term benefit has increasingly functioned to feather the blow of structurally induced job cuts, alongside its previous bridging role during slumps. Whereas short-time money is granted in cases where employment is discontinued temporarily, so that workers keep their jobs and companies their trained labour force, short-time working functions in structural terms as a means of extending employment, even though the jobs have already been lost irrevocably. Employers, of course, will not voluntarily postpone any financially essential or beneficial layoffs[27]; the solutions outlined above have to be negotiated by the works councils. In typical cases, companies are prepared to accept these solutions only if they can then terminate employment contracts by mutual consent, and in this way protect themselves extensively from court action being taken against them by workers. Substitute employers are brought in for this purpose, so-called employment and training companies (*Beschäftigungs- und Qualifizierungsgesellschaften*) that provide temporary employment to short-time workers. In this way, it is even possible for the former employer to terminate employment contracts before the notice period for such termination has actually expired. The company can reduce its workforce size more rapidly in comparison to normal layoffs, while those affected by such moves can nevertheless delay their entry to unemployment for a while. They are no longer in employment and receive short-time money for up to two years. The obvious response is to use this 'structural' short-time working as the first phase in a passage to early retirement, a passage that subseqently continues through the interim phases of unemployment and early retirement benefit as described above.[28]

Because of the reforms that took effect in 1998, the requirements that have to be met before 'structural' reasons for short-time working are recognised have been substantially diluted. On the other hand, attempts have been made to transform the instrument of a 'passive' phase preceding unemployment into an active intervention. Ever since short-time working due to structural factors was officially recognised in labour legislation, in 1988, the law has requested that employers to enable workers to obtain a vocational qualification. Without incentives or sanctions, and due to the predominant use of the instrument as the first stage in the passage to early retirement, it was rarely the case that this legal requirement was actually met in western Germany (Besselmann et al. 1993). In the 1998 labour market policy reform, a new sanction – still too weak, unfortunately – was introduced, according to which short-time money is granted for more than six months only on condition that skilling or some other measure aimed at re-employment is 'envisaged'. However, there are no effective controls on whether they actually materialise or not, or on how many short-time workers take part. Skilling can only be corroborated at present if, in addition to short-time money, the costs for such training measures themselves are also subsidised. This option has existed since 1996 as part of the federal government programme for Objective 4 of the European Social Fund.

In the 1996 –1998 period, the total number of companies operating structural short-time working in Germany was just over 200; the number of people affected was somewhere between 15 000 and 20 000[29]. ESF support was granted for about 3000 people each year (9100 in the 1996 – 1998 period) (Deeke 1999: 51). The extent to which the target group of this instrument was actually reached was somewhat greater than was the case with grants in support of redundancy compensation plans. Data on per capita expenditure and re-employment rates are not available as yet.

On the whole, total participant numbers of around 14 000 within three years for the two instruments of preventive labour market policy that can be deployed in Germany during the 'overt threat' stage of unemployment are not a particularly impressive figure in quantitative terms. Here is another figure for comparative purposes: over the same period, i.e. from 1995 to 1998, the number of jobs in Germany involving compulsory social insurance contributions declined by almost a million. From the microeconomic perspective, such a net change conceals about seven times as many destroyed jobs that are offset by newly-created jobs in other companies. Yet it is by no means a foregone conclusion that those affected can succeed in switching from old to new jobs. The quantitative discrepancy between supply and demand on the labour market is further intensified by the structural discrepancies that exist. This is where preventive labour market policy should have intervened, but the actual response has been more reminiscent of small doses.

4.3 Special features of the situation in Germany, compared to Austria and France

Germany is not the only country in Europe where decisions on the deployment of preventive labour market policy instruments are made during the 'overt threat' phase, with involvement by companies and those representing the interests of social partners. A comparison with other countries highlights the peculiarities of the German approach.

In *Austria*, entitlement to unemployment benefit[30] is extended to a maximum of four years for those periods in which the unemployed worker takes part in reintegration measures after placement by an organisation set up by the collective bargaining parties, whereby unemployment benefit is supplemented (in the form of a 'grant' by the body funding such an organisation). Participants in these 'employment foundations' develop a personal career strategy that generally entails a brief period of further training. For those with the requisite qualifications, degree studies at a university are another option that this maximum four-year entitlement provides. Austria had 78 such foundations in 1997, indicating their relatively widespread occurrence compared to Germany. The re-employment rate is quoted at more than 80% (see ÖSB 1993; Horejs 1998).

In *France*, an employer who lays off workers for financial reasons is obliged by law to offer a 'reorientation contract' (*convention de conversion*) to those affected. If the worker concludes such an agreement, he leaves the company before the termination date and participates for up to six months in employment office schemes instead. The employer pays two months' wages into unemployment insurance. Participants receive a special form of substitute pay that is higher than normal unemployment benefit and non-deductible from later periods in which unemployment benefit is drawn. Support schemes are organised either by technical re-employment units (*unités techniques de reclassement – UTR*) set up by the employment offices, or in re-employment sections (*cellules de reclassement*) within companies. Over the 1996 – 1998 period, more than 100 000 workers took part each year in schemes of this type. Six months after participation had finished, the re-employment rate was just under 50% (see Cloarec 1998; Brégier 1999).

In all three countries, intervention is made as soon as someone loses his job, and collective relations between the victims of corporate restructuring are initially maintained to a certain degree. However, there are differences in the status of participants. In France, a special phase is inserted between employment and unemployment, in which those affected do not qualify as unemployed, but as continuing training participants instead. In Austria, a special sub-category of unemployment has been created. In Germany, in contrast, interventions are made when people are still employed. Where grants supplementing redundancy compensation plans apply, these lead to temporal restrictions on the implementation of measures. In those cases where structurally based short-time working is introduced, the employment relationship is extended in formal terms. Such employment is mostly organised within employment and training companies. Establishing such an employment and training company (if one is not already in place) and transferring the employment contracts in a legally correct manner involves a great deal of time and effort purely aimed at creating a special intermediate status between employment and unemployment. There is a risk that the energies of those involved are dissipated by these efforts, with the result that they leave it at postponing unemployment rather than implementing active, preventive programmes. In the two other countries, social security law provides for a special status between employment and normal unemployment, so there is no need for a separate construction under employment law. Moreover, this intermediate status is bound up with mandatory participation in preventive programmes.

5. SUMMARY AND OUTLOOK

Germany is a newcomer to the field of preventive labour market policy. Innovations in this area were driven by the employment disaster in the wake of German unification and by the deep structural changes that subsequently occurred in western Germany. Since 1998, companies have been provided with two different support instruments from which to choose. Both are little known, and the incentives for companies and workforces to use them are not optimised.

Preventive labour market policy plays a negligible role in Germany compared to the scale in which jobs are lost, or in which people enter a passage that ends in unemployment. The numbers involved in support programmes are lower compared to France and Austria, two neighbouring countries where similar instruments are known, despite the fact that employment trends in Germany are significantly worse.

For all the attempts since 1995 to change direction in this respect, policy is predominated by passive ways of adjusting employment structures. The co-inciding of a phase of accelerated structural change during the 1990s and the ageing of strong birth cohorts made it easier for companies to cut jobs by means of early retirement. Workers in companies with declining workforce size, predominantly male industrial workers, are ending their working lives at an earlier age, while younger and female workers are flowing into those sectors where employment levels are growing.

Of the three possible stages in which preventive intervention programmes can operate, Germany has undertaken systematic efforts only in the middle phase, where there is a 'threat' of unemployment. In both the 'exposure' and 'manifestation' stages of unemployment, there are additional options that have not been utilised to an adequate extent.

NOTES

1. One exception is the QUATRO programme operated by the state of North-Rhine Westphalia, with which company modernisation, including skilling of workers, was supported under Objective 4 of the European Social Fund during the 1994–1999 support period.
2. The predecessor of this policy arose when coping with the labour market repercussions of German unification in the period from 1991 to 1993 (Knuth 1993, 1996 and 1997). However, there were no specific instruments at that time for stage 2 intervention. As a result, 'curative' instruments of labour market policy that had normally been used for people unemployed for some considerable time became options for handling exits from collapsing enterprises formerly owned by the East German state.
3. Eastern Germany is excluded from the statistical analyses in the present chapter because longitudinal time series are only possible and only make sense if they are confined to former West Germany.
4. When unemployment rates are calculated, the denominator is the number of people in employment; non-employed people are not taken into account. In relation to the small number of people in the 60 to <65 age group who still form part of the working popula-

tion, high unemployment rates are then the result. In absolute figures, however, this age group is no longer so significant, as the right half of Figure 5.1 has shown. The real problematic group as far as unemployment is concerned is the 55 to <60 age group.

5.   The data analysis was done by Jörg-Peter Schräpler, Ruhr-Universität Bochum.
6.   Cf. Knuth 1999: 11ff. for details on German employment statistics.
7.   We have included structural steel engineering, machine tools, road and rail vehicles, aircraft and shipbuilding in this broad category.
8.   The previous sample from the same source of employment and wage replacement data was used which covered only the period from 1975 to 1990. The new sample for 1975 to 1995 did not become available before 1999.
9.   The third criterion, which tends to put younger workers at an advantage, is the number of dependent children.
10. 60% of workers in the German private sector are employed in companies in which there is no works council (Wassermann 1999).
11. The other entries into retirement at 65, which still make up around 40% of the total, are women who, because they were classed as non-employed in the second half of their lives, are unable to claim the small pensions to which they are entitled, based on their employment when young, until they reach 65.
12. Although the employment statistics indicate the percentage of employed people who drew unemployment benefit after exiting the labour market – see the above results obtained by Wübbeke in 1999 – the retirement statistics show the proportion of new pensioners who were unemployed immediately beforehand. These figures are not identical, because periods of non-employment may lie between a person's last employment and final retirement.
13. The number of women taking early retirement at 60 has been fairly stable since the early 1970s (cf. figure 5.2).
14. Data for 1995 entries are 159 000 in the West, 111 000 in the East. This development in the East was programmed by a special 'out-of-the-labour-force' status designed to assist the mass exodus from *Treuhand* companies. This status was not statistically counted as unemployment but gave the same entitlement to early retirement at 60 (Knuth and Bosch 1994).
15. Employed women receive a pension at 60 without having to be unemployed first, but are subject to 'equal treatment' when it comes to job cuts.
16. In those companies whose workforce size is declining, laying off older workers without employing younger people does not lead to a younger workforce but to a compression of age structure (see Bender et al. 1999).
17. In 2000, contributions still accounted for about 38% of gross pay, half of that amount being deducted from a worker's gross pay. The other half is paid by the employer on top of basic wage costs.
18. Unemployment benefit is paid for 12 to 32 months, depending on age and the length of time for which contributions were paid. The percentage of pay received is 60%, or 67% if there are dependent children. When unemployment benefit expires, unemployment assistance at 53% of one's former earnings is paid for an unlimited time, but with other household income being offset. When unemployment assistance is adjusted to the pay index, a reduction of 3% is made each year. This means that the rate of pay substitution is actually degressive.
19. One legal way out of this conundrum is to buy real property or to redeem the mortgage for property one already owns, so that rental or mortgage payments are no longer due.
20. Employees who find a new job after losing their old one would have kept the compensation payment in full; the very ones who are reliant on unemployment benefit would have had to accept a deduction, however. Unlike unemployment assistance, unemployment benefit is an insurance payment to which a claim is acquired by paying contributions, regardless of any assets or other income one may have. The envisaged setoff of a certain type of assets or income would at least have meant a change in the system.
21. We must accept a certain delay before we can know whether this conclusion can be generalised and whether it is confirmed by the statistics for entry into unemployment and early pension benefits.
22. About 70% of all German workers are employed in companies with a workforce in excess of 20. That said, employees in small and medium-sized companies often fail to exercise

their right to elect a works council. Unless a works council is in place, there can be no redundancy compensation plan.

23. The German term is '*Betriebsänderung*', meaning a 'change in the objects of a company'.
24. There are no representative surveys on redundancy compensation plans. According to the latest study by Hemmer (1997), compensation payments in the first half of the 1990s amounted to about DM 20 000 on average, but spread across a broad range: 22% of those concerned received less than DM 10 000, whereas 10% received more than DM 75 000.
25. Even if one calculates that about 10% of that figure is too old for preventive support, that about 40% are from small enterprises with no works council, that only a minority of the remainder exits on account of restructuring measures with obligatory compensation plan, and, finally, that many find new employment even without support, this does not alter the fact that the degree to which the new instrument succeeds in reaching its target group has been only a few percentage points up to now.
26. Bender et al. (1999) arrive at a figure of just under 40% immediate re-employment, based on data collected by the IAB random employment sample for the victims of factory closures. Considering the fact that, in the cases we covered that did not involve any total closure, job cuts were made selectively, and that we have data only on those people who joined such schemes for lack of an immediate alternative, then reintegration rates of 50% must qualify as successful. In France, schemes that mostly lasted longer did not achieve a reintegration rate of 50% until six months after participants finished such schemes, when the labour market situation improved and participant numbers declined as a result (Brégier 1999).
27. Short-time working does not exempt companies entirely from labour expenses: vacations and public holidays on which no work would have been done anyway must be paid in full, on top of which companies must pay both halves of the social insurance contributions (the employer's and the employee's), albeit at somewhat reduced rates. Depending on the pay agreement or redundancy compensation plan, a net supplement may also be added to the basic level of short-time money.
28. Before these restrictions were imposed, people in the steel industry, as an example, could effectively stop work at the age of 52, even though their employment did not formally end until they were 54.
29. These are average annual figures. The number of companies and people affected at some time or other during the year is therefore a little higher.
30. Unemployment benefit is granted for a minimum of 20 weeks, rising to 30 weeks after three years of employment and compulsory social insurance payments, to 39 weeks after six years' employment and when the recipient has reached the age of 40.

REFERENCES

Beer, D. (1997), *Participation of unskilled workers in training programmes: paths and barriers in Germany*, Gelsenkirchen: Institut Arbeit und Technik, Projektbericht 1997-10.

Bender, S. and J. Hilzendegen (1995), 'Die IAB-Beschäftigtenstichprobe als scientific use file', *Mitteilungen aus der Arbeitsmarkt- und Berufsforschung*, **28**: 76-95.

Bender, S., J. Preißler and C. Wübbeke (1999), *Betriebliche Determinanten des Generationenaustausches in westdeutschen Betrieben. Eine Untersuchung auf der Basis des IAB-Employer-Employeedatensatzes für die Jahre 1994 und 1995*, Paper presented on the conference 'Generationenaustausch' am 22–23 April 1999 in Bremen. Nürnberg.

Bender, S.; Dustmann, C.; Margolis, D. and C. Meghir (1999a), *Worker displacement in France and Germany*. Unveröffentlichter Manuskriptentwurf

Besselmann, K., G. Machalowski, Ch. Ochs and H. Seifert (1993), *Kurzarbeit und Qualifizierung. Bedingungen und Gestaltungsmöglichkeiten der Kurzarbeit zur*

Nutzung der beruflichen Qualifizierung, Ergebnisse einer Untersuchung im Auftrag des BMA. Bonn: BMA Forschungsbericht Nr. 235.

Brégier, O. (1999), *Les dispositifs d'accompagnement des restructrations en 1998*, DARES: Premières Synthèses 99.09-no. 38.1.

Cloarec, N. (1998), *Le retour à l'emploi après une convention de conversion*, DARES: Premières Synthèses 98.09-no. 39.4.

Deeke, A. (1999), *Vier Jahre ESF-BA-Programm. Die Umsetzung der ergänzenden Förderung zum AFG und SGB III aus dem Europäischen Sozialfonds von 1995 bis 1998*, Nürnberg: IAB-Werkstattbericht Nr. 17 v. 30.9.99.

Hemmer, E. (1997), *Sozialpläne und Personalanpassungsmaßnahmen*, Cologne: Deutscher Institutsverlag.

Horejs, I. (1998), *JobTransfer. Frühzeitige und betriebsnahe Arbeitsmarktpolitik. Modelle und Fallbeispiele aus 5 europäischen Ländern*, Deutsche Kurzfassung. Wien: ÖSB-Unternehmensberatung.

Knuth, M. (1993), 'ABS companies and the potential of labour market policy to promote structural development', *Employment Observatory East Germany*, (8): 3-6.

Knuth, M. (1996), *Drehscheiben im Strukturwandel. Agenturen für Mobilitäts-, Arbeits- und Strukturförderung*, Berlin: edition sigma.

Knuth, M. (1997), 'Active labor market policy and German unification: The role of employment and training companies', in L. Turner (ed.), *Negotiating the new Germany. Can social partnership survive?* Ithaca and London: ILR Press (Cornell University Press), 69-86.

Knuth, M. (1999), *The toll of change. Economic restructuring, worker displacement and unemployment in West Germany*, Gelsenkirchen: Institut Arbeit und Technik, Graue Reihe 1999-07.

Knuth, M. (1999a): 'Senkung der Arbeitslosigkeit durch Ausstieg aus dem Vorruhestand. Gesellschaftliche und betriebliche Innovationserfordernisse im Umgang mit dem strukturellen und demographischen Wandel', in P. Brödner, E. Helmstädter and B. Widmaier (ed.), *Wissensteilung*, München und Mering: Rainer Hampp.

Knuth, M. and G. Bosch (1994), 'Industrial Restructuring and Labour Market Policy in the German Unification Process', in W. Ehlert, R. Russell and G. Széll (eds.), *Return of work, production and administration to capitalism. Europe between restructuring and adaptation*, Frankfurt a. Main et al.: Peter Lang, 86-100.

Mosley, H., Th. Kruppe and S. Speckessser (1995), *Flexible adjustment through short-time work: a comparison of France, Germany, Italy and Spain*, Berlin: WZB discussion paper no. FS I 95-205.

ÖSB Österreichische Studien- und Beratungsgesellschaft (ed.) (1993), *Arbeitsstiftungen und regionale Arbeitsinitiativen als Chancen für Qualifizierung und Beschäftigung*, Tagungsdokumentation, Wien, 3.11.1993. Wien.

Rehfeld, U. (1998): 'Der Arbeitsmarkt: Eckpfeiler für die gesetzliche Rentenversicherung. Anmerkungen aus statistisch-empirischer Sicht'., in INIFES/ ISF/ SÖSTRA (ed.), *Erwerbsarbeit und Erwerbsbevölkerung im Wandel*, Frankfurt/ New York: Campus.

Wassermann, W. (1999): 'Kampf den mitbestimmungsfreien Zonen? Überlegungen zu einer den Bedingungen in Kleinbetrieben angemessenen Weiterentwicklung der Betriebsverfassung', *WSI-Mitteilungen*, **52**: 770-782.

Wübbeke, C. (1999): 'Der Übergang von sozialversicherungspflichtiger Beschäftigung in den Rentenbezug zwischen sozialpolitischer Steuerung und betrieblichen Interessen. Eine Untersuchung der Ursachen des Frühverrentungstrends in Westdeutschland für den Zeitraum von 1975 bis 1990 auf Basis der IAB-Beschäftigtenstichprobe', *Mitteilungen aus der Arbeitsmarkt- und Berufsforschung*, **32**: 102-117.

PART TWO

National experience with preventive labour market policy strategies

6. Corporatist vs. market bargaining processes and foreign investment location: Evidence from Germany and the UK

Philip Raines

1. INTRODUCTION

National industrial relations systems and foreign investors have traditionally been closely interlinked – in understanding the extensive changes to different European labour market frameworks, it is important to assess the contribution of the rise of global foreign investment strategies. While foreign investors have not necessarily been directly responsible for these changes, they have highlighted how greater globalisation of trade and investment has shaped – and in turn been shaped by – industrial relations systems. On the one hand, in having to fit into different local bargaining systems, foreign subsidiaries can display significant differences in their plant bargaining and worker representation arrangements, with the result that human resource management has been decentralised within many multinational groups (UNCTAD, 1994). Although there has been an increasing 'Europeanisation' of bargaining in multinationals – perhaps most visibly in the greater use of European works councils – local plants remain characterised by the local 'colour' of their individualised industrial relations, arising from a mixture of national frameworks and plant-specific traditions (Mueller and Purcell, 1992). At the same time, foreign enterprises act as a conduit for new working practices and labour–management relations into a local economy, whether through emulation by local businesses (in adopting 'good practice') or through direct (and indirect) enforcement of supplier behaviour by investors (Dunning, 1993). The complex interaction ensuing between subsidiaries and their labour market regulatory frameworks can have a variety of outcomes, depending on factors such as the labour relations practices of the multinational's home country, the regulatory framework of the subsidiary country, sector and the multinational group's internal organisation (Ferner, 1994). In all cases though, it demonstrates that investors across the world have become highly attuned to differences in their industrial relations environments.

The relationship is particularly interesting in Western Europe, where a diverse spectrum of industrial relations systems exists – both in the unionisation in the national labour force as well as the centralisation and coordination of negotiations over pay and employment conditions. In some countries – notably Germany – *corporatist* bargaining traditions are supported by powerful legal frameworks in which labour-management relations are institutionalised at national, regional and individual enterprise levels. In contrast, countries like the UK support *market*-based approaches to resolving labour–management disputes, with few proscribed institutions and a strong emphasis on plant-specific bargaining arrangements. In recent years, both systems have come under increasing pressure to adapt to economic integration in Western Europe, as a result of both region-specific processes (such as the completion of the internal market and European Monetary Union) and more global developments (as manifested through greater investment and trade interpenetration of national economies) (Brewster, Hegewisch and Mayne, 1994). In this context, foreign investors have been facilitating agents in promoting restructuring of national and regional economies through changes in their trade and investment activities: questions can likewise be raised about their potential role as agents in the 'restructuring' of industrial relations systems in Western Europe.

At the same time, differences in industrial relations systems also play a role in how multinationals organise their investments. Most directly, local bargaining systems can influence the scale, timing and choice of investment decisions by multinationals. For greenfield sites, considerations of labour market factors – especially the level of skills, overall cost and scope for flexible organisation – are bound up with local industrial relations. For *in situ* investment decisions, the extent and organisation of bargaining arrangements can be significant when companies use the enticement or threat of investment shifts to secure cooperation on contested issues from local workforces. In addition, there is a more indirect yet still visible relationship between industrial relations and investment decisions: where investment decisions are affected by productivity differences between plants, local bargaining practices assume greater significance depending on whether they facilitate or hinder improvements to plant productivity.

To contribute to the debates on these issues, this chapter considers the interaction between different models of industrial relations and foreign investment decision-making. The issue is approached from two perspectives. First, it examines the extent to which investment location behaviour is influenced by differences between corporatist and market-based bargaining processes. Here, the chapter is partly based on research conducted by researchers at the European Policies Research Centre in Glasgow and the Rhine-Westphalian Institute for Economic Research in Essen, funded by a grant from the Anglo-

German Foundation for the Study of Industrial Society (Raines et al., 1999). The study is discussed in more detail by Markus Scheuer, Chapter 2. Second, this chapter reviews the role of investors in altering the bargaining frameworks in which their subsidiaries operate, in particular, whether foreign investment has contributed to convergence pressures in European industrial relations.

2. INDUSTRIAL RELATIONS SYSTEMS AND FOREIGN INVESTMENT LOCATION

Interest in the sensitivity of foreign investors to industrial relations frameworks has increased in recent years, to a large extent, prompted by scares of 'social dumping'. As a global phenomenon, the expression refers to a perception that there might be a systematic 'distortion' of foreign investment towards – all other things being equal – environments where workforces have very limited legal protection and safeguards. While labour standards in Western Europe vary less than they do in other parts of the world, concerns were raised that the differences would nonetheless become more influential with the completion of the internal market. As economic integration created incentives for multinationals to redistribute their investments between different countries, the resulting investment patterns could become more skewed towards locations with relatively low employment protection, putting pressure on other countries to follow suit and triggering an overall lowering of standards. The debate centred around the particular case of Hoover Europe, which shifted production investment in 1993 from France to Scotland, largely because of differences in British and French industrial relations frameworks (EIRR, 1993). Collective agreement restrictions prevented French workers negotiating employment concessions with Hoover whereas Scottish workers were not bound by the same external restrictions on their negotiating flexibility.

Such clear examples of the role of labour market regulation on investment decisions remain isolated though, and overall, there has been little evidence that investors have systematically pursued social dumping strategies in Western Europe (Raines, 1998). Indeed, few other examples can be cited, suggesting that the specific circumstances surrounding the Hoover incident were unusual. Given the type of sectors associated with Western European production investment decisions – particularly electrical and mechanical engineering and motor vehicle production, where the skills level of the workforce and labour costs tend to be more important factors than levels of employment protection – investors are unlikely to gain consistently from long-term arbitrage behaviour. However, while employment protection levels are rarely the dominant factor in investment decisions, they can still be a major influence in combination with other determinants. This is especially evident when examining one aspect of the national employment protection regime: bargaining systems. Significant evidence has emerged that investors are often highly sensitive to the impact of industrial relations differences on production – and ultimately, investment – strategies. For example, in a 1992 study of US plant managers, Karnani and Talbot found that 'labour practices and regulations' could be decisive factors in determining future investment decisions (as quoted in Cooke and Noble, 1998). Similarly, multinational subsidiaries in the UK emphasised the importance of the regulatory environment on human resource management in their location decisions (Marginson et al., 1995).

What is less clear is *how* different industrial relations systems influence location behaviour. A variant of the social dumping hypothesis has argued that multinational companies tend to favour locations that provide the least constraints on how management conducts business, often interpreted in terms of an investment shift towards places with weak unions and few collective bargaining restrictions on individual plant autonomy (Ferner, 1994). Examining investment flows through regression analysis, Cooke and Noble (1998) concluded that there was a strong negative correlation between the level of US direct investment capital in a foreign country and the coverage of collective bargaining agreements. The argument appears to be reinforced by the propensity of many investors to establish non-union sites: for example, a study of inward investors in North-East England by Peck and Stone (1992) showed that 66% of inward investors had non-unionised workforces, compared to only 38% of indigenously-owned plants. Indeed, the UK's success in attracting inward investment has been consistently linked to cycles in its approaches to industrial relations: during the 1970s, when the country was known for aggressive union activity, investors were reluctant to establish in the UK (and in a few cases, existing investors withdrew), while in the 1980s, with extensive deregulation of working practices and the enforced weakening of union power, investors were increasingly attracted by the country's new reputation for 'flexible' working arrangements (Dunning, 1993).

However, other research has questioned the extent to which strong union activity and extensive collective bargaining dissuades investors. Within the US, Mair, Florida and Kennedy (1988) concluded that the evidence that investors are systematically attracted to locations where unionisation is weak appears limited. Another study of US foreign production abroad found little statistical association between bargaining systems and levels of FDI, though perhaps crucially, the variable here was union penetration (rather than collective bargaining coverage, as in Cooke and Noble (1988); Karier, 1995). Again, using the example of the UK, while the majority of foreign investors may support no-union agreements, groups of investors have expressed different preferences: for example, Japanese investors have largely been characterised by their support for single union sites (Watanabe, 1993; Oliver and Wilkinson, 1989).

Similar ambiguity surrounds the link between industrial relations, productivity improvements and investment activity. In this context, the two industrial relations systems set out here have been defended and criticised from various perspectives, in terms of both the strength of bargaining institutions at plant level and the impact of wider collective bargaining arrangements. In *corporatist* systems, strong workforce representation within individual plants can provide a collective focus in the workforce for conflict resolution. Not only can it assist negotiations by a more efficient means of articulating labour interests and responses to management proposals, but it can also expedite the implementation of decisions by creating a hierarchy and single point of internal authority in local workforces. *Market*-based approaches can also offer advantages to companies aiming to increase productivity. The presence of strong local and collective bargaining institutions can result in restrictive work rules, more strikes, higher wage claims and increasing misallocation of labour (McConnell and Brue, 1989). A market system has the appeal of maximising enterprise decision-making, achieving productivity gains through the threat of job losses on individual workers' incentives to accept new working arrangements and reduced remuneration.

The empirical evidence supporting the claims of either industrial relations approach has not been conclusive. While Brown and Medoff (1978) found the presence of unions to have raised enterprise productivity in a landmark study, research over the last two decades has come down in support of both systems (for a review, see McConnell and Brue, 1989). Buchele and Christiansen (1992) concluded that the advantages of both systems can be 'activated' depending on whether overall industrial relations can be characterised by consensus or conflict. Indeed, Addison and Chilton (1993) have gone further, arguing that it may not be possible to assess the different systems because of the heterogeneity of industrial relations and the role of too many exogenous variables. As a result, an intricate picture emerges of the interaction of local industrial relations, enterprise bargaining and foreign investment.

3. GERMANY AND THE UK: INDUSTRIAL RELATIONS SYSTEMS AND FDI PATTERNS COMPARED

Although investor attitudes to both corporatist and market approaches to industrial relations remain ambiguous, when examining the operation of the two systems in Western Europe, connections between bargaining structures and foreign investment appear more evident. These links are exemplified by Germany and the UK: both countries not only demonstrate features at different ends of the corporatist-market spectrum of employment regulation, but they have also had differing – and, it has been argued, closely related – successes with regards to inward investment attraction.

Germany has exhibited a highly stable approach to employment issues, distinguished by institutional consensus, strong collective agreements and a universal commitment to social cohesion. As a 'corporatist model', it is both relatively centralised and bounded by industrial relations institutions and national regulations. At its heart, the system is based on the provision of common and equal minimum standards in exchange for worker commitments to refrain from industrial actions to disrupt work. To achieve this, a number of mechanisms encourage industrial relations consensus. At national level, a legal framework sets the scope for negotiating wages and working practices through a collective bargaining system, in which regional and sectoral associations of employers (representing the majority of employers) negotiate with trade unions on industry-wide agreements. At enterprise level, 'co-determination' exists through the statutory requirements for works councils – which have extensive rights in setting local pay and working conditions within those agreements – and worker representation on supervisory boards. In addition to these delegated areas of joint negotiation, works councils have important rights to information about and consultation of major corporate decisions. Compared to other European countries, the institutions at the two levels have clearly defined roles designed to complement each other (Hassel, 1999).

By contrast, the *UK* has been seen as the principal European example of decentralised and deregulated labour markets. In this 'market model', the regulatory framework is markedly weaker. There are no industrial relations institutions comparable to the collective bargaining and co-determination features of the German system. While the power of trade unions has historically been strong in the UK, their relations with employers have been piecemeal and *ad hoc* – in many cases, differing on an enterprise by enterprise basis – so that it has not generated the same level of consensus as in Germany. Traditionally, the government has pursued minimal intervention in employment issues – especially in legislative terms – while increasingly advocating a policy of settling wage and working conditions at enterprise level. However, under the Conservative government through the 1980s and early 1990s, a concerted effort was made to reduce union power overall, diminishing the remaining national institutions for bargaining. The result has been the restriction of a national level framework to a relatively liberalised regulatory system and a diversity of bargaining arrangements existing at local level.

As statistical reports show, the more centralised and consensus-based approach to industrial relations in Germany appears to be reflected in historically fewer industrial conflicts (see also Table 2.1 this volume). In the 1989–93 period, Germany lost only 20 days per year to strike action, considerably less than the 70 days in the UK. In both countries though, the incidence of strikes has been declining in recent years. The fall is most dramatic in the case of the UK, where the absence of extensive industrial relations conflict has been achieved less by finding mechanisms for resolving disputes – as in Germany – than by removing the ability of one of the disputants to prosecute aggressive industrial action.

There is some evidence that companies may be sensitive to the different 'models' of workforce flexibility and industrial relations systems in both countries. As a whole, the UK has been highly successful in attracting internationally-mobile investment: not only has it been the main foreign direct investment location in Europe, but it continues to be the world's second largest recipient of FDI after the US (UNCTAD, 1998). While the country's relatively low labour costs tend to more frequently cited, foreign investors have listed the importance of the UK's 'flexible' workforce and industrial relations arrangements as key factors in their decisions (Montagnon, 1997). Indeed, a low level of labour costs has been linked to limits on the ability of workforces to press wage demands because of weak union power (McConnell and Brue, 1989). Traditionally, Germany has also been a major destination for FDI – it has the second largest stocks in Europe – but its inward flows have declined sharply in recent years, leaving the country with one of the lowest FDI-to-GDP ratios in Europe (UNCTAD, 1998). While to a large extent offset by better productivity performances, higher wages in Germany have been associated by investors with strong bargaining institutions at local and national level (Kahraß, 1997). Moreover, investment inflows have been apparently dwarfed by massive outflows, prompting the so-called 'Standort Deutschland' debate over whether Germany industry is 'hollowing out' (Tüselmann, 1995). While it has been argued that German statistical collection methods may be exaggerating the 'crisis' (Döhrn, 1996), there has been a rising volume of anecdotal evidence suggesting that Germany's reputation for high labour costs and labour market rigidities has not only dissuaded investors from locating but has also accelerated outward investment by German companies (Flaherty, 1997; Sadler and Amin, 1995).

4. GERMANY AND THE UK: CORPORATIST AND MAR-
KET BARGAINING APPROACHES COMPARED

To investigate these issues, the study undertook original survey work through
a series of company case studies in Germany and the UK (Raines et al.,
1999). It had several objectives: to identify the role of labour market factors
– particularly labour market flexibility - in influencing investment in Germany and the UK; to determine whether differences in national regulatory
frameworks and industrial relations have determined the type of workforce
flexibility prevailing in both countries; and to assess the importance of labour
market flexibility as an investment location factor. As part of the research,
face-to-face interviews were held with senior executives in investor companies, including German-owned enterprises (investing in the UK), UK-owned
enterprises (investing in Germany) and 'other'-owned enterprises (investing
in both). Altogether 46 interviews were conducted with manufacturing facilities in both countries, yielding a sample set of 31 multinational groups. Investors were selected from two sectors in which manufacturing investment in
Germany and the UK has been relatively extensive: automotive engineering
and chemicals.

The results of the study are discussed in more detail in Chapter 2. For the
present chapter, the study is of interest with respect to investor attitudes to
differing industrial relations and bargaining structures in the UK and Germany. The impact of differing systems on investment behaviour was only
one of several issues in the project, which aimed to examine how investment
activity has been shaped by the need for many businesses to increase their
workforce flexibility. As part of the study, companies were asked to rank
different labour factors by their importance to both the business and their
investment decisions. Where two firms in the same multinational group were
interviewed – the parent firm and the subsidiary – only the answers for the
parent were used to avoid double-counting (producing a sample of 31 cases).
Using a weighted value system, a scored ranking of factor was produced:
while such methods cannot provide very accurate estimations of the relative
significance of different factors, they could indicate broadly which factors
tended to be valued most by firms.

As the table below illustrates, it is clear that three types of labour factors
were most significant to investors in general:

- *labour costs*, both direct (in terms of wage levels) and indirect (such as
  employers' insurance premiums);
- *skilled labour*, both its availability in the surrounding labour market and
  the level of skills among the firm's workforce); and

- the *'flexibility'* of the workforce, a widely defined concept embracing numerical flexibility (the ability to change the size and composition of the workforce), temporal flexibility (the ability to alter working time) and functional flexibility (the ability of individual workers to move between tasks and take on additional responsibilities).

Table 6.1: Importance of different labour market factors (weighted averages)

	Firms investing in Germany	Firms investing in the UK	All firms
Availability of skilled labour	1.78	1.09	1.29
Direct wage costs	1.11	1.50	1.39
Indirect labour costs	1.00	1.23	1.16
Workforce flexibility	1.45	1.50	1.49
Level of employment regulations	1.00	0.87	0.91
Industrial relations	0.89	0.87	0.88

Sample: 31 cases.

More telling differences emerged when separating the results for firms investing in Germany (both UK- and 'other'-owned) and investors in the UK (both German- and 'other'-owned). Firms investing in Germany valued workforce skills above all other factors, whereas UK firms tended to place a great priority on wages and indirect labour costs. This would tend to reinforce the traditional picture of Germany attracting investors with its highly-skilled workforce and the UK's principal attraction being the low level of its overall labour costs. However, for both sets of enterprises, achieving greater workforce flexibility was also a priority.

Few companies in the survey felt that industrial relations in either country had presented them with significant restrictions; indeed, in no case did investors identify the factor as a determinant of their initial investment decisions. Moreover, trade union influence was recognised as being dependent on a series of local variables, especially in the UK, where the strength of union influence was often dependent on the existence – or absence – of local traditions of industrial conflict. While many firms reported union and worker resistance to company efforts to change working practices in both countries (as part of efforts to increase workforce flexibility), in very few cases did such conflict appear to jeopardise management plans. As a result, hardly any of the investors in the survey attempted to standardise their industrial relations practices across different subsidiaries, instead allowing different arrangements as long as they did not conflict with management objectives. Indeed, in spite of its potential for conflict, investors in both countries supported some form of centralised worker representation within individual plants as it facilitated the process of bargaining.

For investors in both countries, differences at local level could often be greater than those at national level. In the UK, the level of trade union influence varied enormously, much more than in Germany (as might be expected in a 'market' system). In older industries, long-established plants often reported a history of negotiating with single unions - characterised in some instances as 'stormy', in others as cooperative - whereas among newer investments, many firms had non-unionised workforces. In the majority of cases, local union quiescence was typical, and several firms did remark on how the changes in trade union legislation over the past two decades had 'improved' the industrial relations climate. Similarly, views on the industrial relations system in Germany were mixed. Several smaller companies found the strong presence of larger trade unions in their activities restrictive, and wanted greater freedom to set wage rates at company level rather than by wider collective bargaining. For example, one German automotive supplier in the interviews considered IG Metall's campaign for a 35-hour week to be interfering with the company's own industrial relations practices. Larger firms tended to support the influence of unions, describing their relations in some cases as 'co-management', though principally at local level. In fact, many works councils were viewed as increasingly identifying with company management rather than their trade union, notably where plant survival was at stake.

Overall attitudes to industrial relations systems were shaped by how they affected the general 'flexibility' of the workforce (the importance of which factor can be seen in Table 6.1). When questioned in detail about workforce flexibility, companies identified a range of aspects they found important, including the abilities to: vary working time (either through changing the working week or arranging unusual shifts); hire fixed-term employees without incurring large additional costs; re-assign workers between different jobs, entrust workers with additional tasks; and combine different employees into flexible production teams. In this respect, investors showed significant interest in the *capacity* of individual sites to increase workforce flexibility over the long-term, and recognised that local industrial relations was an important feature in achieving – or limiting – this.

As a result, while initial investments were not significantly affected by industrial relations systems in both countries, local industrial relations practices could influence *follow-up* investments. Differences in workforce performance were sometimes significant in the distribution of incremental investment between existing plants. In one German-owned multinational producing automotive parts, the need to restructure the group had raised the importance of productivity as a factor determining plant survival. In order to reduce excess capacity, one plant in Europe (in neither Germany nor the UK) had already been closed because of its poorer productivity performance. The UK plant realised that it could not compete with other plants in the group on a cost basis because of its relatively small size, hence, it had to improve productivity through increasing the flexibility of its workforce, allowing it to handle shorter and more complex production runs. The ability to mobilise the local workforce to make the necessary changes without external interference was seen as critical.

A similar situation was found in a German-owned chemicals multinational which was considering how to restructure the group, again with a view to reducing excess capacity. As before, the UK plant was instituting a series of changes in working practices in order to improve its ranking ahead of a group review of plant productivity, and again, workforce compliance was seen as a significant factor. Both these and similar firms tended to be multinationals where plants manufactured relatively similar, standardised products. Where excess capacity existed in the firm, there were pressures on individual plants to reduce costs and raise productivity as production could be transferred to other manufacturing units in the group. In multinationals where plants specialised in particular product areas, such obvious closure threats were less likely to emerge.

At its most extreme, the threat of closure or diverted investment was used in a few instances to extract workforce concessions. Occasionally, the threat was explicit, as when one of the German automotive suppliers noted that the threat of shifting production from one of its smaller plants in Germany to an existing UK site forced the works council to agree to new shift and overtime pay arrangements. In other cases, though the threat was not direct, local management still reacted to fears of an imminent decision on restructuring within the group by maximising their flexibility. While commentators have noted that 'closure' threats often lack credibility – because of the 'sunk costs' issue (Enderwick, 1985) – it was sufficiently plausible to persuade worker representatives on several occasions among the sample companies. For example, this was a factor in the case of another UK subsidiary of a German-owned automotive investor, where the local unions agreed to changes in working time in order to strengthen the plant's chance of survival. Perhaps most interestingly, the threats were often not expressed by local management as part of a wider multinational bargaining strategy, but a reflection by the subsidiary of its own vulnerability to investment shifts; in this respect, management and labour interests could come together in indirect competition with other subsidiaries.

Overall, while the study found national-level differences in industrial relations systems had limited investment impacts, many investors placed considerable emphasis on plant-level bargaining arrangements and the ability to adapt to production and market changes quickly. Investors wanted conditions which would expedite the introduction of new working practices; in practice, this usually meant factors influencing the ability and willingness of their workforces to adapt to new production systems. Strong workforce representation at a plant level was regarded as an important factor influencing both such ability and willingness. Where wider collective agreements reinforced the role of local bargaining, investors favoured the system; where they interfered, investors were more critical.

These results concur with other studies. Analysis of German multinationals in the UK suggest that there has been little transfer of German working practices in worker consultation or training to the subsidiaries in the UK (Edwards, 1998). Similarly, Muller (1998) found that in spite of the regulated German system, US multinationals reported that there was adequate flexibility in the industrial relations of their German subsidiaries to meet their management objectives. In his study, examples were cited of foreign subsidiaries which had 'opted out' of collective bargaining agreements, but maintained local works councils, even when they were absent in the investor's home country. In the context of the German system, while recognising the difficulties of their collective bargaining system in allowing organisational flexibility for individual enterprises, German companies applauded the works councils (Wever, 1995). They provided strong enterprise-level groups for securing workforce agreement to implementing bargaining decisions. Indeed, the use of works councils in some countries has been seen as a means of limiting the influence of collective bargaining, in some cases, potentially circumventing existing union power (Rogers and Streeck, 1994). Moreover, as noted in the research presented here, such local arrangements could be attractive to investors. In their research, Cooke and Noble (1998) also found a strong association between works councils and levels of US foreign investment, whereas collective bargaining had been negatively related.

5.   CONCLUDING REMARKS

On the basis of our study, empirical evidence points to the limited role that differences in industrial relations systems have in systematically influencing foreign investment patterns in Western Europe. While investors noted broad differences between corporatist and market-based systems, neither appears to have consistently restrained investors in their labour–management relations. Enterprises reported a diversity of industrial relations arrangements in both countries, suggesting that there is considerable degree of flexibility within the two systems. Overall though, investors seem determined to achieve the same outcomes irrespective of the systems within which they operate: a com-

bination of strong local bargaining structures and consensual industrial relations. As a result, while they have tended to be attracted to market-based
systems because of the fewer constraints from a lack of collective bargaining,
and to corporatist systems because of the virtues of work councils, investors
have been able to produce comparable industrial relations results in both
countries. Indeed, what appears to have been the deciding factor in these circumstances was the degree of consensus between workforce and management in individual plants.

The evidence here highlights the complex connections between different
aspects of industrial relations systems and investor behaviour, particularly the
relationship of bargaining arrangements at local and supra-plant levels. A
close reading of other studies reveals similar conclusions. Cooke and Noble
(1998) found that US investors seemed to be drawn towards both environments where collective bargaining is limited but works councils are preva-
lent. Buchele and Christiansen (1992) concluded that the extent to which
local industrial relations have been antagonistic is a more significant factor in
productivity changes – and so ultimately, investment decisions – than the
strength of labour representation. Herein may lie an explanation for the apparently mixed trends in research regarding investor reactions to different
industrial relations systems, as investors find different aspects of the various
systems appealing. Investment is sensitive to these differences, but only insofar as the combination of local circumstances can maximise individual enterprise efforts to alter working arrangements to maximise productivity. While
several factors are at work here – perhaps most importantly, workforce skills
– the bargaining autonomy of single plants appears to be the key consideration among investors.

This raises the second set of questions outlined in the introduction: Does
shifting foreign investment activity affect the operation of industrial relations
systems? If multinationals are attracted to particular features of certain systems, what pressure – either directly or indirectly – are they exerting to diffuse these features more widely through Western Europe? By favouring local
bargaining and eschewing collective bargaining, are investors encouraging a
broad convergence between corporatist and market-based bargaining systems? The influence of multinationals in this context should not be exaggerated: while they can provide a catalyst to more widespread changes because
of their coercive and trend-setting roles as large firms operating within local
economies, their importance lies mostly in demonstrating how the internationalisation of business activity can shape industrial relations practices
within different systems. To illustrate these effects, it is worthwhile examining recent trends in the automotive industry, where there has been considerable greenfield foreign investment into Western Europe over the last two

decades as well as increasing pressures to redistribute existing investment because of excess capacity problems in the industry as a whole.

The role of *greenfield* investments is particularly visible in the case of the UK, which has been host to the majority of non-European automotive investments in Western Europe over the last two decades. Here, new investors – notably Japanese car companies – have often changed local industrial relations arrangements by spreading new working practices. The clearest example of this in recent years has been Nissan, whose plant in Sunderland has been an emulated model of new approaches to enterprise-level industrial relations. These include the development of a single-union site, the breakdown of traditional craft/job definitions among workers and a workforce relatively willing (or at least acquiescent) to adapt to changing production requirements (Garrahan and Stewart, 1991). The diffusion of Japanese investor working practices has been a notable feature of the automotive and electronics sectors in the UK, as indigenous companies have rapidly adopted different aspects of their approach (Morris and Imrie, 1992; Oliver and Wilkinson, 1989).

Similarly, investment decisions involving existing car manufacturing plants have also had an impact on industrial relations. The importance of industrial relations consensus in affecting investors' attitudes has already been discussed, but such consensus can in turn be influenced by investment decisions. In the case of the UK, some automotive multinationals have been willing to carry through threats of lost incremental investments to secure workforce concessions. US companies such as Ford and General Motors have made more active use of differences in plant productivity to press for changes in workforce flexibility. General Motors was the first major manufacturer to introduce a continuous, round-the-clock shift system following a review of its production system in the late 1980s, using productivity improvements in one plant as pressure to secure agreements in the other plants (Mueller and Purcell, 1992). The company explicitly linked further investment at its Ellesmere Port plant in the UK with changes in working practices and bargaining procedures (Wells and Rawlinson, 1994). Ford carried through on an investment threat, ironically 'punishing' its UK plants following a prolonged strike in 1990 at its Halewood site by shifting promised investment to one of its German plants (Hudson, 1995).

In Germany, similar multinational pressures have had implications for collective bargaining. In 1994, Mercedes-Benz decided to locate a new engine factory at its existing German site of Untertürkheim, but only after securing a flexibility deal with its workforce which included longer and more flexible working time (to maximise plant operation) through a system of annualised hours. This was viewed as necessary to the investment decision, as management had been considering locating the factory in Alsace, where wage costs were up to 30% lower (EIRR, 1994). Another decision on the construction of a different type of engine was also made by the company in favour of an existing German location – Rastatt – but only when the German workforce was able to make concessions on shift payments and the use of paid holiday time for training in order to bring its overall costs closer to a rival site in the Czech Republic (Income Data Service, 1996). Comparable exposure to the competitiveness of other locations influenced the agreement of greater flexibility in working time between plant workforces and management in BMW, Opel and VW (Schamp, 1995; EIRR, 1995). In these and similar cases, investment decisions were used to influence local workforce bargaining outside (though not necessarily in contradiction to) collective bargaining arrangements (Mueller, 1996).

Hence, for both corporatist and market approaches to labour-management relations, foreign investment activity has placed minor, but nonetheless convergent pressures on systemic differences within Western Europe. On the one hand, it may have partially weakened collective bargaining processes: while multinationals are unlikely to be responsible for any fundamental changes to corporatist approaches, they have acted to increase the scope of local workforces to strike individual deals more tailored to specific enterprises. In the case of Germany, the pattern of behaviour fits into a wider corporate dilution of the collective bargaining system and increasing pressure for more decentralised arrangements (Hassel, 1999). On the other hand, many multinationals appear to favour the operation of strong (but cooperative) bargaining institutions at local level, in some cases fostering them in industrial relations systems where they may be lacking. It has been argued that the strength of existing national labour market institutions will ultimately provide strong breakers on industrial relations convergence across Europe as a result of such inward investment (Smith and Elger, 1997). Nevertheless, the effects noted here have been to create stronger enterprise-level ties among workforces – in some cases, encouraging common interest with local management – while potentially diminishing the sense of common interest with workforces in other companies, indeed, with other enterprises within the same multinational group.

REFERENCES

Addison, J. and J. Chilton (1993), 'Can we identify union productivity effects?', *Industrial Relations*, **32**, 124-132.

Brewster, C., A. Hegewisch and L. Mayne (1994), 'Trends in European human resource management: signs of convergence', in P. Kirkbride (ed.), *Human Resource Management in Europe: Perspectives for the 1990s*, London: Routledge.

Brown, C. and J. Medoff (1978), 'Trade unions in the production process', *Journal of Political Economy*, **84**, 355-378.

Buchele, R. and J. Christiansen (1992), 'Industrial relations and productivity growth: a comparative perspective', *International Contributions to Labor Studies*, **2**, 77-97.

Cooke, W. and D. Noble (1998), 'Industrial relations systems of US foreign direct investment abroad', *British Journal of Industrial Relations*, **36**, 581-609.

Döhrn, R. (1996), 'Direktinvestitionen und Sachkapitalbildung - Statistische Unterschiede und ihre ökonomischen Implikationen', *RWI-Mitteilungen*, **47**, 19-34.

Dunning, J. (1993), *Multinational Enterprises and the Global Economy*, New York: Addison-Wesley.

Edwards, T. (1998), 'Multinational companies and the diffusion of employment practices: a survey of the literature', *Warwick Papers in Industrial Relations*, **61**.

EIRR (1993), 'The Hoover affair and social dumping', *European Industrial Relations Review*, **230**, 14-20.

EIRR (1994), 'Industrial relations and industrial location - a case study of Mercedes-Benz', *European Industrial Relations Review*, **244**, 12-15.

EIRR (1995), 'Landmark deals in the German car industry', *European Industrial Relations Review*, **261**, 12-13.

Enderwick, P. (1985), *Multinational Business and Labour*, London: Croom Helm.

Ferner, A. (1994), 'Multinational companies and human resource management: an overview of research issues', *Human Resource Management Journal*, **43**, 79-102.

Flaherty, N. (1997), 'The billion dollar bait', *Corporate Location*, January/February, 16-17.

Garrahan, P. and P. Stewart (1991), *The Nissan Enigma: Flexibility at Work in a Local Economy*, London: Mansell.

Hassel, A. (1999), 'The erosion of the German system of industrial relations', *British Journal of Industrial Relations*, **37**, 483-505.

Hudson, R. (1995), 'The Japanese in Europe', in R. Hudson and E. Schamp (eds), *Towards a New Map of Automobile Manufacturing in Europe?*, Berlin: Springer.

Income Data Services (1996), 'Das Gegenschäft ist Standort Deutschland', *IDS Focus*, **79**, 13-17.

Kahraß, K. (1997), 'Investment down but competitiveness up', *Corporate Location*, July/August, 48-51.

Karier, T. (1995), 'US foreign production and unions', *Industrial Relations*, **34**, 107-17.

Mair, A., R. Florida and M. Kennedy (1988), 'The new geography of automobile production: Japanese transplants in North America', *Economic Geography*, **64**, 352-73.

McConnell, C. and S. Brue (1989), *Comparative Labor Economics*, 2nd edition, New York: McGraw-Hill.

Marginson, P., P. Armstrong, P. Edwards and J. Purcell (1995), 'Extending beyond borders: multinational companies and the international management of labour', *International Journal of Human Resource Management*, **6**, 702-19.

Montagnon, P. (1997), 'The right skills are in the right location', *Financial Times*, 6 October.

Morris, J. and R. Imrie (1992), *Transforming Buyer-Supplier Relations: Japanese-Style Industrial Practices in a Western Context*, Basingstoke: Macmillan.

Mueller, F. and J. Purcell (1992), 'The Europeanization of manufacturing and the decentralization of bargaining: multinational management strategies in the European automobile industry', *International Journal of Human Resource Management*, **3**, 15-34.

Mueller, F. (1996), 'National stakeholders in the global context for corporate investment', *European Journal of Industrial Relations*, **2**, 345-68.

Muller, M. (1998), 'Human resource and industrial relations practices of UK and US multinationals in Germany', *International Journal of Human Resource Management*, **9**, 732-749.

Oliver, N. and B. Wilkinson (1989), 'Japanese manufacturing techniques and personnel and industrial relations practice in Britain: evidence and implications', *British Journal of Industrial Relations*, **27**, 73-91.

Peck, F. and I. Stone (1992), *New Inward Investment and the Northern Region Labour Market*, Employment Department Research Series, **6**, London: Employment Department.

Raines, P. (1998), *Labour Standards and Industrial Restructuring in Western Europe*, Employment and Training Papers, **17**, Geneva: International Labour Office.

Raines, P., R. Döhrn, R. Brown and M. Scheuer (1999), *Labour Market Flexibility and Inward Investment in Germany and the UK*, London: Anglo-German Foundation.

Rogers, J. and W. Streeck (1994), 'Workplace representation overseas: the works council story', in R. Freeman (ed.), *Working under Different Rules*, New York: Russell Sage Foundation.

Sadler, D. and A. Amin (1995), '"Europeanisation" in the automotive industry', in R. Hudson and E. Schamp (eds), *Towards a New Map of Automobile Manufacturing in Europe?*, Berlin: Springer.

Schamp, E. (1995), 'The German automobile production system', in in R. Hudson and E. Schamp (eds), *Towards a New Map of Automobile Manufacturing in Europe?*, Berlin: Springer.

Smith, C. and T. Elger (1997), 'International competition, inward investment and the restructuring of European work and industrial relations', *European Journal of Industrial Relations*, **3**, 279-304.

Tüselmann, H.-T. (1995), 'Standort Deutschland - is Germany losing its appeal as an international manufacturing location?', *European Business Review*, **95**, 21-30.

UNCTAD (1994), *World Investment Report 1994*, United Nations Conference on Trade and Development, New York: Division on Transnational Corporations and Investment.

UNCTAD (1998), *World Investment Report 1998*, United Nations Conference on Trade and Development, New York: Division on Transnational Corporations and Investment.

Watanabe, S. (1993), 'Growth and structural changes of Japanese overseas direct investment: implications for labour and management in host economies', in P. Bailey, A. Parisotto and G. Renshaw (eds.), *Multinationals and Employment: The Global Economy in the 1990s*, Geneva: International Labour Office.

Wells, P. and M. Rawlinson (1994), *The New European Automobile Industry*, London: St. Martins Press.

Wever, K. (1995), *Negotiating Competitiveness: Employment Relations and Organizational Innovation in Germany and the US*, Boston: Harvard Business School Press.

7. Danish labour market policy since 1994 – the new 'Columbus' egg' of labour market regulation?

Henning Jørgensen

'You can do it the American way, or you can do it the Danish way.' Those were the options for a successful strategy for labour market regulation expressed by Allan Larsson, Director General of EU's DG-V in 1999, and Larsson and the EU exclusively favoured the Danish way. Denmark is currently seen as leading the most visionary and successful labour market policy in Europe and the way of creating employment. At the turn of the century, unemployment has been reduced to 5%, the lowest level in Denmark in 24 years, and next to Norway and The Netherlands, also the lowest in Europe. Sweden, once the pioneer in labour market policy, has lost steam and reprogrammed its efforts. This has led to unusually high unemployment levels, something Sweden has never known, not even during the worst crisis in the 1980s. The Danish development and innovative policies in the 1990s attract increasing international attention. Many see Denmark as a model country – a reputation that matches the Danish Social Democratic-led government's self-image.

But is there basis for this strong optimism? Has Danish labour market policy suddenly found the Columbus' egg of labour market regulation, while most other European countries are struggling with continuing high and structured unemployment and clearly less effective political efforts on the labour market? The answer is not simple and there are several steps on the way to a substantiated answer. While this chapter does not pretend to identify each step as a proposed, tentative answer, it will present brief outlines and different views and opinions. The relation between activities and steering is central, where regionalised labour market policy and corporatisation of policy formation and implementation are characteristic traits of Danish policy developments in the 1990s[1].

1. RATIONALES IN LABOUR MARKET POLICY

Most policy fields have an inner core of rationalised conceptions about problems and measures that may solve these problems. The relation is usually formulated in a causal chain, a policy theory, which actors in the field know and, largely, share (Parsons 1995). Most fields require, at a minimum, a proven relation between problems and possible solutions. In any case, it is normal to trace the rationale in policy implementation back to such a policy core or cores, which often deal with problem complexes.

It is not that simple in the case of labour market policy, which is shaped, to a large extent, by practical experience and power struggles. In one sense, it is justified by the fact that conditions in the labour market are unstable and subject to cyclical changes, which means that measures must constantly adapt. Problems cannot be solved efficiently by inflexible, detailed laws and administrative rule steering in a machine bureaucracy. But in another sense, if short-term power struggles and organisational self-interest are allowed to dominate, the actual needs to solve the problems in the labour market are neglected. There is a schism between activity design and activity steering that deserves a spot on the political agenda: what are the options in terms of efforts and measures, how do we implement them, and how do we evaluate the outcomes of the policy measures?

In short, labour market policy is always conflict ridden, plagued by special interests, and ineffective. This is not to say that these measures cannot be analytically rationalised, but, fundamentally, this cannot happen in an interest-free space. There is a struggle over causal theory and practical influence in this field. Many actors and lines of interests cross each other: employers versus employees, including internal fractions on each side, state versus municipalities, etc. Still, open struggles are the exception, because many measures have gained institutional ground and stability, and also because the actors have learned, over time, to gauge other actors' intentioned 'rationality' in behaviour and experience. Historically, an understanding has been established that the goals of labour market policy concern economy as well as welfare, and that a trade-off between these two does not necessarily have to take place.

Labour market discourses typically focus on the schism between the vantage point of economic growth, according to which unfilled positions may hamper production and development, and a social and welfare-political vantage point that favours security for all and special assistance for victims of socially created problems. Since the early 1980s, this discursivation has been a constant in labour market policy developments in Denmark (see Bredgaard and Jørgensen 2000), the very same period when the bourgeois governments, since 1982, headed the parliamentary policy design. Attempts to steer policy developments in a more neo-liberal direction intensified this dilemma. The chances of designing measures that could simultaneously improve the way the labour market functions *and* strengthen employee security and income compensation claims were seen as slim. Sometimes, perhaps, the actors in the labour market saw policy issues as a zero sum game and not as a positive sum game. This makes it easier to get into a distribution struggle which politicises measures and implementation.

The occasional lack of order and respect in relation to employment measures has not improved the policy implementation in an active way, and the unemployed might get the idea that labour market policy was forced in the direction of support and control elements. Companies want a highly qualified and highly motivated labour force and they are interested in avoiding cost increases. Job seekers have to find productive and preferably lasting and well-paid work, and they want a social and economic safety net extended underneath them. Unions want generous unemployment support to keep the unemployed from underbidding the collective agreements (Ibsen and Jørgensen 1979). Employers are interested in cost control and moderate demands from employees, which are promoted by strong competition among employees. The state has fiscal interests in diminishing the burden on the taxpayers, but also a political interest in making the parties participate in policy implementation and a peaceful labour market[2]. However, the high politicisation counteracts this.

At first glance, it might be difficult to spot the equalising and non-partisan common denominator in the labour market policy. This perception was strengthened significantly when the unemployment rate rose by 50% from 1987 to 1993, when it exceeded 12%. In contrast, the inclusion of the first systematic rights concerning the education of unemployed from 1984/85 in the policy implementation, increased the awareness that the perceived trade-off in the policy was partly false: betting on more than short-sighted measures to increase the potential for re-integrating the unemployed and to strengthen qualifications in the employed labour force was exactly what was needed to expand and develop capacities that would benefit the development of the labour market[3]. Throughout the 1990s, this conception gained strength as a professional and political belief that enhancing the quality and motivation of the labour force makes more sense in labour market policy than short-sighted emergency solutions.

Analytically, the rationales in labour market policy can thus be split into three sub-groups, identified by capacities contained in the different activities:

- *productive capacities*: utilise existing potential to ensure increased efficiency in the many transactions in the labour market and its current mode of function.

- *welfare capacities*: include political reason in definitions of fair support of those who make up the active labour force (including currently unemployed), and
- *evolutionary capacities*: are rooted in activities aimed at developing and expanding productive potentials in a more and more knowledge-based society. As knowledge becomes a still larger part of products and services, labour market-related measures aimed at increasing competencies and motivation also become more important, just as the boundaries to other selective policy types, e.g., industrial, educational and social policies, become blurred.

The actual organisation of activities and measures varies according with the institutionalisation of policy elements, volume and local conditions for actors and implementation. Since 1994, when Danish labour market policy became regionalised, the significance of this diversification has increased (Hansen et al. 1997). One thing that cuts across the wealth of policy and administration practices is the labour market political organisation of *four basic functions: allocation* (matching demand and supply; measures and service in relation to companies; job provision; counselling and information); *education* (improve competencies to strengthen employed as well as unemployed – this has grown into a strong policy priority in Denmark in the 1990s); *employment measures* (activities and initiatives to re-integrate the unemployed in the open labour market); and finally: *support* (economic support of the unemployed through income compensation in accordance with politically determined guidelines). The first three functions comprise the active elements in a country's policy implementation, the fourth function is the passive element. From the mid-1970s through the 1980s, passive expenditures for unemployment benefits and early retirement pension (implemented in 1979) made up 75% of labour market-related government spending. In absolute terms, Denmark spends many resources in this area, almost 6% of GDP. The passive part is still the largest, but since 1993/94, the active part has been upgraded to the point that the passive expenses now make up less than two thirds. The great volume of active measures has paid off, as we will discuss below.

2. INSTITUTIONAL TRAITS IN DANISH LABOUR MARKET REGULATION

It is difficult to comprehend labour market regulation independently of established institutions, which are not only influential in giving incentives to or prescribing behaviour but which are also significant for the filtration/mediation of interests. Firm institutionalisations, which are part of the path dependencies of the Danish labour market, are referred to in this section before the regionalisation of policy in the 1990s is presented.

In Denmark, the *unemployment insurance system* is particularly significant for the labour market policy – and also for the way the unions recruit and interpret interests. Based on an, in theory, liberal help-to-self-help principle, registration in and payment to the unemployment insurance fund have become the criteria for entitlement to assistance and support during unemployment. It is fair to say that 'hygienic principles' have formed, according to which people are classified as 'good wage earners' (members of an unemployment insurance fund) or as mere 'proletarians' (non-insured). This often leads to social constructions, also at the administrative level. Likewise, Danish legislation is built on this separation, and different authorities deal with different target groups: the public employment service (*Arbejdsformidlingen*, AF) system and the labour market parties in the regional labour market councils (*Regionale Arbejdsmarkedsråd*, RAR (see below)), which primarily take care of the unemployed with insurance; and the local, politically governed, systems, whose target group is social welfare clients (non-insured). From the end of the 1970s, Danish labour market policy was primarily focused on preventing unemployed persons with unemployment insurance from being dislodged from the unemployment insurance system. The unemployment benefit eligibility period was, therefore, extended to up to 9 years, at its maximum. In the 1990s, the eligibility period was reduced to currently 4 years, after which the unemployed person will be transferred to the municipal social assistance system.

Early on, an *organised regulatory system* was created in the Danish labour market. The so-called 'September Accord' in 1899 laid the groundwork for the usually peaceful collective bargaining and for the subsequent juridical regulation of the system. Collective responsibility for policing agreement was formed, and employers, organised in the Danish Employers Confederation (*Dansk Arbejdsgiverforening*, DA), and employees, organised in the Federation of Danish Trade Unions (*Landsorganisationen i Danmark*, LO), recognised each other as legitimate bargaining partners. The state recognised the parties' collective autonomy, but through supplemental legislation and since 1933 also through state intervention in the collective agreements, the state has established itself as a normally non-intervening actor, but at the same time also as umpire and potential intervenor, in case the organisations are unable to solve conflicts on their own (Ibsen and Jørgensen 1979). Compromises have deep historical roots in Danish industrial relations and in parliamentary developments. Also *corporatism* is more than 100 years old[4]. Interest organisations have a very strong position in Denmark, and the development of the welfare system and labour market regulation is based on a partnership model. Historically, Denmark has established institutions that influence the orientation and actions of actors; this has created feedback mechanisms which, in turn, strengthen institutional regulation. A special policy style has evolved that stresses participation by organisations and a collective culture.

In accordance with the institutional heritage, the new steering system and implementation arrangements in the labour market policy are, in fact, corporative. But despite the spirit of consensus that permeates the process norms, conflict is still a possibility: the threat of open, industrial clashes must be present to make negotiations real. Approximately every 12 years since WWII, Denmark has experienced general strikes or general lock-outs, when the voluntary regulation by concerned parties has failed to produce viable results, which to the members means acceptable results.

Labour market policy will always be characterised by the contrasting relations from which the policy springs, but degrees of conflict/consensus and more or less intelligent use of policy instruments can actually ease tensions and divisions. Policy prioritisation and implementation attempts in the labour market corridor[5] must also take place in a hilly landscape of interests. There is a parallelogram of forces in which the supply and growth forces are interlocked with security-based welfare demands. It is tempting, because the best way to handle and reduce these perceived tensions is normally to endow the decision makers who are close to the changing reality with competencies and means to program and implement measures. As 'affected parties', they possess special resources and considerations which can be employed procedurally, and interest interpretations and preferences can be changed once again. Management by objectives has become complicated, because there is no single, overall objective for labour market policy which, parallel with a private company's clearly organised goal hierarchy can establish a vertical relation between strategic, tactical and operational levels (Dalsgaard and Lassen 1997). Working with labour market policy becomes a matter of vertical and horizontal coordination, more than of top-down steering. Historically, a *zone of compromise* has grown into a powerful factor in the labour market corridor, and it makes this work a lot easier. The powers of capital, organisations and government are interbalanced in a cooperative, Danish fashion. A kind of deliberate democracy model is in use.

The pool of knowledge, reason and legitimacy potentially possessed by representatives for capital and labour when they manage to work together as a decision making body is the argument for the labour market parties' participation in the leadership of authorities. In addition, interest organisations save parliament and administration the enormous amount of time they would otherwise have to spend on finding and storing political information and situational advice in connection with decision making. Active participation by the organisations makes decisions and implementation quick, flexible and, in terms of information and acceptance, more adequate (Jørgensen 2000). In other words, institutionalising participation by the interest organisations contributes to this. One of the most important policy tasks is designing good institutions. Excluding the parties from participation would make the relationship between the labour market authorities and the actors on the labour market more naked and power driven. The interest organisations obtain permanent influence on public policies and administrative norms, which makes them accountable. When the organisations obtain access and official status as representatives, their resource bases and the processes, the trade-offs, are also affected. Representation by organised interests definitively redefines the democratic contents in public decisions because, ideally, the 'affected parties' are both represented and accountable; this also justifies corporatism as a precondition for the success of Denmark's active labour market policy in the 1990s. The parties have been able to qualify – or hamper – policy design through both political and administrative channels.

In order to understand Danish policy developments in the past seven years, we have to go back to the relationship between labour market policy and the general economic policy implementation. Since the end of the war and up through the 1980s, a Keynesian policy course was followed, in which especially restrictions on demand prevailed in particular. The period 1976–94 was characterised by unsynchronised relations, in contrast to the Swedish developments (based on the Rehn-Meidner model).

In 1993/94, attempts were made to obtain stronger synchronisation of policy planning in an expanded *policy mix* that upgraded labour market policy once again. However, leaving behind a pure Keynesian policy development makes sense, because total demand regulation that aims at economic equilibrium does not take into account existing divisions, segmentations and sub-labour markets. Manoeuvres must be diversified and adapted to local conditions to successfully handle the many sub-imbalances that emerge, to mobilise available labour power and avoid bottlenecks and inflationary pay increases. Economic-political models would argue in favour of selective, specific measures adapted to local and regional conditions accompanied by coordinated measures and timing in relation to the general stabilisation policy. Synchronisation in relation to the general economic policy was partly contained in a demand-regulating fiscal and tax policy which, at the same time, was able to prevent a growth in unemployment and promote mobility and occupational change. The main ingredients were a kick-start of the economy in 1993/94 through a tax reform, a new fiscal policy and a quickly adopted labour market reform. However, policy implementation has not only focused on lowering unemployment at the given unemployment level; it also contains a desire to activate the potential labour force that is otherwise not present on the labour market. The Danish service sector is very strong and offers a variety of job opportunities; activation measures are most successful in the private sector.

Denmark has the highest rate of participation in the labour market for all age groups in the EU. The participation rate for women is remarkable; it has nearly doubled since 1960 when the participation rate was around 40. Unlike other countries, the improved employment rate is not a result of more part-time jobs. On the contrary, the employment rate has increased while the share of part-time jobs has been significantly reduced. Denmark has become a nation of 'workaholics'! Still, Denmark has managed to keep those with a non-Danish ethnic background out of the labour market! The reluctance of employers and labour to admit immigrants and refugees to the labour market – to put it in diplomatic terms – has created barriers and a suboptimal utilisation of available labour resources. Discrimination is manifest. This is a serious problem which labour market policy has not been able to solve. In other words, Danish labour market policy is not an all-round success!

3. REGIONALISATION OF LABOUR MARKET POLICY

The purpose of making labour market policy an independent policy type in the 1960s was to make a transition from an effort motivated by social policy, which primarily consisted of economic compensation for loss of income, to a targeted and programmed policy. The parole was a transition from passive or reactive to active labour market policy (inspired by Swedish policy formation). The goal to make labour market policy active could only be realised if the state simultaneously increased its consensus-making resources. The only way to do this was to include the labour market's interest organisations in the planning and implementation of the policy. An influence and decision system, established in 1969/70, had the power to integrate affected organisations and to assist in expanding the state's scope of action. A central tribunal, The National Labour Board (*Landsarbejdsnævnet*), and 14 regional labour market tribunals (*Arbejdsmarkedsnævn*), divided according to the counties' administrative borders, functioned until 1993 as an interest mediation system and as an administrative organisation, the latter within a strong, central steering committee.

The 1993/94 labour market reform provided the regional freedom and independent economic means that enabled – even necessitated – independent regional strategies for the labour market. A transition was made from organisation around a functional principle of ensuring vertical integration of labour to a territorial principle centred on the regional and local labour market. The principles of organisation affect both policy formation and implementation. Regionalisation creates tensions in the policy, since labour market policy in historical origin and justification is founded on functional principles. It also counterbalances the centralisation of the labour market organisations. The functional capacity and balances of the entire labour market used to be in focus, but after 1994, things became more complicated. Territorial elements became central – even though it is obvious that no labour market or problem structure stops at regional administrative borders. So, are the problem, policy and administration sides coherent after 1994? Has Denmark established adequate policy frames? First, we must answer the question of whether it makes sense to regionalise policy formation and implementation.

If the effect is that central decision makers feel liberated from the responsibility of fighting unemployment, it is very risky to regionalise labour market and employment policy. To prevent undermining of regional measures, reliable push and pull effects must exist. A *dual strategy* for the state's labour market measures should be a requirement: first, the government must lead a policy that improves employment opportunities so that the general economic policy can flank selective measures; second, the latter must be regionalised. Under these conditions, regionalisation may be implemented expediently with the following objectives:

- a *stronger regional targeted policy*, based on analysed and demonstrated needs and potentials;
- a *more regional diversified policy* aimed at matching local problem structures to measure and resource structures; and
- a *stronger regionally programmed and implemented policy* aimed at including decentral actors in cooperation, which can simultaneously increase acceptance of labour market programmes.

A recommendation of regionalisation does not mean that regional policies should be decoupled from a central formulation framework. It must continue to exist as a part of strategy determinations contained in the policy mix. But if we see regionally targeted, diversified and effected measures, their system character may obtain a greater operational value. In such cases, local custom tailoring is better than ready-to-wear issued from Copenhagen!

The path Denmark chose to follow in 1994 is one of an intra-regional policy type centred on actors' attempts to combat local imbalances. One alternative would be a policy frame that enables several inter-regional measures through separate assistance to exposed regions, diversification, uneven distribution of resources and instruments, etc. Here, the goal would be to overcome imbalances and distribution among regional labour markets. The chosen intra-regional policy type concentrates on the situation in the local labour market and the local actors' efforts to reduce goal conflicts. In addition, the policy must also be delivered to citizens and industry; that involves policy adoption and target formation issues that need special attention (Schmid et al. 1996). Dependency on well-functioning policy networks and implementation structures is very high. Organised negotiation should not turn into organised obstruction!

4. THE REFORM COMPLEX IN 1993/94

This background had to be considered when a new labour market policy was designed in 1993. Roughly, the labour market reform consisted of a new activation system, leave schemes and the creation of a new institutional set-up through regionalisation of the steering system (cf. Box 7.1).

Box 7.1: Personal action plan and active labour market policy instruments

The *personal action plan* is a contract between the public employment service and the unemployed person. The personal action plan forms the basis of activities to be followed by the unemployed person as well as an evaluation of the consequences if the individual refuses activation (i.e., loss of unemployment benefits). The action plan is formulated before being used by the active labour market policy instruments.
Besides placement activities in connection with ordinary (non-subsidised) work, the *following instruments can be used in the elaboration of a personal action plan*:

Information and guidance
Subsidised employment (job training) with public or private employers
Individual (specialised) job training for unemployed persons who cannot be placed in job training in ordinary workplaces
Pool jobs[6] (subsidised employment for unemployed persons who are qualified for unemployment benefits), which are jobs in the public sector of up to three years' duration for the long-term unemployed. The main goal of the pool jobs is to create more permanent jobs in priority fields or in which there is a need for a higher level of services (i.e., child or elder care)
Education/training in the ordinary education/training system or as part of a specially organised activity adapted to the background of the unemployed persons concerned
Job rotation, where the leave taken by an employed person is combined with the recruitment of an unemployed person for job training
Special, tailor-made training activities, other specially organised activation activities (experiments) and voluntary and unpaid activities such as social, cultural, sports or environmental activities (all three instruments only for unemployed person receiving social assistance)
A combination of the above instruments
Other instruments (for both employed and unemployed) include:
Educational/training leave for special training courses
Parental leave

Contrary to international de-corporatising trends, the Danish reform actually strengthened the role of the social partners, especially at the regional level. The large-scale measures in the reform concerned an earlier effort directed toward the potential long-term unemployed and generally more tailored measures for the individual unemployed person and for the regional labour market. Each unemployed person became entitled to *a personal action plan* that forms the basis of activation measures (e.g. education, job training) and is made in agreement with the public employment service.

Increased influence by labour market organisations (employees and employers), decentralisation and a more flexible and responsive administration would form the main steering rearrangements. Despite the OECD's recommendations (1993), the passive part of the labour market policy was retained at a very generous level on an international scale. Significant changes were made, such as limited duration of unemployment benefits, no retaining of unemployment insurance from participation in job training and a tightening of the criteria for job availability, e.g., widening mobility criteria (Jørgensen et al. 1998/99).

By 1994, Danish unemployment had reached a record high of more than 343000 full-time unemployed, corresponding to more than 12% of the labour force (see Table 7.1).

Table 7.1: Labour force, unemployment and employment in Denmark, in thousands, several years

	1990	1992	1994	1996	1998
Labour force	2907	2910	2908	2872	2868
Em-ployed	**2674**	**2626**	**2585**	**2649**	**2699**
Men	1454	1426	1396	1444	1465
Women	1219	1200	1189	1205	1234
Unem-ployed	**272**	**318**	**343**	**246**	**183**
Men	124	149	164	116	81
Women	148	169	180	130	102

Source: Danmarks Statistik: Statistisk Ti-årsoversigt, 1999 [Statistics Denmark: Statistical Ten-year Review]

The structural composition was such that, while 775 000 persons were affected by unemployment in 1994-95, nearly half of them had an unemployment rate of less than 0.3. In contrast, the group of long-term unemployed, with an unemployment rate of over 0.7, constituted half the calculated number of full-year unemployed (cf. Ministry of Finance 1995: 291). Unemployment was especially characterised by a large and, until 1994, increasing number of long-term unemployed. The rise in unemployment, with an increasing number of long-term unemployed, was further described as an expression of hysteresis and marginalisation problems. The phenomenon of hysteresis expresses the fact that the level of structural unemployment increases as a result of the increase in the number of long-term unemployed. Considering the definition of structural employment, this makes reduction of unemployment more difficult. Figures on the development in the size of the labour force, employment and unemployment during the 1990s are presented in Table 7.1.

In 1993, widespread anxiety among politicians and economists in Denmark over the rapidly growing unemployment rate resulted in a consensus to slow down this development via an expansive fiscal policy. The rising unemployment curve had to be broken. However, the political-economic exercise consisted partly in increased demand by easing the fiscal policy, in that the structural unemployment problem at the same time had to be combated with labour market policy measures to hinder increasing inflation problems. Thus, a combination of general and selective measures was needed. The law on active labour market policy, which took effect on 1 January 1994, was intended to ensure this.

Table 7.2: The unemployment rate in Denmark, in %, several years

	1988	1990	1992	1994	1996	1998	1999
Aver-age	**8.7**	**9.7**	**11.3**	**12.3**	**8.9**	**6.6**	**5.6**
16-24	9.2	106	11.5	11.1	6.8	4.2	3.8
25-34	11.6	12.8	14.8	14.9	11.3	8.0	..
35-54	6.9	7.6	9.3	10.5	7.7	6.1	..
55-59	9.4	10.5	13.0	16.8	9.9	9.0	..
60-66	7.5	9.4	9.7	13.6	15.5	8.9	5.1

Sources: Figures for 1999 are from September 1999 and seasonally adjusted (Statistics Denmark, Statistical News, 1991, Vol.41). Danmarks Statistik: 'Statistisk Tiårsoversigt', 1999 [Statistical Ten-year Review]

The policy combination was definitely a success. After 1994, Denmark has experienced a dramatic turnover. As seen in Table 7.1, the number of employed grew by approximately 114 000 between 1994 and 1998 and the number of unemployed has been reduced by nearly 50% since 1994 to 183 000, or 6.6%

of the labour force in 1998. Unemployment continued to fall throughout 1999, and is also expected to fall slightly in 2000, though at a slower pace. Moreover, the marginalisation problems observed in 1994 due to the increase in long-term unemployment are apparently also starting to resolve themselves, in that the number in this group has fallen significantly since 1994 and was estimated at 40 000 persons in 1999 compared to 160 000 in 1994 (cf. Ministry of Finance 1999). There is some controversy regarding the fall in long-term unemployment, due to the fact that many long-term unemployed are still occupied in active labour market measures and not in ordinary jobs. Furthermore, it is becoming increasingly difficult to continue to bring down the number of long-term unemployed, because the remaining group is poorly qualified and has very long periods of unemployment. However, as seen in Table 7.2, it is quite amazing how successful the combat of youth unemployment in particular has been.

Table 7.3: Average number of participants in active labour market measures (1994-1998); number of persons in thousands

	1994	1995	1996	1997	1998
Total	*256*	*293*	*305*	*294*	*298*
Subsidised employ-ment	60	51	49	49	46
Leave	51	82	63	47	43
Education	23	17	23	24	27
Other active measures	2	3	3	4	5
Early retirement	119	138	167	171	177
Not informed	0.3	0.2	0.3	0.2	0.3

Source: Danmarks Statistik: Statistisk Årbog, Div. årgange [Statistics Denmark: Statistical Yearbook]

In connection with the passive part of labour market policy, an array of active measures and instruments were added in 1994. These new instruments are presented in Box 7.1. As indicated, some of these are only available to the unemployed entitled to unemployment benefits. Public efforts are also made to stimulate a 'behavioural change' in unemployed individuals. Active participation and motivation on the part of the unemployed person are required, and measures must be extremely responsive to individual needs and the dynamics of the local labour market. In 1997, approximately 12 000 personal action plans were prepared each month. Table 7.3 above shows the quantitative use of the main instruments in the active labour market policy.

It is important to note that one of the secrets behind the reduction in unemployment in Denmark since 1994 is that *participants in active labour market policy measures are not registered as unemployed in official statistics*. All in all, almost half a million persons in Denmark were without regular employment in 1998 (183 000 persons registered as unemployed and 298 000 persons in active labour market policy measures). Excluding those in early retirement schemes, who may be conceived as voluntarily unemployed, the actual number of unemployed amounted to 306 000 in 1998. The Danish labour market consequently harbours a considerable amount of hidden unemployment (up to 40% more than the official statistics).

As seen in the table, the use of active instruments, after the introduction of the labour market reform, reached its highest point in 1996 with a total average of more than 305 000 persons engaged in active measures. According to OECD (1998), participant inflows as a percentage of the labour force could be estimated at 19.4 % in 1995. This figure includes 9.2%, being employed adults engaged in training, and they should not be included as participants in active labour market measures, as is the case in the table, which constitutes the official Danish statistics.

In general, the use of active instruments has been decreasing throughout the period in line with unemployment (mainly due to a fall in the number of participants in subsidised employment by nearly 14 000 between 1994 and 1998). This also holds for leave arrangements, which have become considerably less popular after the eligibility rules and leave benefits were tightened during the last three years. The big gender difference regarding use of leave instrument is another important point to emphasise. In the opposite direction, attention has to be drawn to the massive growth in early retirement arrangements. Early retirement rose from approximately 119 000 in 1994 to more than 177 000 in 1998. This means that, in a period with very good job opportunities, 58 000 chose to leave the labour market. Politically, this has recently drawn attention to the possibility of bringing some of these people back to the labour market through education and more flexible working conditions. The potential labour supply shortage in the next 5-6 years has suddenly popped up as a new theme on the labour market agenda.

Table 7.4 shows the distribution of participants in active labour market policy instruments. The importance of skill enhancement is clearly reflected in the table, as education has increasingly become the most commonly applied and popular activation measure. Though the total use of active instruments has increased each year since 1995, the number of participants in ordinary job training has fallen successively each year in line with unemployment. But individual job training has increased by 50%, indicating that those who have remained unemployed throughout the period have been much more difficult to re-employ.

Table 7.4: The distribution of participants in active labour market policy measures, 1995-1998

	1995	1996	1997	1998
Job training	26 098	20 443	16 829	16 502
Individual job training	10 856	13 317	13 960	15 249
Pool jobs in municipalities	-	2059	6638	6237
Voluntary, unpaid activities	494	372	284	280
Enterprise allowance	14 045	12 427	11 245	7783
	20 632	26 376	27 818	31 923
Education				
Total	*72125*	*74 994*	*76 774*	*77 974*

Source: Danmarks Statistik: Statistiske Efterretninger. Arbejdsmarked. Div. årgange. [Statistics Denmark: Statistical News: Labour Market]

To account for the dual Danish system of labour market policy, Table 7.5 shows the number of people activated through the public employment service and the municipalities.

*Table 7.5: Number of participants in active measures, activated through the public employment service (AF) or the municipality**

	1995	1996	1997	1998
Public employment service	44 606	45 741	47 471	46 484
Municipalities	26 532	28 322	28 692	31 010

Source: Danmarks Statistik: Statistisk Årbog [Statistics Denmark: Statistical Yearbook, 1995; 1996; 1997; 1998; 1999]
* This does not account for the total number of unemployed in active measures, as some arrangements are provided through law by application and some through the educational system.

As seen, the public employment service has throughout the period been activating around 60% of the unemployed persons. In 1998, public expenditures for labour market programmes amounted to 5.6% of GDP. Expenditures have dropped from nearly 7% in 1994 to the current level, mainly due to decreasing expenditures for passive measures, e.g., unemployment benefits. While the public sector (the state, the 14 counties and the 275 municipalities) has been the key responsible actor in implementing the activation policy, the private sector has remained sceptical of participation in activation.

4.1 Integration and continued marginalisation

Adding to the acclaimed success of the current Social Democratic-led govern-ment, one of the major social and structural problems in the Danish labour market since the 1970s, namely youth unemployment, seems to have disap-peared in the late 1990s. The registered youth unemployment rate has been reduced to one third since 1993, and young people currently have the lowest unemployment rate of all age groups. One important explanation for the decline is the radical Youth Unemployment Programme in 1996, which was directed towards unemployed, low-educated youths, and in 1999 extended to also cover unemployed young people with education. Youths without formal education who have been unemployed for 6 of the last 9 months are offered 18 months specially designed vocational education during which unemployment benefits are cut by 50%. Refusal to participate results in a loss of unemployment benefits and transferral to the social assistance system at a much lower income rate (for a detailed description, see Bredgaard and Jørgensen 2000). Even though the discursive framing and legitimisation of Danish youth unemployment policies experienced a 'fortunate moment' in the late 1990s in the form of positive economic conditions and employment opportunities, shrinking youth cohorts, expansion of educational capacity and admission rates, the youth unemployment programme has undoubtedly been influential in lowering youth unemployment, at least in the short run (Bredgaard and Jørgensen 2000; Jensen et al. 1999; Nord-Larsen 1997). The programme significantly increased the effective labour supply of, in particular, short-term unemployed youths. However, there seems to be a general tendency towards a tripartite polarisation of young people. The majority is well integrated on the labour market and has benefited from both the improving employment situation and the youth unemployment programme, a smaller group is loosely coupled to the open labour market and floats in and out of activation and regular employment, while a minor, but hard-core group is becoming increasingly excluded from open employment. Unlike the two other groups, this last group of marginalised youths can neither be 'enticed, sanc-tioned nor sermonised' into regular employment or education, but requires much more differentiated, individualised, costly and time-consuming measures to be integrated into the labour market.

The tendency towards polarisation of young people seems to be a reflection of a general development in the Danish labour market. As seen in Table 7.6, the positive economic conditions since 1994 and improving employment situation have also set off a quite considerable growth in the number of people outside the labour force.

Table 7.6: Persons outside the labour force receiving social welfare benefits, 1994 and 1998 (age 15-66 years), in thousands

	1994	1998
*Temporary absence from the labour force**	*231*	*226*
Early retirement schemes	*392*	*454*
Transitional allowance	8	35
Early retirement pay	111	142
Pre-pension	267	273
Other pensions	6	4
Outside the labour force	*623*	*680*

Source: Ministry of Finance 2000.
* Persons who are temporarily absent from the labour force comprise persons on leave, recipients of educational benefits, childbirth benefits, sickness benefits, social assistance and recipients of rehabilitation benefits.

Early retirement and pre-pension schemes are causing a considerable drop in the size of the labour force. As more than 100 000 persons shifted from unemployment to employment between 1994 and 1998, 62 000 persons entered into early retirement schemes and left the labour force. Throughout the recession in the 1980s, a significant number of people were excluded from the labour market by means of, for instance, pre-pension. These people are now locked into the social benefit system outside the labour force and lack the qualifications for re-integration in the labour market at a point where available labour is in short supply. Coupled with the changing demographic situation, labour supply problems are emerging: The youth cohorts will continue to shrink until at least 2005, as the proportion of older people grows.

As Denmark approaches full employment, the political and public eye increasingly focus on the potential and future labour supply problems of the firms and public institutions. The demand side has never been in political focus in Denmark.

5. ASSESSMENT OF THE RESULTS OF ACTIVATION

If the overall picture of policy results is positive, we also have to reserve judgement for the remaining tasks of reintegrating marginalised groups. The interests of these groups have not yet been pushed to the foreground – and certainly not by the labour market organisations. It cannot be denied that some activation instruments may have had negative side effects ('windfall profits'). There are no precise, analytical accounts, only indications. Critics of the activation offensive will furthermore claim that the unemployed (and the unemployment statistics) are only getting short-sighted help. Are the critics right?

This question is not easy to answer. Ideally, regular and continuous follow-up ought to take place. This is not the case, but there are two evaluations, one from 1995/1996 (Langager 1997) and one from 1997 (Arbejdsmarkedsstyrelsen 1999), so we can calculate the employment effect in this 18-24 month period. Table 7.7 shows the status of the so-called *short-term unemployed* (i.e., people who have been activated in the first half of the unemployment period).

Table 7.7: The labour market status of the short-term unemployed 6-18 months after activation (persons with unemployment insurance)

	1995/96*	1997**
In ordinary employment	36%	51%
In ordinary education	1%	8%
In activation	17%	11%
Unemployed	38%	27%
Outside the labour force	7%	3%
Total	99%	100%

*   6-18 months after the end of an activation offer.
**   7-10 months after the end of an activation offer.
Source: Arbejdsmarkedsstyrelsen, 1999; Langager, 1997

While 36% found ordinary employment in 1995/96, more than 50% re-entered the open labour market in 1997. At the same time, more people have joined ordinary education. This constitutes a significant improvement of the activation results among the short-term unemployed, a development that has been facilitated by an economic upturn and earlier activation. The status of the long-term unemployed is somewhat different, as shown in Table 7.8.

Table 7.8: The labour market status of the long-term unemployed 6-18
        months after activation (persons with unemployment insurance)

	1995/96*	1997**
In ordinary employment	23%	19%
In ordinary education	1%	7%
In activation	25%	54%
Unemployed	35%	27%
Outside the labour force	17%	3%
Total	101%	100%

*   6-18 after the end of an activation offer.
**   6 months after the end of an activation offer.
Source: Arbejdsmarkedsstyrelsen 1999; Langager 1997.

As Table 7.8 shows, the employment effect has diminished, whereas the education percentage has increased. Significantly more people are placed in activation, probably because of the expansion of the activation period since 1996. However, it is obvious that the long-term unemployed tend to stay in a situation where they have problems finding employment. Among the unemployed with insurance, the short-term unemployed are best off.

Table 7.9: The labour market status of social assistance recipients 6 months
        after activation

In ordinary employment	23%
In ordinary education	21%
In activation	26%
Unemployed	29%
Total	99%

Source: Weise and Brogaard 1997

There is only one status for the unemployed under the municipal social assistance system. The employment status is calculated six months after activation, as shown in Table 7.9.

We encounter patterns similar to the long-term unemployed with insurance. 44% have found ordinary work or education, which is positive, but among social assistance recipients, education beats employment. It is obvious that 'creaming' has taken place, so that those with the most resources have escaped first. Therefore, a new status would reveal that the group of persons without active help has become 'heavier'. Likewise for the unemployed with insurance, among whom the strongest were helped early on – typically placed in private job training, which then, in turn, scores the best evaluation results. Public job training cannot demonstrate similar positive effects. One reason is that the public sector functions as a backstop in connection with activation and that public jobs are usually created as extraordinary jobs in order to solve this task. Municipal activation is not for 'clingers'! The combined, estimated employment and education effect for those short-term unemployed who have been through activation in the AF/RAR system is approximately 60%, compared to under 50% for people in municipal activation. In addition, around one third has not left their predicament, and remains unemployed.

Statistical studies based on the 'fixed effect' method have also established that the pure effect numbers, presented above, represent a not so great reduction in gross unemployment (between 5 and 15%). It is highly likely that some short-term unemployed would have found employment, also without activation (Langager 1997). However, *effect-based evaluations usually omit other successes, such as increased self-esteem and self-confidence, better vocational preparedness and qualifications* which, in the long term, improve their situation on the labour market. Activation has a multitude of effects, and positive as well as negative side effects must be included in calculations. It seems evident that the quality of activation projects needs to improve and that greater patience in individual efforts is required.

Activation is *a right and an obligation*, now split into an unemployment benefit period of one year and an active period of three years. The sooner activation can start, the greater the chances of forging a lasting contact between the unemployed and the open labour market. But early activation costs a lot of money and requires a high investment of resources at the implementing levels. Since 1997, more unemployed have been subjected to measures in the active period instead of in the early unemployment benefit period. This development continues, as shown in Figure 7.1. The large annual fluctuations in the activation effort are primarily attributed to activity planning at educational institutions, which normally have a minimum of activities during the summer. And since education is the most important activation instrument, this becomes very visible in the statistics. The scope of activation partly conceals the fact that the authorities are under pressure – also economically – to give up on very early activation (within the first year), partly that the system is now geared to reach a goal of 75% activation measured by the duration of the active period. The AF system has not yet succeeded in this. The actors – politicians, administrators and organisation – are very focused on goals in activities.

Figure 7.1: Participants in measures of active labour market policy with different status

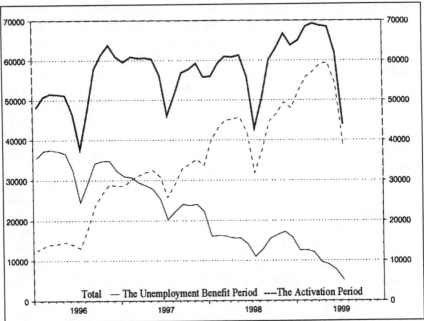

This could also be called political impatience. And along with administrative modernisation, output and efficiency goals have become very prominent. The labour market policy has been pushed ahead in order to achieve a large volume in efforts so that short-sighted measures will cause a fall in recorded unemployment and increased efficiency in public authorities. More and cheaper activation programs are, it seems, a goal in itself. This means that, relatively speaking, elements in more long-term strategies, e.g., massive education and skill enhancement, are somewhat downgraded.

The labour market reform of 1994 was a clear-cut commitment to an active policy stance. With more than 10% of the labour force engaged in active labour market policy measures, this commitment has, apparently, manifested itself. Activation and skill enhancement are key concepts in the Danish approach to fighting unemployment. But the provision of active measures in quantity does not guarantee success. Therefore, the Danish labour market reform also focused on what could be called crucial design and resulting implementation features as a key to quality and positive results. Regionalisation was also a further step towards private interest government in labour market policy. This induces a test of the willingness of private actors to find compromises and to contribute to the ability of labour market policy to develop and implement strategies.

6. POLICY IMPLEMENTATION

You cannot assume that policies can be designed in close association with intentions and results. You also have to consider actor interests, networks and implementation processes. It has become evident that political-administrative interventions are not only produced with reference to the control ambitions of central actors, and that performances can seldom exhibit the degree of agreement with the intentions implied by optimistic policy models. Therefore, the question concerns the degree to which political administrative interventions and their processual and institutional preconditions can, in fact, be designed and steered. An exhaustive discussion of this issue is not within the scope of this chapter (see, instead, Jørgensen and Larsen 1997), but it signals a need for a closer examination of the more concrete experiences of implementation when evaluating the apparent success of Danish active labour market policy. It is thus not only a question of choice of policy instruments, steering resources and causal theory, but basically it can also be one of actor interests, exercise of power, discursive activities, narrow-minded actor horizons, and the actions of the parties involved. In this context, there is a clear need to examine more closely the implementation-related conditions as an explanatory variable in the success of Danish labour market policy.

In substantive terms, earlier labour market policy measures lacked a larger responsiveness toward both regional and individual problems concerning job matching and re-education. In relation to the latter, there were problems with motivation and active participation by unemployed clients. The effort was rule governed, and unemployed persons received help only after mandatory waiting periods and specific deadlines in the legislation. Generally, experience in the sphere of labour market policy has shown that it is difficult to formulate and design policies that meet the needs for flexibility, responsiveness and, hence, also the right measures for each observed problem. Politically and administratively, it has thus been extremely difficult to formulate precise laws and regulations centrally which would achieve the desired effect, unless they were intended to be purely symbolic and pseudo policies.

Where activation was formerly a way to earn a renewed right to receive additional unemployment compensation, the activation process now offers only the possibility of re-education. Besides a more flexible effort in accord with the needs of the local labour market, one of the intentions behind the reorganisation is prevention of long-term unemployment. The goal is to give those who are most likely to end up in long-term unemployment an activation offer early in their unemployment period. Yet, during the last three years, this goal has not been reached.

In the domain of steering, the Danish tradition of corporatist arrangements was strengthened, simultaneously with a significant regionalisation of competence in designing activation efforts for the unemployed. Fourteen regional labour market councils were established in 1993/94 in which the labour market organisations (employees and employers) occupy two thirds of the seats, and the regional/local authorities (county and municipalities) the remaining one third. Private interests are institutionalised as part of public authority (cf. Figure 7.2).

Figure 7.2: Organisation of Danish labour market policy

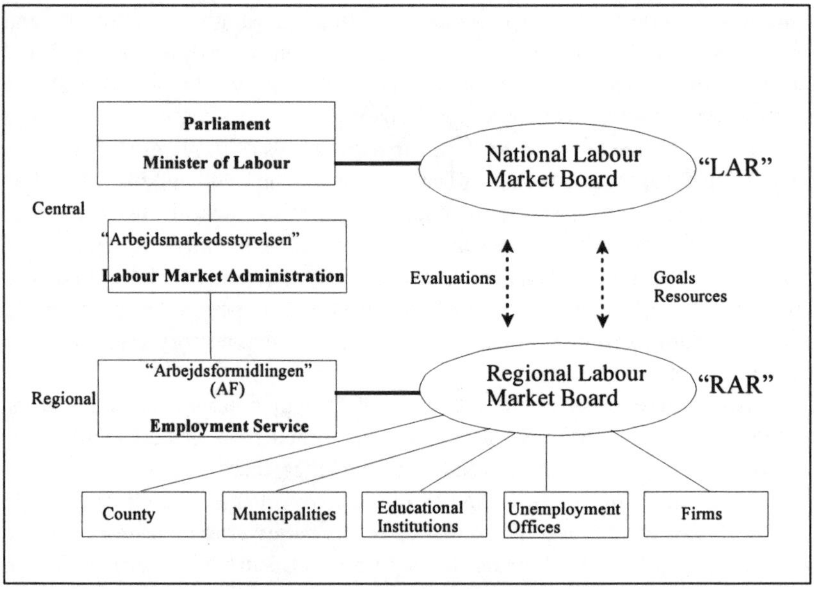

The labour market councils establish priorities and plan their activities in accordance with regional needs. That is, within certain relatively broad, centrally established frameworks, they set priorities as to who should receive an offer of activation, and what types of activation options will be made available (e.g., job training, education, etc.). Hence, it is a matter of setting a regional strategy. The public employment service facilitates the councils and assumes the function of 'main executor' of the effort, and the reform has given the employment service (AF) a fundamentally altered role: measures for unemployed persons and the labour market must now be based on more concrete assessments rather than on automatic rules. With the regionalisation and reorganisation of the content of the effort, however, implementation and thus organisation of the activation sequence can occur only in coordination with regional enterprises, regional authorities (counties), local authorities (municipalities), unemployment offices (the social insurance system), and educational institutions. In terms of steering, the labour market policy effort has thus become increasingly based on network coordination - both social and institutional in form (Larsen et al. 1996; Jørgensen & Larsen 1997; Jørgensen 2000).

When the political competence to design the effort is applied regionally, a field of tension emerges vertically between the central and regional political levels. A visible result of this tension is that the employment service (AF), as main executor of the effort, tends to retain its traditional bureaucratic form with relatively strong central control. This is another problem for successful implementation. The central level is formulating goals and result demands on a quantitative basis, thereby focusing on effectiveness and efficiency. The desire for a certain volume in the system is in conflict with the need to secure quality in efforts. The result is a partial 'roll back' in relation to the regionalised and need-oriented activation measures. And a result of the great focus on productivity and efficiency criteria is AF's 'creaming' of the unemployed. The 'weak' unemployed, so to speak, take too many resources from the system. Instead, the unemployed person's resources are to a high degree decisive in determining the character of activation and training given.

7. CONCLUDING REMARKS

Denmark has turned around after 1994: from an economy plagued by negative developments and high unemployment, Denmark has reached the highest employment rate in Europe and has reduced unemployment to one of the lowest in Europe. The labour market policy has had a key role in the new policy mix in which the selective measures have been redefined, including strengthened regionalisation and participation by interested organisations. The ability of the labour market corridor to produce useful results as far as policy and labour market are concerned has been put to the test. Decentral strategy and policy decisions and implementation processes have had to adapt different considerations to each other and empower the capacities that constitute the basic rationality in labour market policy. Policy developments involve coordination of cognitive understandings, actions and institutional conditions. Processes and results become very dependent on self-coordination and corporatist policy formation. The fourteen regions have designed different types of activation regimes with three mutually connected, intended conditions: policy priorities, actor interaction and linkage results. Coordination demands have an impact on policy operation, and that means the connection to a collective output.

In terms of policy results and processes, the reform has not been a fiasco – on the contrary. The policy shift from 1994 is ambitious, both on the demand side and the steering side, but the results speak of a synchronisation between the general economic policy and selective measures, which has helped the labour market function better. This has not triggered a wave of inflation, not even now, when the unemployment rate is approaching 5%. The Danish economy is top-tuned and strong with low interest rates, surplus on public budgets and on the balance of payments.

The principles of a greater targeted and tailored effort to provide activation offers adjusted to both the labour market and to the individual needs of the unemployed person have shown themselves to be effective in allocation and education of labour. The effort has become essentially more flexible and responsive toward the various problem types, just as incentives and motivation for active participation in activation measures have increased regionally, locally and among the unemployed. The social partners play a decisive role in corporatist policy formation and implementation. Acceptance of policy goals and measures has also been secured. Administrative corporatism works in Denmark.

There are, however, continued growing implementation problems, which means that a movement away from the original intentions behind the policy has begun in Denmark. This is due to problems in finding the right balance in the relations of competence between central and regional levels, partly insufficient regional policy formation capacity, some lack of coordination in network cooperation at the regional level, conversion problems in the public employment service in relation to working in a subjective, assessing fashion, and finally, general resource problems at the operational level in relation to the costly need orientation. If we look at the implementation problems alone, none of them seem unsolvable. The problem is, however, that the system is expected to operate according to political intentions within no time. This can also be attributed to the high level of politicisation of labour market policy. The result has been political interventions in 1995, 1996 and 1999, which in reality has increased the distance from the original principles for the effort, as well as new demands on the system for an 'output' equal to the one prior to the transition to the regionalised and need-oriented activation effort. Focus had been on quantity rather than quality.

The central goal and frame steering will prioritise the quantitative and administrative demands for results, where the corporative organs' attempts at qualitative consideration easily get squeezed. But if corporatively constructed organs are, in reality, drained of their contents, they will collapse like card houses. If decisions and influence are removed from corporative bodies, the state will lose not only legitimacy, but also knowledge, time and consensus, all losses which will be very difficult to surmount.

In spite of the positive results after the noticeable policy shift in 1994 towards a more active labour market policy in Denmark, there has been a 'roll-back' tendency to earlier bastions in the labour market policy. Government and parliament seem to be a bit confused at the moment as to further development of activities and policy arrangements.

The lesson of the Danish experiences refers to both a theoretical renewal and more practical measures. As to the theoretical understanding of selective political interventions, I propose substituting coordination concepts for steering concepts. Policy results are not made through vertical steering, but through *a mixture of decentral, network-based coordinations and vertical processes of implementation* (Jørgensen and Larsen 1997). The forms of coordination are social and institutional in character, and they can be performed in a positive or a negative way (Scharpf 1993). They are found in all stages of the policy cycle, which should not be seen in any respect as causal, linear and one-dimensional. The question of good coordination is not simply one of steering resources, information, causal theory and institutional set-up, but basically one of actor interests, influence, mutual understanding, trust, and learning. Network co-operation must be seen as a necessary, but not sufficient condition of successful policy developments. Collective intelligence, time, strategic management and standards for policy implementation and coordination are decisive. *The solution to design problems lies in the processes themselves - in interaction, under-standing and learning.* Uniform standardisation and central control of decentral implementation processes and arrangements must be avoided. Attention must be drawn to both the decentral interaction processes and to the policy rationale. Coordination should be explained by norms, networks and cooperative actions. Multi-level regulations must be identified, and here institutionalised participation in both policy making and implementation by the social partners must be considered most positive - even though the interests of the 'outsiders' some-times are forgotten, when 'insider' interests are at stake. Denmark still has groups of persons who are not integrated in the labour force. Unemployment is not eliminated.

A decentral activation regime has been created around the attempts to redesign the activation efforts and labour market interventions in Denmark. The regime is decentral, cooperative, network based and need oriented. It is process oriented rather than program strategic and, as a consequence, the choice of strategy and instruments should not be understood as a professional or manage-ment-determined design issue only. Incentives in a policy programme might be overvalued these days. One must also be able to explain why and how changes of preferences and priorities occur in the use of policy instruments. In practice, Denmark seems to have found workable policy parameters. Competitive employment and labour market policies are rested in the coordination of public policies and private collective actions. Both evaluations and economic indicators speak of positive results. The lesson is that a policy must be both economically reasonable and politically and institutionally feasible. This also involves the cultural and political heritage - traditions, which cannot be exported. Not everyone can do it the Danish way! We must also remember that successful activation is not the whole story of a good labour market policy. Questions on imbalances in supply and demand, job creation, preventing discrimination, and regulative measures are relevant too.

Christopher Columbus made his discoveries without knowing where he was. Behind the great explorer was a human being who longed for home. Perhaps he did not know who he was either. But this is a source of beautiful dreams. They could be a parallel to the Danish government's visions and plans for Denmark as a 'model country'.

NOTES:

1. I am thankful to Thomas Bredgaard, research fellow at CARMA, Aalborg, for his helpful comments and assistance in structuring the data material for this chapter.
2. A typical trait of the Danish labour market is that the state carries a large part of the financial burden of unemployment benefits. People pay a membership fee to be covered by the unemployment insurance fund, but as taxpayers, all wage earners pay the costs of labour market policy through a general gross tax, the labour market contribution. From 2000, the employers do not contribute at all.
3. No doubt labour market policy, with its many-sided attention to allocation policy and welfare policy, is closest ideologically to the labour movement. Full employment has been the main priority of the united labour movement since WWII, following a Keynesian-inspired view of economics. Economists have, with reference to the Philips curve, attempted to convince us of the correlation between price increase rate and unemployment rate. The actual choice of dot or position on the curve has not been a safeguard against a strong goal conflict among the considerations. The politicians' choice has been strongly determined by cycles. In Sweden, there has been talk of a stronger rationalisation in policy implementation; the so-called Rehn-Meidner model (Hedborg and Meidner 1984) for a non-inflationary full employment economy has contributed to a common understanding of considerations and policy definitions with active labour market policy as a corner stone. Since 1991/92, this common understanding has been disintegrating.
4. The first corporative administrative body in the Danish labour market was already established in 1898 (Nørgaard 1997). Since then, participation by organised interests in councils, boards and commissions has become the rule rather than the exception. In addition to administrative cor-poratism, we have political corporatism where organised interests are consulted or participate in general policy formation.
5. The term 'labour market corridor' describes the nationally developed relation between the primary power (organisation of production and distribution) and the secondary power in society (born from collectively won agreements or legislation that regulates the exercise of power (cf. Jørgensen 1985, chap. 2). In Denmark, the labour market corridor is highly institutionalised, but it also has normally voluntaristic elements. The state guarantees welfare benefits, services and infrastructure and establishes frames through labour market legislation.

6. Since 1994, adjustments and changes of the activation system have been effected through the yearly Finance Acts; from the beginning of 2000,pool jobs and public job training are merged into one instrument and the enterprise allowance scheme has been repealed.

REFERENCES

Arbejdsmarkedsstyrelsen (1999), *Surveyundersøgelse af effekten af* aktivering *i dagpengeperioden*, København: AMS. [The Danish Labour Market Authority: *A survey of the effects of activation in the unemployment benefit period*]

Bredgaard, T. and H. Jørgensen (2000), 'Denmark: Combating Youth Unemployment in the 1990s', in I. Richter (ed.), *Youth Unemployment - What do other countries do? Programmes for vocational training and employment in Europe*, München: Leske + Budrich, Deutsches Jugendinstitut (forthcoming).

Dalsgaard, L. and Morten Lassen (1997), 'Politikdannelse og brugere - kvalitetsvurderinger på hjemmehjælps- og aktiveringsområdet', in P. Gundelach, H. Jørgensen and K.K. Klausen (eds.), *Det lokale - Decentral politik og forvaltning*, Aalborg: Aalborg Universitetsforlag. ['Policy formation and users - assessments of quality on home help and activation']

Hansen, C., F. Larsen, M. Lassen and H. Jørgensen (1997), *Ta' teten i arbejdsmarkedspolitikken*, Aalborg: CARMA, Aalborg University and LO Denmark. [*Take the lead in labour market policy*]

Hedborg, A. and R. Meidner (1984), *Folkhemsmodellen*, Stockholm: Rabén og Sjögren.

Ibsen, F. and H. Jørgensen (1979), *Fagbevægelse og Stat*, Bind 1 og 2, Aalborg: Aalborg Universitetscenter. [*The labour movement and the State*]

Indenrigsministeriet (1998), *Udlænding '98*, København. [Ministry of the Interior: *Foreigners '98*]

Jensen, P., M.S. Nielsen and M. Rosholm (1999), *The Effects of Benefits, Incentives, and Sanctions on Youth Unemployment*, Aarhus: Centre for Labour Market and Social Research (CLS), Working Paper 99: 005, Aarhus University.

Jørgensen, H. (1985/86), *Arbejdsmarkedsnævn i arbejdsmarkedspolitikken - Forvaltning mellem stat og marked*, I-II, ATA-Projektet, Aalborg: Aalborg University. [*Regional Labour Market Councils - Administration between State and Market*]

Jørgensen, H. (2000), *From deregulation to co-regulation. Neo-corporatism and its contribution to a theory of coordinated labour market regulation*, Paper prepared for the proceedings of the IIRA World Congress, Tokyo (forthcoming).

Jørgensen, H. and M. Lassen (eds.; 1992), *Efter Zeuthen-Rapporten*, CARMA yearbook 1992, Aalborg: CARMA, Aalborg University. [*After the Zeuthen report*]

Jørgensen, H. and F. Larsen (1997), *The Blessings of Network Steering? Theoretical and Empirical Arguments for Coordination Concepts as Alternatives to Policy Design*, Aalborg: Working Paper no. 9, Department of Economics, Politics and Public Administration, Aalborg University.

Jørgensen, H., F. Larsen, M. Lassen and J. Stamhus (1998/99), 'La politique active du marché du travail au Danemark: réforme du marché et décentralisation' ['Active labour market policy in Denmark: Labour market reform and the problems of decentralisation'], in J.C. Barbier and J. Gautié (eds), *Les Politiques de l'emploi en Europe et aux Etats-Unis*, Paris: Presses Universitaires de France.

Jørgensen, H., F. Larsen and M. Lassen (1999), *Styr på Arbejdsmarkedspolitikken – Forslag til nyt styringssystem på arbejdsmarkedspolitiske område*, Aalborg: CARMA, Aalborg University. [*Steering the Labour Market Policy – Proposals for a New Labour Market Steering System*]

Langager, K. (1997), *Indsatsen over for de forsikrede ledige*, København: Socialforskningsinstituttets (SFI) rapport 97:20. [The Danish National Institute of Social Research: *The efforts for unemployed with insurance*]

Larsen, F., C. Hansen, H. Jørgensen, M. Lassen, B. Bagge and H. Höcker (1996), *Implementering af Regional Arbejdsmarkedspolitik*, Aalborg: CARMA, Aalborg University. [*Implementation of Regional Labour Market Policy*]

Ministry of Finance (1995/96; 1998/99), *Finansredegørelsen*, København: Finansministeriet [*Financial Report*]

Noergaard, A.S. (1997), *The Politics of Institutional Control: Corporatism in the Danish Occupational Safety and Health Regulation & Unemployment Insurance 1870-1995*, København: PhD Dissertation, Politica.

Nord-Larsen, M. (1997), *Ungeindsatsen start*, København: SFI report. [The Danish National Institute for Social Research: *The Start of the Youth Unemployment Programme*]

OECD - Organisation for Economic Cooperation and Development (ed. 1996/1999), *Employment Outlook*, Paris: OECD.

Parsons, W. (1995), *Public Policy: An introduction to the theory and practice of policy analysis*, Cheltenham: Edward Elgar.

Regeringen (1999), *Danmark som foregangsland - Arbejde og Service*, [*Denmark as Model Country – Labour and Service*]

Scharpf, F.W. (1993), 'Positive und negative Koordination in Verhandlungssystemen', in A. Héritier (ed), *Policy-Analyse. Kritik und Neuorientierung*, Opladen: Westdeutscher Verlag, 57-83.

Schmid, G., J. O'Reilly and K. Schömann (eds.; 1996), *International Handbook of Labour Market Policy and Evaluation*, Cheltenham, UK and Brookfield, US: Edward Elgar.

Weise, H. and H. Brogaard (1997), *Aktivering af kontanthjælpsmodtagere - en evaluering af Lov om kommunal aktivering*, København: SFI-rapport 97:21. [*Activation of social assistance recipients - An evaluation of the Law on municipal activation*]

8. Cooperative labour market policy in Eastern Germany

Reinhard Penz

1. INTRODUCTION

The liberal theory of economic policy can be considered – to express it pointedly – to be dominated by essentially one issue: where and how are individual interests to be integrated into the policymaking process (Buchanan, 1975/84)? Since individual interests should be realised, according to liberal values, and given the empirical evidence confirming that interests must be politically organised in large societies, the problem raised is how organised interests are to be integrated into the policymaking process (Streek and Schmitter 1996; Wegner 1998). A basic scepticism prevails on the liberal side: first, organised interests do not represent the actual needs of members (the principal-agent problem); second, such interests attempt and attempting on the political level to gain and/or defend certain privileges at the expense of others (Eucken 1952/90; Streit 1988). The results, especially in advanced economies, are the familiar symptoms of economic sclerosis: restricted competition, high rates of taxation and government spending, inequitable distribution and weak growth.

The opposing argument holds that collaboration between politicians and organised interests is precisely where opportunities to escape such dead-ends are created (Commons 1934/90; Scharpf 1992). Advocates of collaborative policy processes pin their hopes on 'innovation through cooperation' (Hayden 1993; Mayntz 1993). A further argument they put forward is that, when fundamental political decisions are to be made, the only way to guarantee the legitimisation effect from which long-term stability is generated is by engineering a broad consensus within society (Penz 1999; Pies 1998).

Undeterred by such theoretical debates, cooperative forms of economic policymaking have been extensively practised in Germany for some considerable time. In the heyday of German Keynesianism, 'Concerted Action' (*konzertierte Aktion)* was a commonplace, subsequently followed by the *Kanzlerrunden* – top-level, multilateral talks moderated by the Chancellor himself. For example, a number of voluntary agreements on environmental protection have been concluded in recent years. Ongoing talks aimed at reaching an energy consensus are currently being held; in eastern Germany there are 'Round Tables' on a wide diversity of political issues (from anti-immigrant violence to shop opening hours); an 'Alliance for the German Film' is planned, and 'Alliances for Jobs' are operating at all levels of local government. In eastern Germany, in particular, the dominant strategy is one of 'cooperative labour market policy'. The latter is manifested not only in the various 'macrocorporatist' alliances, but also in local self-governing bodies at the (meso-) levels of employment offices, *Land* employment offices and the Federal Labour Office, where government, industry and the trade unions are represented equally. This chapter centres on experience gained in Saxony-Anhalt with the 'Alliance for Jobs, Training and Competitiveness'. Thus, this contribution will offer answers to the following question: what conclusions can be drawn from this experience with regard to the theoretical dispute over cooperative policymaking processes referred to above?

The chapter is structured as follows: in the next section, I discuss some ideas on reforming the social welfare state from the perspective of institutional theory, leading to the basic notion that cooperative policymaking processes are essentially a rational mode of social policy reform. The following section describes the benefits of cooperative procedures as they are discussed in political science, in particular; after that the liberal critique of corporatism is elaborated in rough outline. The line of argument is then applied to the operative field of labour market policy (in the narrower sense of 'employment promotion'), whereby the basic features of labour market policy in Saxony-Anhalt are taken as exemplary for the strategies adopted in all eastern German states. The next section looks at the experience of the 'Alliance for Jobs, Training and Competitiveness' in Saxony-Anhalt, against the theoretical background elaborated in the chapter. It becomes apparent that a process of cooperative labour market policy is compelled to abandon the narrower field of 'employment promotion'. The chapter ends with a summary.

2. INSTITUTIONAL REFORM OF THE SOCIAL WELFARE STATE

The core problem with *fundamental* reforms in the social welfare state stems from the fact that individual citizens or entire sections of the population be-come worse off due to the erosion of rights and possessions, compared to periods of political normality (Rösner 1997). The resultant political conflicts that can be expected must be embedded in institutional frameworks if they are to be handled in a rational way. Institutional reforms necessarily involve considerable frictions, since they not only modify formal legal structures, but also impinge upon the routine way of life and moral attitudes of people at the same time (Bush 1988; March and Olsen 1984). This is politically relevant, because culture changes more slowly than the system of laws (Krasner 1984; Penz 1999). In the current dispute over social justice, in particular, the powerful impacts exerted by subjective perceptions of political decisions becomes strikingly apparent.

In recent years, the view that the social welfare state generates the very problems it is supposed to solve has been gaining currency. The social welfare state does not eliminate the employment crisis, it is claimed, but exacerbates that crisis with false incentives, excessive regulation and high social security contribution levels (Berthold and Hank 1999). Reconstructing the historical development of the German social welfare state is necessary if we are to gain a deeper understanding of the reforms required. This chapter is not the place to provide such a reconstruction. We shall therefore confine ourselves to reconstructing the relevant design principles on which the german social welfare state is based. Only then do the political options become apparent – the principles by which the selection of options should be guided, and above all (the focus of interest in this context) the appropriate political procedures for achieving the desired ends (Cowen 1990; Eggertsson 1997). On the other hand, any attempt to derive policy prescriptions from abstract theoretical constructs is bound to fail in everyday political reality. Specific notions of economic order must always be implemented in a specific 'historical moment' (Eucken 1952/90).

In very condensed form, the German social welfare state is characterised by the following features (Offe 1998):

- The predominant social security systems – unemployment, medical, pension and nursing care insurance – are based on the principle of a compulsory insurance system regulated by central government. The state also guarantees the continued existence of the social insurance system by paying obligatory subsidies to balance any budgetary deficits. A certain economic status leads inevitably to membership in the collective of those insured. In one's role as a citizen of the country, one is only afforded protection in the form of welfare assistance from the secondary social security system. The latter is need-based and financed from normal tax revenues.
- The social security system provides protection against risks that arise during a normal employment biography, by minimising the differential between income from gainful employment and transferred income in situations of non-employment (unemployment, sickness, old age). The 'equivalence principle' dominates here, i.e. the idea of claims being

based on earned income – as a normative entitlement in any case. Security for the needy as well as distributive equity play a subordinate role and are safeguarded by means of transfer payments or the taxation system. However, it is a historical fact that the equivalence principle is frequently undermined in the various parts of the social insurance system.

- The financing collective, comprised of all insured persons, also exercises the self-governing rights of the insurance funds. This leads to complex institutional arrangements. There are some democratic elements, such as the elected bodies that supervise the insurance bodies. However, the system is dominated by corporatist structures based on the social partners, one example being the self-governance of the 'Federal Labour Office' (*Bundesanstalt für Arbeit; BA*). This self-governance serves to bolster the legitimacy of political and organisational decisions within the separate social insurance systems. At the same time, it is designed to disconnect such bodies from temporary conflicts over the distribution of wealth and property.

All three design elements, and the ensuing institutional arrangements, have for a considerable time been subjected to the following critique (Offe 1998; Berthold and Hank 1999):

- The German social security system provides collective insurance only against the standard risks faced by those with a certain economic status, and leaves little scope for individual initiative to safeguard one's own future.
- Its inadequate focus on real needs generates distributive inequality. Benefits may be provided to people who are protected on a subsidiary basis.
- Solving distributional problems and pursuing employment policy goals through the vehicle of social insurance funds leads to the equivalence principle being hollowed out by benefits that are otherwise alien to the particular form of insurance. Examples include the family allowance system and the inadequate consideration of individual risks in the statutory medical insurance system, the early retirement scheme instituted after German unification as an instrument of employment policy, occasionally active labour market policy as a whole, and more recently the introduction of elements into the pension system involving a baseline pension rate.
- The orientation of the social insurance systems towards a citizen's 'income-earning role' means that certain socially useful activities that consolidate the social and cultural cohesion of a political community are,

from a financial standpoint, treated unfavourable when compared to 'standard' employment.

- In a situation of persistent underemployment and an ageing population, the social security system as it is presently financed is not viable in the long run.
- The institutional logic based on self-governance by social partners renders the German social security system inflexible and incapable of self-reform.

Demands for systematic changes to the social welfare state, aimed at a 'basic income, independent of employment, as a civil right' and at more 'privately funded insurance against individual risks' are based on the foregoing description of the status quo. Basically, any social system, and in general any economic order, will attempt to meet the demands of *diverging* notions of equality. The very concept of *social justice* is devoid of content and has to be specified in detail. An initial approach stems from the idea of *equitable exchange or performance*. This principle, based on the liberal theory of contract, demands equivalence between performance and counter-performance in all contractual relations between individuals and/or between individuals and a collective body (Buchanan 1975/84; Pies 1998). However, this principle is flanked by that of *need-based equity*, which, as a principle of natural law, derives certain rights and material entitlements from the citizen's role in society and his or her specific life situation. The problem of social justice becomes even more complicated when one adds *distributive equity* as a further component. How can we define an equitable distribution – as the reduction of distributional differences between the rich and the poor, or as improvement of the relative position of the poor in comparison to other systems of economic and social order (Rawls 1971/96)?

As already mentioned, the equivalence principle plays a major normative role within the German system of social security, especially in pension and unemployment insurance, in which entitlements depend on the duration of employment and the amount of income earned (Offe 1998). Basing entitlement on gainful employment, rather than defining it as a basic level of security provided as a kind of civil right, is intended to act as an incentive to enter employment that is subject to compulsory social insurance. The country's citizens are supposed to participate in the creation of wealth within the economy. In contrast, the statutory system of medical insurance is dominated by need-based and distributive aspects – the relevant laws stipulate that greater contributions do not entitle one to a higher level of care. Unemployment assistance (received when entitlement to unemployment benefit expires) involves a hybrid of equivalence- and need-based criteria, while welfare assistance is purely need-based.

Given the changes occurring in the world of work, there is much to be said for the idea, often raised in this connection, of a basic social security level for everyone regardless of employment, combined with greater individual provision against risks (Offe 1998). From a normative perspective, this involves a redefinition of responsibilities in respect of the various equity/justice principles: in future, state-organised and/or collective security systems are to be based solely on the principle of need-based equity and are to interpret the solution to the distribution issue – outside the taxation system – as one of securing a minimum income. Compliance with the equivalence principle is to be achieved exclusively with private forms of social security (Berthold and Hank 1999).

As in almost every dispute over economic issues, this one, too, is concerned at root with the relationship between *efficiency and equity*. In this case, the cardinal issue is the relationship between two norms: first, the norm for an *equitable* form of social security against the risks encountered during an employment biography (unemployment, sickness and ageing) that guarantees a certain income; second, the norm for an *efficient* labour market, according to which market clearance and Pareto efficiency, especially among the low-skilled, can be ensured only if wages are linked to productivity (as a necessary but insufficient condition). In borderline cases of transfer accumulation by families, the two norms can become opposing principles.

On closer analysis, however, the distinction between efficiency and equity does not appear to hold (Penz 1999). Ultimately, the two norms are different means for achieving one and the same end: safeguarding or extending the options available to individuals for participating in society, and hence for achieving social recognition – firstly with collective security for those in phases of non-employment, secondly with open labour markets accessible to all. Accepting this argument raises again the following question: what form must a feasible reform of the social welfare state take if it is to minimise potentially counter-productive impacts on the meso level (Pies 1998)?

I do not intend to discuss these proposals at this juncture. The crucial issue, as I see it, is to find appropriate *procedures* for reforming the system (Buchanan 1975/84; Willke 1992). Any reform must conform to the principle of institutional feasibility. This means that the legal frameworks resulting from historical development, as well as the cultural mentalities and moral justifications associated with those frameworks, must be taken into consideration in a political transformation process (Commons 1934/90; Penz 1999). Generating a normative ideal is of no use. We are not referring here to the *implementation and transition problems* that are often bandied around in this context, but to cooperative shaping of institutional change at the very level where problems are identified, and potential solutions discussed and decided.

3. THE MEANING AND PURPOSE OF COOPERATIVE POLICYMAKING PROCESSES

The starting point for the idea of cooperative economic policy lies hidden in the fundamental pluralist conviction that *politics* is constituted by competition and by the subsequent balancing of interests within society. The immediate consequence is that the function of democrats is by no means to generate a 'volonté generale'. Their importance consists in their organising a legitimate balancing of interests. Ultimately, the core concern is not the 'common welfare' but rather a 'parallelogram of interest' (Fraenkel 1974).

From the outset, this conception of politics and policymaking harbours severe theoretical and practical problems, relating primarily to the fact that weak, long-term and general interests are systematically under-represented in political competition. The problem is that interests within society are inadequately organised or organisable. This led *neo*-pluralists to concede the necessity of a 'non-controversial sector' encompassing fundamental, commonly held and institutionalised convictions that tame competition, take weakly represented interests into account and provide scope for considering the common welfare (Fraenkel 1974).

In the 1970s, this long-prevailing neo-pluralist conception was developed in a decisive way to arrive at the idea of *liberal corporatism* or *neo-corporatism* (Streek and Schmitter 1996). The term corporatism was used to describe in theoretical terms a particular trend in liberal societies that had been categorially undefined to date: the fact that chambers, federations, parties, churches and other intermediary organisations represented their concentrated interests not simply as lobbies in the political process, but also discharge, in exchange for certain privileges, additional functions in the political communication of interests.

The path taken by liberal societies led from the *representation of interests* mode to the *mediation of interests* mode (Streek and Schmitter 1996). The state provides a regulatory legal framework and privileged access to political decision-making processes for relevant intermediaries; it also assigns the political business of constituting and mediating interests to these self-governing bodies. The list of privileges and delegated decision-making powers is long: compulsory membership in chambers, protection against competition (e.g. for craft trades, welfare organisations, etc.), self-governance in the social insurance systems, autonomy in collective bargaining, tax privileges for political parties, etc.

The counter-performance accrues to the state, it is argued: more detailed, control-centred knowledge for the legislative process, support from intermediaries in implementing its laws, simplification of the otherwise confusing diversity of interests, as well as additional, extra-parliamentary legitimisation for its actions (Mayntz 1993; Scharpf 1992). We recognise the form of political exchange as the granting of privileges against assistance with the business of political control. The image of a *negotiating democracy* ensues from this (Commons 1934/90; Scharpf 1992).

This concept of a second-level interventional state, a corporatist Keynesianism that seeks to avoid the technical problems associated with first-level control by integrating from the outset the cooperation and coordination of macroeconomic policymaking fields (monetary, fiscal and wage policies) and the players involved in this structure, has been the strategic counter-image of neo-liberalism ever since. It now celebrates a renaissance, as 'cooperative economic policy' or 'macro-corporatism', in the 'Alliance for Jobs' or the 'European Employment Pact' (Berthold and Hank 1999).

How can the usefulness of this process be described in theoretical terms? It is essential to distinguish here between processes and their outcomes. In the course of the process, those involved (be they individuals or corporate bodies) should state their basic assumptions, seek common goals, create objectively adequate solutions and in this way generate options for consensus (Ostrom 1990; Scharpf 1992). The various stages in the process can be described as follows:

- those involved formulate interests, rather than positions,
- they reveal their theoretical assumptions,
- they jointly develop definitions of the problems in hand,
- they agree on (abstract) values and (specific) objectives,
- on the strength at which they are able to speak in rational terms about adequate instruments, and
- they agree on a solution to the problems they face.

Different qualities of consensus are conceivable as far as results are concerned. These extend from simple 'negative coordination' (Scharpf 1992) for preventing externalities, to gains from collaboration as a consequence of resolving dilemmas and establishing a win/win situation (Sen 1979), to deliberation and the discursive convergence of the knowledge, theories, values and moral convictions of the persons concerned (Lowe 1965/84).

This rosy view of cooperative policy processes has naturally had its critics, especially among liberal economic theorists.

4. THE LIBERAL CRITIQUE OF CORPORATISM

The baseline of liberalism's critique of corporatism is the idea of *Ordnungspolitik*: individual interests are best served when the state concentrates on providing a general framework of rules to ensure that market prices reflect preferences and scarcities so that resources are exploited in the most productive way, and hence that needs are efficiently satisfied or, put differently, that a *socioeconomic optimum* is ensured (Eucken 1952/90).

The prerequisites of this in market theory were originally defined as the 'perfect competition' market form, and later in the concept of optimal intensity of competition. What is not disputed is the distortion of competition caused by market access barriers, and there is little controversy about the importance of concentration and company size. In the dynamic variant, the specific market form plays no further role. In the latter case, it is important to safeguard a society's capacity to develop through 'competition as discovery process' (Hayek 1978). The evolutionary goals of a national economy are more likely to be found in the rate of innovation or the rate at which per capita GNP increases than in the efficiency of a particular allocation system.

The quintessential element in this line of thought for our present subject-matter is the following: by nature, organised interests pursue the political goal of rent-seeking, i.e. negotiating restrictions on competition that operate in their own favour (Buchanan 1975/84). The political exchange (establishment of control, in return for privileges) is made at the expense of third parties, the *outsiders* (Berthold and Hank 1999). A popular example in this respect is provided by the Craft Trades Regulations (*Handwerksordnung*) and collective bargaining agreements for entire industries and regions, whose institutional characteristics operate, so the hypothesis at least, to reduce efficiency and the capacity of society to develop (Wegner 1998). Liberal political theorists are also worried that parliamentary democracy might be eroded by burgeoning corporatism; this explains their warnings about the legitimisation of state institutions declining over the long term.

However, since the functional fact of organised interests can scarcely be denied, i.e. that federations and the like are indispensable, economic theorists are also compelled to take an empirical stance vis-à-vis the phenomenon, beyond any normative prejudices or misgivings they may harbour. This is manifested in 'New Political Economy', or 'public choice theory'. The starting point for analysis is the behaviour of politicians, bureaucrats and lobbyists. These 'agents' maximise their own interests rather than those of the general public and fail, above all, to respect the interests of their 'principals': the citizens (Pies 1998).

This has consequences for the efficiency of political exchange and hence for a negotiating democracy:

- negotiations are dominated by interest-based distortions of information,
- there are serious problems regarding representation (principal/agent problem 1: members vs. federation heads),
- legitimisation problems arise (principal/agent problem 2: citizen/sovereignty vs. politicians),
- the problem of inadequate knowledge for control is exacerbated by the greater complexity of decision making in cooperative processes,
- *rent-seeking* behaviour occurs at the expense of the negotiating parties (when information is asymmetrically distributed),
- *rent-seeking* behaviour occurs at the expense of external parties (people affected, but not represented at the negotiating table).

From the perspective of public choice theory, these factors lead to the danger of negotiating democracies becoming sclerotic (ossified) and incapable of development (Berthold and Hank 1999). For the partners within corporatist procedures, *rent seeking* at the expense of others substitutes (in a rational way) for the search for market opportunities and political innovations (Wegner 1998). The results are inefficient expansion of governmental activities, fiscal exploitation of citizens (the Leviathan hypothesis) and weakening viability of a society (Buchanan 1975/84).

The normative consequences of the public choice approach are to tame the Leviathan by constitutional rules (rules for constraining budgets) and the removal of policymaking fields from the democratic (negotiation) process: e.g. monetary, currency and collective bargaining policies. The normative basis is provided here by the liberal concept of the inalienability of (financial) constitutions being approved on a consensual basis: taxation of citizens can only be legitimated in a general way according to the *principle of unanimity*; taxation based on financial capability is ethically unacceptable for a liberal economist (Buchanan 1975/84).

Despite the emphasis on basic 'consentability' (*Zustimmungsfähigkeit*) as a liberal democratic principle, (Penz 1999) economists consider 'policy-remote' institutions to be the most appropriate for realising the principle. In the following, I trace this intuition with reference to the 'Alliance for Jobs, Training and Competitiveness' in Saxony-Anhalt. Firstly, I examine the principles and structure of labour market policy in Saxony-Anhalt.

5. LABOUR MARKET POLICY IN SAXONY-ANHALT

The following observations concentrate on the 'secondary labour market'. Instruments explicitly centred on target groups and on training/skilling are excluded, by and large. The description below serves to illustrate the specific employment policy background to the 'Alliance for Jobs' in Saxony-Anhalt. As the subsequent section shows, the 'Alliance' goes beyond that framework as far as content and outputs are concerned.

In periods of high unemployment, the secondary labour market is an imperative element in employment policy. In order to assess the benefit of the government-supported labour market for the economy as a whole, it does not suffice to analyse isolated financial impacts or to draw up balance-sheets on labour market integration. All impacts within the economic system have to be taken into account. This means that gross expenditure for supporting the second labour market must be reduced by the alternative costs of unemployment. The total fiscal costs for the registered unemployed in the Federal Republic of Germany amounted to DM 166 billion in 1997. This amount is obtained if one takes into consideration not only the additional expenditure as a result of unemployment but also the lower revenue generated from taxes and social insurance contributions. If these alternative costs are included, the total net fiscal costs of active labour market policy in the government supported labour market is around 30% of the gross costs of any measure.

The decisive factor in the macroeconomic evaluation of these additional costs is how they are financed – by social insurance contributions, direct taxes, indirect taxes or borrowing? Different impacts on employment will result, depending on the specific impacts on the economic system. This is a broad field of analysis, but one thing is certain: financing such support from social insurance funds is a dubious approach for both labour market *and* fiscal policy.

The situation is even more complex on the benefits side of the supported labour market. The employment impacts, in the narrower sense, are uppermost, of course: the government-supported labour market improves the employability of unemployed workers, in compliance with pillar 1 of the European Employment Guidelines. This improves their placement chances in the primary labour market. This 'bridging' function performed by the secondary labour market is corroborated by various evaluation studies and the reintegration balance-sheets drawn up by the Federal Labour Office. There are also structural impacts deriving from two sources: first, important infrastructural effects are generated for Saxony-Anhalt via the specific fields in which the supported labour market measures are deployed; secondly, they represent major investments in the human capital of workers.

Whereas the short-term relief provided by the supported labour market is measurable to some extent, assessing the long-term structural impacts is problematic. An adequate evaluation is thus difficult to obtain. The problem is all the more serious in that the long-term, investment component of active employment promotion is actually the most important. A look at the history of active employment promotion in the Federal Republic of Germany shows that it was originally an instrument, explicitly focused on structural change, for combating mismatch unemployment, and by no means an instrument for boosting economic growth in general – i.e. short-term relief for the labour market. This idea must be pushed more intensively in future.

The supported labour market also performs a key social function. Financing employment rather than unemployment is an ethical imperative. The long-term impacts of unemployment on society – most clearly evident in the socialisation problems of highly disadvantaged groups in the labour market and which in some cases can lead to criminality – can only be prevented by activating unemployed people through suitably designed employment promotion schemes. Thus, the government-supported labour market is also an instrument for stabilising democracy. If labour market policy is understood in this sense and unrestricted in its objectives by an all-too-narrow interpretation as a 'bridge to the primary labour market', it will be open to the perspective of giving certain groups with minimal placement chances an opportunity to perform socially meaningful tasks on a long-term basis.

5.1 Policy frameworks at federal level

The effectiveness of Saxony-Anhalt's labour market policy is heavily dependent on the legal and financial framework created by decisions at federal government level. Labour market policies cannot be effective unless the conditional framework is consistent. Both policy-implementing bodies and the workers receiving support need security of planning before they can develop long-term perspectives for action. Short-term actionism does not lead to success and in the long run is not conducive to public support of active labour market policies.

In recent years, the Federal Labour Office has provided substantial funds for employment promotion. More than two-thirds of all job-creation finance goes to the states of eastern Germany; more than 90% is spent on structural adjustment measures. Saxony-Anhalt receives around 20% of each. However, the precise figure depends on the amount of cofinancing that Saxony-Anhalt puts up for these instruments.

5.1.1 Job-creation schemes (Arbeitsbeschaffungsmaßnahmen – ABM)
In absolute figures, Saxony-Anhalt received DM 1.09 billion from the Federal Labour Office for labour market reintegration measures in 1998 (in the following, reference is mainly to 1998 figures, since those for 1999 are still provisional); this were cofinanced by Saxony-Anhalt with DM 102.7 million. If job-creation schemes meet special regional interests, the *Land* provides a higher level of support amounting to a maximum 10% of wage costs. The Federal Labour Office provides additional grants to the same amount (Sec-

tion 266 SGB III – Book III of the Social Security Code). The *Land* can thus control the quality and structural policy thrust of job-creation schemes. Saxony-Anhalt's guidelines contain regulations that ensure preference for women (higher levels of support). By this means, a high female participation was recorded in the publicly supported labour market.

The activities of the *Land* also influence the quality of job-creation schemes, due to the fact that, in some cases, no scheme would have materialised had it not been for the support provided by the government of this land. The employment offices also manage their budgets for reintegration measures according to the volume of cofinancing they receive. Recent years have seen a shift in support towards continuing training. This also suggests that the volume of cofinancing is not sufficient.

Up to 1999, there was considerable discontinuity in the amount of support given to job-creation activities by labour market policymakers at federal government level. The marked decline in support and funding in the period up to spring 1998 was followed by a strong increase engendered by additional federal funding and the weakening of legal restrictions on support provision. In 1998, the number of people in job creation schemes in Saxony-Anhalt fell to around 13 500 on average during the first quarter, only to rise again to around 43 000 in the last quarter. Over the year, the average number of people receiving this kind of support was 27 438. Cycles like this, arising from different legislative periods, are detrimental to the quality of labour market policy. It has to be emphasised once again that labour market policy is not an instrument for boosting or controlling the economy. Unfortunately, however, the immediate statistical impact of active employment promotion on the number of people registered as unemployed, and hence on the unemployment rate as well, leads to this instrument being misused on many occasions for politically motivated control of the national economy. The number of people in support schemes has stabilised in the meantime and in Saxony-Anhalt will range between 25 000 and 30 000 in future.

The marked decline in the job-creation domain was mainly due to the tougher eligibility criteria for such measures in the industrial field. The generally applicable principle is that job-creation schemes are eligible only on the condition that they be entrusted to business enterprises. Only in certain circumstances can a scheme be carried out on an independent basis by the support body.

Setting up a particular scheme under the award procedure is much more complicated than if a support body organises it. In addition, the necessary involvement of chambers and industry federations in approving an exception to the rule and allowing a support body to implement a scheme in the industrial sector leads to enormous bureaucratic barriers. It was not until a letter of interpretation was sent by the Federal Ministry of Employment and Social

Order to the Federal Labour Office that this restrictive regulation on actual practice was watered down again.

5.1.2 Structural adjustment measures (SAM)

When the German Social Security Code III (SGB III) was introduced in 1998, measures for productive employment promotion (wage grants – *Lohnkostenzuschüsse*, or LKZ for short) under Sections 242s and 249h of the Federal Employment Promotion Act were replaced by support for structural adjustment measures (SAM) under Sections 272-279 and 415 SGB III. Accordingly, wage grants for East German companies (Section 249h (4b) of the Employment Promotion Act) were replaced by SAMs (Sections 272 ff. and 415 SGB III). Support bodies implementing structural adjustment measures can receive grants for employing workers if the measure helps to create new jobs that compensate for job losses at local level, and if people referred by the employment office are recruited. The latter are eligible for support if they become unemployed or are threatened by unemployment, if they meet the criteria for unemployment benefit and unemployment assistance prior to being referred, and cannot be placed in jobs within the foreseeable future unless they are referred in this way.

Measures eligible for support in the East German states are those for improving and preserving the environment, for improving the social services, in youth aid, amateur sport, independent cultural work, for preparing and implementing the protection of monuments, for urban renewal, and for improving the residential environment. The amount of support paid is calculated on a lump-sum basis in proportion to the average cost per person of unemployment benefit and unemployment assistance, including contributions to social insurance. This means that expenditure on SAMs is equivalent to the costs for passive compensation of lost earnings. These costs do not come under the funds for reintegration, and hence are on average neutral for the Federal Labour Office.

SAMs for East German companies (SAM OfW; '*SAM Ost für Wirtschaftsunternehmen*') enable extended support to be given to additional employment in East Germany industry. The eligibility criterion is that the employer neither reduce the number of employees during a minimum period of six months prior to receiving support, nor that the number be reduced during the support period, and that training is provided to employees as long as employment is subsidised. Financial assistance for a 'SAM OfW' measure is limited to one year.

On average in 1998, 8677 people were sponsored in SAM projects in Saxony-Anhalt, and 20 408 in companies. This means that around 2% of all workers in Saxony-Anhalt (not counting those in job-creation schemes and SAM projects) received a wage grant under SAM OfW. The open access provided to all unemployed people, thus far without any target group focus, suggests that it is unlikely that SAM OfW support for additional employment in companies induces any substantial deadweight. Moreover, SAM OfW often conflicts with wage grants focused on particular target groups. Another aspect is that the eligibility criterion stipulating a constant number of employees during the six-month period prior to support is too restrictive for our *Land*, since the structural problems faced by Saxony-Anhalt mean that only few companies can meet this requirement.

Saxony-Anhalt supports SAM projects that serve the special interests of the *Land* as a whole, paying an extra DM 1100 a month for a female worker and DM 800 a month for a male. Half these rates are paid in the case of private support bodies. In total, around DM 162.9 million flowed into SAM project support from the Federal Labour Office (saved unemployment benefit), while around DM 94 million to Saxony-Anhalt came from federal government funds (saved unemployment assistance). These figures are highly dependent on the volume of cofinancing provided by Saxony-Anhalt. In 1998, the *Land* spent DM 94.2 million on cofinancing SAM projects. Cofinancing is therefore a good instrument with which Saxony-Anhalt is able to channel external funding to the *Land* in the form of support for SAM projects aimed at improving the employment situation.

5.1.3 New eligibility criteria imposed by the Second Act Amending Social Security Code III (Zweite SGB III-Änderungsgesetz)

The Second Act Amending Social Security Code III (SAA-SSC-III) came into force on 1 August 1999. The most important new regulation affecting job-creation schemes relates to the new legal foundations consolidating the previously informal practice of diluting the priority granted to subcontracted measures, as opposed to self-managed measures: for certain target groups particularly in need of support, it is now possible for measures to be implemented by support bodies acting on their own initiative. Examples include measures involving social work support, or measures for old people and the seriously disabled. The employment offices decide whether it might be inappropriate to subcontract a measure due to lack of interest on the part of companies, or the fact that the financial conditions are not acceptable. In such cases, the measure in question can be implemented on an independent basis by support bodies instead. The trade and industry federations must be consulted on this point.

To bolster preventative effects in the publicly supported labour market, the SAA-SSC-III stipulates that an eligibility criterion for accessing job-creation schemes is to be re-introduced, according to which the person concerned must have been unemployed for only six of the last twelve months. Experience has shown that if a worker is among the long-term unemployed, i.e. has been out of work for more than 12 months, the impact of these instruments is often curtailed. Placement risks (advanced age, low skills, poor health) that could lead to long-term unemployment can be identified at a very early stage, which means that active employment promotion should be applied immediately.

The SAA-SSC-III also stipulates that SAM support for additional employment in (East German) companies be focused on workers who are particularly in need of support, in order that deadweight be prevented. Furthermore, in those employment exchange districts with a particularly high level of unemployment, structural adjustment measures lasting up to five years are avaible to the unemployed over 55.

This is a response to the fact that, in some regions, older unemployed people over 55 have virtually no chance of finding work. It makes little sense to make these people alternate between support measures and the dole queue when they are unable or unlikely to rejoin the primary labour market. Here, the 'bridge to the primary labour market' has to be replaced by a 'bridge to retirement'. This means it is necessary to develop additional instruments, designed for long-term operation, that enable these people to have a secure transition to retirement by doing useful community (or other) work, in a way that maintains their human dignity. A start was made in Saxony-Anhalt on 1 February 1999, when a pilot project was launched for ten women aged 55 who can then retire after the project has run its five-year term.

To enable greater flexibility in structural policy, the Second Act Amending the Social Security Code III also extended the list of fields in which structural adjustment measures can be applied. The scope of application was also extended to the whole of Germany. One more field of support was added to the previous ones mentioned above, namely 'Improving Infrastructure for Business, Including Improvements to Tourist Infrastructure'. New investment options for cofinancing, also with long-term impacts on employment levels, are thereby created and should be exploited as much as possible.

5.2 Criteria for supplementary *Land* support in the second labour market

Job-creation schemes receive additional support from Saxony-Anhalt only on the condition that their specific content matches the guidelines laid down by the *Land*. The priority areas covered by the guidelines for enhanced support from *Land* funds for job-creation schemes are the following:

- environmental remediation and infrastructural improvements,
- tourism,
- landscape management and nature conservation,

- youth aid and social services,
- jobs in advisory positions and in projects for unemployed people and
- promotion of culture, protection of monuments.

This accords with the general provision in Section 260 SGB III, which specifies that measures for improving the social infrastructure or the environment should be given preferential support. The *Länder* are free to choose the particular fields to which they grant extra support. Since mid-1998, the amount of assistance has consisted in up to 10% of the eligible wage costs, plus supplementary support to the same amount from the labour administration.

All job-creation measures, including the funds put up by Saxony-Anhalt itself, are approved and financed by the labour administration in accordance with the administrative agreement concluded with the Federal Labour Office. Monitoring support is the responsibility of the State Office for Employment Protection (*Landesamt for Arbeitsschutz* – LAS) in Dessau. This ensures, at the operative level as well, that cofinancing is granted only to those measures in which the state of Saxony-Anhalt has a special interest. The priority fields for support are based on the objectives of other government departments, so that supported bodies are able to acquire external, third-party funding through this channel as well.

The quality of structural adjustment measures is assured by approvals being granted by the *Land* itself. This is normally done by the LAS; in exceptional cases, approval can be granted by the responsible government department. An additional filter is that it is now necessary for a positive verdict to be given by the local government body with local and substantive responsibility. The *Land* guidelines specify the priority support areas in the following fields:

- improving the environment,
- social services and youth aid,
- increasing access to popular sport,
- independent cultural work,
- preparing measures to protect monuments,
- protecting urban monuments,
- improving the residential environment and
- improving the infrastructure for business, including improvements to tourist infrastructure.

The guidelines, review of applications and the statement of position by local government all ensure that only those measures in which the *Land* has a particular interest are actually supported. Efforts are also being made, as part of the regionalisation process, to increase local government responsibility for the approval of measures.

5.3 Strategic priorities of the *Land*'s policies for the second labour market

The strategic goals of the government in Saxony-Anhalt are to increase the precision and efficiency of policy instruments in the publicly supported labour market, and to reinforce the budding links with the regional and industrial policy field. In line with the employment guidelines of the European Union, the government of Saxony-Anhalt has specified the following general aims:

- Improving the employability of workers
- Promoting entrepreneurship
- Fostering the adaptability of companies and their employees
- Promoting equal opportunity on the labour market

The labour market strategy of the state government must be focused on quality improvements in the *effectiveness and efficiency* of policy instruments. In operative terms, this means getting involved at federal level in the forthcoming procedures for fundamental reform of the SGB III, as well as exploiting the control options presented by the *Land* programme of supplementary support, on the one hand, and implementation in certain fields of action, on the other.

If the effectiveness and efficiency of policy instruments is to be boosted, they have to be deployed with a *greater target-group focus* whenever this is feasible and rational. Consideration must be given to the special importance attached, to both investive measures and measures to improve the regional economic structure in the state's guidelines on job-creation schemes and structural adjustment measures. The latter cannot normally be achieved with a target-group focus alone. The skills and qualifications of participants are prioritised, especially in projects with ambitious targets. However, wage grants of the kind provided under SAM OfW (without confinement to specific target groups) produce deadweight and distortions of competition, which is why the legislative changes are so important.

With regard to the European Employment Guidelines, the government of Saxony-Anhalt is striving to *design support measures* in the second labour market so that they have greater *preventative impact*. Placement risks (advanced age, low skills, poor health) that could lead to long-term unemployment can be identified at a very early stage, which means that active employment promotion should be applied immediately. Six months of unemployment within a 12-month period is a time criterion that makes good sense as a point of reference.

One key imperative that future reforms in the publicly supported labour market must satisfy is to exercise control over support programmes in a *more flexible and decentralised way*. Independent support is an important marker in this respect. As a general principle, labour market policy must now enter a phase of financial and legal consolidation and consistency, especially as regards the publicly supported labour market. In the fundamental reform of SGB III, now in the pipeline, these aspects must be taken into account. Continuity of legal foundations is absolutely essential if active labour market policies are to operate properly. Continual amendment of federal laws causes major uncertainties for support providers and avoidable discontinuities in the number of people at the receiving end. This means that the instruments must be so designed that they will take effect in different labour market constellations. The conclusion to be drawn from this is that the regulations in SGB III be worded in more general terms, and that more scope be given to those applying the law at the operative level.

6. COOPERATIVE LABOUR MARKET POLICY: THE 'ALLIANCE FOR JOBS, TRAINING AND COM-PETITIVENESS' IN SAXONY-ANHALT

In the Employment Guidelines of the European Union, involvement of social partners is seen as an essential feature of modern labour market policy. In Saxony-Anhalt, labour market policy has always featured efforts to use the knowledge of social partners and institutions within the *Land* in shaping and executing its various programmes. The following benefits are associated with a strategy of cooperative labour market policy:

- control of the labour market is becoming more informed, and hence more effective
- the legitimacy of labour market policy decisions is enhanced by the consensus achieved with the social groups involved
- the social partners are put in a position where they can overcome dilemmas and achieve gains through cooperation
- the integration of different standpoints and interests generates potential for creative solutions

Since early 1999, this cooperative strategy has been given a new mantle in the shape of the 'Alliance for Jobs, Training and Competitiveness'. This history of the alliance began with an initiative launched in the Saxony-Anhalt parliament, before it was then actively embraced by the state government. Once the political level was convinced that a separate alliance for the *Land* made sense – a renewed attempt at national level has just been started, and a number of other *Länder* are pursuing such alliances – suitable priority areas were identified and selected. The choice was by no means easy, given that the core issues had to be specific to Saxony-Anhalt and due to the systematic dependence of *Land* policymaking on pre-givens at national and European level. The following, now familiar institutional structures were adopted: the alliance is headed by the actual round table itself; the participants are supported by the 'Steering Committee', while working parties at the bottom of the hierarchy – and workgroups below them – conduct the core political business of mediating between conflicting interests.

Three working parties were formed, mirroring departmental structures: training issues managed by the Ministry of Culture, whereby an existing workgroup was integrated; in the Ministry for Trade and Industry, a working party on promoting medium-sized companies was established; in the Ministry of Employment, activities were concentrated on problems in the 'work and social welfare' field, in a 'Generational Employment Pact' emphasising the notion of distributive equity. The first session of the latter working party collated the potential issues; workgroups were then set up to address 'Promoting Part-Time Employment', 'Older Workers' and 'Dismantling Overtime'. Additional workgroups on 'Combating Clandestine Work and Illegal Employment' and 'Jobs for Youth' have meanwhile been added. As one can see, these activities go far beyond the normal confines of labour market policy. Three working parties were formed, mirroring departmental structures: training issues managed by the Ministry of Culture, whereby an existing workgroup was integrated; in the Ministry for Trade and Industry, a working party on promoting medium-sized companies was established; in the Ministry of Employment, activities were concentrated on problems in the 'work and social welfare' field, in a 'Generational Employment Pact' emphasising the notion of distributive equity. The first session of the latter working party collated the potential issues; workgroups were then set up to address 'Promoting Part-Time Employment', 'Older Workers' and 'Dismantling Overtime'. Additional workgroups on 'Combating Clandestine Work and Illegal Employment' and 'Jobs for Youth' have meanwhile been added. The fact that a subordinate role is played in a jobs alliance at *Land* level by the classical measures of labour market policy is explained by the legislative competence of federal government in this particular field.

The problem of *representation* was initially solved along familiar lines of social partnership. Not surprisingly, it is important to ensure approximate parity in the number of representatives from each side, at least in the principal decision-making bodies, whereas this aspect was handled less rigidly at the workgroup level. However, 'alliance round tables' and 'steering committees' have been enlarged, in terms of the diversity of the parties involved, by adding representatives from the chambers, local authorities and the labour administration. Whereas the Saxony-Anhalt government sent delegates for each of the four hierarchical levels within the alliance (cabinet members, secretaries of state, department heads and section heads), the social partners were not always able to follow suit because they did not have the same organisational depth.

In the working party on the 'Generational Employment Pact', parity of the social partners was less rigid from the outset due to participation by representatives from the chambers of trade and industry, the craft trades chambers and the state employment office. This strategy of involving as many relevant social actors as possible, has proved effective in practice and was further extended. The workgroup on 'Dismantling Overtime' organised a workshop with representatives of companies in Saxony-Anhalt in order to integrate their specific experience into the alliance; the workgroup on 'Combating Clandestine Work and Illegal Employment' is attempting to cover the complex material through the diversity of its membership (trade supervision and regulatory offices, factories inspectors, labour administration, the department of public prosecution, principal customs offices, federations of local authorities, pension insurance institutions, regional commissions, craft trades chambers and various ministries).

All in all, five different fields of interest have been worked on so far, all of which come under the broader topic of 'labour market policy'. What can be said about the results?

6.1 Promoting part-time employment

The workgroup on *Promoting Part-Time Employment* focused first of all on the empirical facts. According to the Companies Panel of the IAB (Institute for Employment Research at the Federal Labour Office), part-time employment accounts for 17% of all jobs in Eastern Germany, and 24% in Western Germany. The Saxony-Anhalt Labour Market Monitor has calculated that 131 000 women and 40 000 men in the state are in part-time employment. Looking at the sectoral distribution of these figures, there is a strong concentration of part-time jobs in education, the retail trade, health, other services and public administration. There is both involuntary part-time employment in compliance with collectively bargained rules, as well as involuntary full-time employment due to the lack of part-time jobs. According to the microcensus, both parents in 46.8% of all families work full time in East Germany, whereas the figure in West Germany is only 16.3%.

The workgroup also discovered that there is no specific preference for part-time employment in SGB III, and that all wage grants can be provided without regard to the number of working hours. Since the *Land* guidelines under the Act Amending Social Security Code III were up for debate anyway, an obvious option was to provide greater support to the creation of part-time jobs in *Land* programmes and with supplementary grants to Federal Labour Office programmes. A directive has been drafted on this issue, but it has not yet been adopted by the 'Alliance Round Table'.

The trade unions, in particular, have emphasised that sufficient potential for more part-time employment would exist if barriers to promotion were eliminated, if links were forged to support programmes for women, if all company and hierarchical levels were integrated, and if part-time working were made voluntary, with an unrestricted right to return to full-time employment. Employer representatives, too, saw definite opportunities for more part-time employment if transferrable pilot projects were set up, if temporary grants were available for making the changeover, if advisory services on part-time employment were improved and if the promotion of part-time working were publicised more intensively. In this sense, the workgroup will be monitoring two pilot projects on such advisory services, and will focus in the near future on public relations issues in connection with part-time employment.

6.2 Older Workers

The *Older Workers* workgroup also began by conducting a summary analysis of the status quo. There are currently about 75 000 workers over 55 in jobs involving compulsory social insurance; approximately 60 000 are registered as unemployed and approximately 16 000 unemployed people over 58 no longer appear in the unemployment statistics. According to the German Institute for Economic Research (DIW), 87% of all those entering retirement in eastern Germany (in 1997) were either women or unemployed people; the figure for these two categories in western Germany was only 44% by comparison.

The workgroup identified the long-term unemployed over 55 as the main problem. Although improved support in the field of structural adjustment measures – five-year programmes as a 'bridge to retirement' – is a useful option for this group, major quantitative impacts are unlikely to materialise. To respond to this problem, the workgroup developed a model for *transitional benefit*.

The latter envisages transitional benefit being paid to the long-term unemployed over 55 years of age, to the same amount as their entitlement to unemployment benefit, until the earliest date at which they can draw a (possibly reduced) pension. Linked to this is a withdrawal from the labour market and the extinction of any claim to active employment promotion. The latter refinances the extra expenditure generated by the supplementary benefit as compared to unemployment benefit. The Alliance Round Table accepted this proposal.

The workgroup also concerns itself with part-time working in old age. The re-enactment of the *Altersteilzeitgesetz* (the law governing part-time working in old age – AltzG), which comes into force on 1 January 2000, integrates key demands raised by the alliance in Saxony-Anhalt (see also Chapter 5 by Knuth in this volume):

- The changeover to part-time employment in old age will be possible in future for workers who are already in part-time employment.
- Companies with more than 50 employees do not have to provide evidence of a vacancy-filling chain. It suffices if they employ one new worker of any sort, and trainees can be employed as well, not just people registered as unemployed.
- Companies with more than 50 employees are analysed on a functional entity basis. This means there has to be an internal successor and a new recruit within the specific functional entity (accounting, production, sales, etc.). In departments or divisions with less than 50 employees, the regulation for small companies is applied. Implementation orders put these rules into effect.

In Saxony-Anhalt there are currently around 1400 people who are eligible for this type of support, of whom half are already in part-time old-age employment, the other half being cases where such employment is blocked for some reason. 650 people in part-time old-age employment receive DM 200 in additional benefit from the *Land* (capped to 90% of full-time net pay); advance decisions on support have been granted in another 400 cases. The potential number of people eligible for part-time old-age employment, i.e. the number of employees with compulsory social insurance and aged 55 or more, is around 75 000, primarily in the building, health, housing, public service and agricultural sectors. Since Saxony-Anhalt has 67 400 companies with less than 50 employees – constituting 96% of all companies in Saxony-Anhalt – the *Land* profits to an above-average extent from the aforementioned means for facilitating the re-filling of such jobs in SMEs. The workgroup was agreed that the new laws taking effect on 1 January 2000 will lead to greater use of the AltzG regulations in Saxony-Anhalt.

In the meantime, a workgroup organised by the *Land* employment office has focused on two further-reaching aspects in this respect. Firstly, there is a plan systematically to examine potential multiplier pathways for spreading information about the support provided for part-time old-age employment. Secondly, the workgroup is examining options for reducing the deductions made from retirement pensions of those who switch to part-time employment. For example, they plan to find ways of applying *Land* support schemes in this area; the 'partial pension' option is to be emphasised, and the transfer to pension funds of payments under redundancy compensation schemes will be discussed.

6.3 Dismantling Overtime

The *Dismantling Overtime* workgroup first carried out a number of studies based on the IAB Companies Panel. The overall finding was that the number of hours' overtime worked in Saxony-Anhalt is in decline. Within this total, there is a visible shift from paid to unpaid overtime. Paid overtime is mainly worked in companies with a workforce of 100 – 499 (around 1.74 million hours in 1998); far less overtime is now worked in smaller companies, whereas the figure for large companies (500 employees and more) was around 460 000 hours in 1998. On a sectoral basis, overtime is concentrated in manufacturing, the construction industry, transport and communications, and other services (including restaurants, education and training centres, the health services and legal advice). The total volume of paid overtime in 1998 was around DM 5.8 million. Assuming average annual working hours per capita to be 1564 hours, this total is equivalent to around 3800 full-time jobs.

The latter figure was assessed by the workgroup to be decidedly relevant, although the findings did not lead to any immediate conclusions regarding policy instruments. Above all, it is unclear at this aggregated level whether production conditions in companies and the amount of work available actually permit such overtime to be converted into full-time jobs. First, overtime can arise in higher-skilled jobs for which there may be no appropriate supply on the labour market. Secondly, overtime is worked sporadically and cannot be forecast; consequently a permanent full-time job is not an option, and temporary employment is not easy to organise. Furthermore, the IAB Companies Panel only enquired into the total number of overtime hours and paid overtime hours actually worked, thus concealing any further differentiation. This prompted the idea of gathering more precise information, at a workshop conducted with representatives of Saxony-Anhalt companies, on the factors giving rise to overtime and the options for dismantling it.

The picture produced by the workgroup's investigations up to that point was then supplemented by reports from the company representatives. The main factors preventing the reduction of overtime in order to create more employment include:

- the unforeseeable, short-term or seasonal occurrence of overtime,
- the need for a flexible buffer in the volume of hours worked,
- the excessive financial risk associated with employing new people to cover the volume of overtime,
- the generally poor or at least uncertain economic situation,
- the widespread introduction of working hours accounts and hence the tendency toward transitory overtime
- and the lack of skills among the unemployed.

The problem is further exacerbated by the fact that, to an increasing extent, companies are achieving greater flexibility of capacity utilisation that they require by making more use of part-time employment, temporary employment contracts, contracted labour and farming out of work and services.

Nevertheless, there remains a certain volume of paid overtime and that, as one company representative expressly emphasised, is financially inefficient in view of the declining productivity of employees and higher labour costs. Failing to discuss possible instruments for dismantling this 'residual overtime' would therefore be financially irrational. The further discussion focused on the possibility of temporarily employing suitably skilled unemployed people in order to reduce the volume of permanent overtime (especially predictable, seasonal overtime). The social partners and the labour administration were encouraged to continue exploring the options in this area.

6.4 Combating Clandestine Work and Illegal Employment

After what were sometimes heated discussions, the workgroup agreed upon the following package of measures:

A joint circular order on Combating the Grey Labour Market and Illegal Employment will be drafted by the state ministries responsible, where the objective is to ensure a common and practical knowledge base among the relevant authorities and cooperating institutions. This will lead to improved cooperation between the governmental and social actors involved with this issue. The prerequisite, however, is better staffing in the authorities that monitor such practices, especially the trade supervision and regulatory authorities.

With financial participation by the craft trades chambers, pilot projects for combating illegal employment will be carried out in the city of Halle and the rural district of Eisleben, whereby special investigators (probably ex-police officers) are to be recruited by the responsible authorities. This offer on the part of the craft trades chambers applies to all rural districts and municipal boroughs. The special employment office units for combating clandestine work will perform an intensified coordinating function. A key element here is to integrate 'grassroots experience' on the part of trade supervision and regulatory authorities into the substantive and conceptual work in this field.

Efforts must be made to introduce European rules for reciprocal enforcement of fines imposed on illegal employment; the state government must support activities at European level to develop policies in this regard. Thought should be given to launching a central register that documents offences pertaining to illegal employment and/or against the law governing subcontracted labour. What is also needed is better informational work on the social significance of the grey economy, and educational campaigns aimed at highlighting the damage it causes to society.

6.5 Jobs for Youth

This workgroup focused initially on evaluation and possible proposals for redesigning the federal government's 'Jump Programme' for combating youth unemployment. The results were then fed into discussions conducted in September at the Federal Ministry for Employment and Social Security in Berlin. As work proceeded – after a summary analysis of the employment situation for young people in Saxony-Anhalt – the workgroup agreed to focus in future on publicising support schemes, on collective bargaining policies at the second labour market threshold and the related issue of adequate starting salaries, using the part-time old-age employment law to promote youth employment, the lack of equal opportunity between the sexes in certain occupations, the growing problem of youths having no school-leaving certificate, and on the continuing evaluation of 'Jump'.

7. SUMMARY

Let us recall the most important points of dispute around the theoretical question this chapter sought to answer. Cooperative policy processes lead to

- informed control, or to strategic distortions of information (the 'knowledge' problem)
- greater integration of interests within society, or activation of principal-agent problems (the 'representation' problem)
- improved legitimisation based on consensus among groups within society, or to decision making being disconnected from parliament, the body with real sovereignty (the 'legitimisation' problem)
- creative solutions via discourse, or to the structural conservatism of the consensus principle (the 'innovation' problem)

- gains from collaboration, or to rent-seeking behaviour (the 'efficiency' problem)

It is too early as yet to give serious answers to these questions – if answers can indeed be given. At the *knowledge level*, neither major gains nor strategic distortions of information can be identified. The atmosphere is very open as far as information flow is concerned, without the decision-makers obtaining a more enlightened state of knowledge. The question of *representation* is solved organisationally, without problems. From my position, nothing of empirical significance can be said about principal–agent problems in the federations. However, declining membership on both sides (and the weakening grip of collective bargaining agreements) is leading, of course, to major problems for our understanding of democracy. In the case of 'transitional benefit' (*Übergangsgeld*), a broad *legitimatory basis* was indeed created within the 'Alliance', yet parliament was initially involved as a mere recipient of information. However, the reason here is that the initiative was aimed at influencing policymaking at federal government level. Agreements within such alliances cannot ignore the legislature.

The question of how or whether autonomous knowledge for problem-solving (alliances' *innovatory power*) develops in this cooperative process, a benefit frequently referred to in theoretical debate, cannot be answered yet on the basis of experience so far. Initially, meetings tended to be organised in a moderating style by the ministries involved, so that representatives of the various groups could have space to put forward their views, ideas and proposals. As time went on, previous work to describe the employment situation, specify the problems and identify solutions were mainly provided by the representatives of the ministry and the *Land* employment office. There was therefore a risk that the negotiations would degenerate into a set of hearings of oversized proportions. This was contrary, of course, to the intended purpose. Yet there were interests on both sides that pointed in this direction – first, the limited inclination of interest groups, by nature, to assume responsibility for society as a whole; secondly, the political pressure to produce fast results. At least the anticipated barriers to consensus have not arisen, and the process has its merits in the dissemination of solutions and associated knowledge, at least.

One major advantage of cooperative labour market policy is the greater social acceptance and legitimisation accorded to the resultant decisions – an aspect that impacts, in theory at least, on the *efficiency – and stability –* of political regulation (Penz 1999). Before it can do this, however, it is essential to get all stakeholders around the same table, as far as organisationally possible. The implication is that one has to go beyond the usual involvement of employers' federations and trade unions. This has been achieved in Saxony-

Anhalt. According to the principle of fiscal equivalence, there should be congruence between decision maker, financer and user collectives, since otherwise there is a risk that burdens will be shifted to non-involved outsiders. There is already an awareness that this ideal situation can only be achieved to an approximate extent in any representative democracy. In Saxony-Anhalt's 'Alliance for Jobs, Training and Competitiveness', the governmental actors are responsible for taking over-arching aspects into consideration and ensuring that the interests of non-participants are not ignored. However, when decisions have been adopted unanimously, the problem as to how these decisions are to be presented in public and in the parliamentary process is considerably reduced. This is the attraction of such processes for policymakers; at the same time, however, the question of democratic legitimacy and welfare efficiency is rendered even more acute. Experience in Saxony-Anhalt has provided confirmation of the latter problem.

The separate points can be subsumed under the more general question as to whether cooperative processes, as a mode of policymaking, enhance the capacity of society to develop, or tend rather to ossify it. There is probably no general answer to this question, since cooperation as a political process must always harmonise with an *institutional setting* that is pre-given (Hayden 1993; Penz 1999). To summarise, we would say that all actors are still learning how to handle such processes in a rational way. If they fail, and the whole idea is submerged in the currents of everyday German corporatism, the critics will be proved right and the 'Alliance for Jobs' will have no future.

REFERENCES

Berthold, N. and R. Hank (1999), *Bündnis für Arbeit: Korporatismus statt Wettbe-werb*, Tübingen: Mohr.

Buchanan, J.M. (1975/1984), *Die Grenzen der Freiheit. Zwischen Anarchie und Leviathan*, Tübingen: Mohr.

Bush, P.D. (1988), 'The Theory of Institutional Change', in M.R. Tool (ed.), *Evolutionary Economics*, Armonk: Sharpe, 125-166.

Commons, J.R. (1934/1990), *Institutional Economics. Its Place in Political Economy*, New Brunswick: Transaction Publishers.

Cowen, T. (1990), 'What a non-Paretian welfare economics would have to look like', in D. Lavoie (ed.), *Economics and hermeneutics*, London: Routledge, 285-298.

Eggertsson, T. (1997), *The Old Theory of Economic Policy and the New Institutionalism*, Jena: MPI zur Erforschung von Wirtschaftssystemen.

Eucken, W. (1952/1990), *Grundsätze der Wirtschaftspolitik*, Tübingen: Mohr.

Fraenkel, E. (1974), *Deutschland und die westlichen Demokratien*, Stuttgart: Kohlhammer.

Hayden, F.G. (1993), 'Institutionalist Policymaking', in M.R. Tool (ed.), *Institutional economics: theory, method, policy*, Norwell: Kluwer, 283-331.

Hayek, F.A. v. (1978), 'Competition as a Discovery Procedure', in F.A. v. Hayek, *New Studies in Philosophy, Politics, Economics and the History of Ideas*, London: Routledge & Kegan Paul, 179-190.

Krasner, S.D. (1984), 'Approaches to the State. Alternative Conceptions and Historical Dynamics', *Comparative Politics*, **16**, 223-246.

Lowe, A. (1965/1984), *Politische Ökonomik. On Economic Knowledge*, Königstein/Ts.: Athenäum.

March, J.G. and J.P. Olsen (1984), 'The New Institutionalism: Organizational Factors in Political Life', *American Political Science Review*, **78**, 734-749.

Mayntz, R. (1993), 'Policy-Netzwerke und die Logik von Verhandlungssystemen', *Politische Vierteljahresschrift*, **24**, 39-56.

Offe, C. (1998), 'Der deutsche Wohlfahrtsstaat: Prinzipien, Leistungen, Zukunftsaussichten', *Berliner Journal für Soziologie*, **8**, 359-380.

Ostrom, E. (1990), *Governing the Commons. The Evolution of Institutions for Collective Action*, Cambridge: Cambridge University Press.

Penz, R. (1999), *Legitimität und Viabilität. Zur Theorie der institutionellen Steuerung der Wirtschaft*, Marburg: Metropolis.

Pies, I. (1998), 'Liberalismus und Normativität: Zur Konzeptualisierung ökonomischer Orientierungsleistungen für demokratische Politikdiskurse', in P. Klemmer, D. Becker-Soest and R. Wink (eds.), *Liberale Grundrisse einer zukunftsfähigen Gesellschaft*, Baden-Baden: Nomos, 45-78.

Rawls, (1971/1996), *Eine Theorie der Gerechtigkeit*, Frankfurt am Main: Suhrkamp.

Rösner, H.J. (1997), 'Beschäftigungspolitische Implikationen des Globalisierungsphänomens als Herausforderung für den Sozialstaat', in R. Hauser (ed.), *Reform des Sozialstaats I*, Berlin: Duncker & Humblot, 11-43.

Scharpf, F.W. (1992), 'Koordination durch Verhandlungssysteme: Analytische Konzepte und institutionelle Lösungen', in A. Benz, F.W. Scharpf and R. Zintl (eds), *Horizontale Politiverpflechtung: Zur Theorie von Verhandlungssystemen*, Frankfurt am Main: Campus, 51-96.

Sen, A. (1979): 'Rational Fools: A Critique of the Behavioural Foundations of Economic Theory', in F. Hahn and M. Hollis (eds), *Philosophy and Economic Theory*, Oxford: Blackwell, 87-109.

Streek, W. and P.C. Schmitter (1996), 'Gemeinschaft, Markt, Staat – und Verbände? Der mögliche Beitrag von privaten Interessenregierungen zu sozialer Ordnung', in P. Kenis and V. Schneider (eds), *Organisation und Netzwerk. Institutionelle Steuerung in Wirtschaft und Politik*, Frankfurt am Main: Campus, 123-164.

Streit, M.E. (1988): 'The Mirage of Neo-Corporatism', *Kyklos*, **41**, 603-624.

Wegner, G. (1998), 'Wirtschaftspolitische Reformen und Interessenwahrnehmung – ein Dauerkonflikt?', in P. Klemmer, D. Becker-Soest and R. Wink (eds.), *Liberale Grundrisse einer zukunftsfähigen Gesellschaft*, Baden-Baden: Nomos, 79-93.

Willke, H. (1992), *Ironie des Staates. Grundlinien einer Staatstheorie polyzentrischer Gesellschaft*, Frankfurt am Main: Suhrkamp.

9. The territorial dimension of modern industry and the scope of regional industrial and labour market policies

Riccardo Cappellin and Luigi Orsenigo[1]

1. INTRODUCTION

The diffusion of industrial development at the interregional and international level in Europe during the last decades points out a clear and sustained shift from few old industrialised regions to various new regions, due to the very different performance in terms of employment and output of the single regions and countries. The last two decades, with the advent of the 'post-fordist' era and under the pressure of major technological revolutions, have also been characterised by profound changes in the forms of organisation of firms and industries. The vitality of systems of small firms strongly rooted in specific geographical areas has attracted the attention of scholars and policy makers, spawning an enormous variety of interpretations and contributions. In a closely related way, industrial economists have rediscovered the fundamental importance of the territorial dimension of productive and innovative activities, while regional economists have rediscovered and absorbed the suggestions coming from the developments in the economics of innovation and technological change.

'Industrial districts' have been identified in almost any country in Europe and have stimulated the development of a large number of studies. A major result of this research effort has been to gradually overcome the original approach, which was considering this as an, albeit virtuous, exception to the general paradigm, determined by very specific factors relevant in delimited areas and mainly having a non economic but rather social and cultural character (Cappellin 1998, Steiner 1998). In fact, economic literature, starting from the specific case of the 'industrial districts', has identified factors and processes, which have a general relevance and which are increasingly important in any sector and in any area of the modern industrial economies. An important question is that of originally redefining the most appropriate geographical framework for the design and the implementation of the industrial policies. Traditional instruments of national industrial policy, such as the financial incentives or the market regulation (Balloni et al. 1998), can not be efficiently managed at the local level. They are not capable of effectively tackling the problems of the small and medium firms, which represent a large share of European industry, or the relationships between the process of industrial development and the labour market and the territorial environment, as these policy fields clearly require decentralised policy decisions. On the other hand, even the regional level may be too wide in order to intervene effectively in very different local contexts. A new approach to regional industrial policies is emerging in Europe, leading to a widening of the traditional perspective of these policies, which have essentially considered measures aimed at single firms, and promoting a better integration of industrial policies with the labour market problems, the territorial and transport organisation and the change in the institutional framework.

In this chapter, we discuss some recent important changes in the forms of industrial organisation at the territorial level and some broad implications for regional industrial policies. Whilst the discussion refers to the case of the Lombardy region, we believe that the essence of the argument may have a wider generality, as it raises basic issues and problems that apply to a large variety of circumstances. Starting from this background, we discuss how the concept of industrial district may not be adequate to analyse and guide policy making in productive systems like Lombardy. We argue that it is extremely important to define precisely the concept of 'production district' and of 'local production system', which may be most appropriate with respect to the specific characteristics of the economy and of the territory of an already developed region and which may take into consideration the recent evolution of the relationships among the firms and of the production technologies in the international experience.

In particular, different concepts, like regional systems of innovation, milieux innovateurs, learning regions and the like, seem to converge in suggesting that the origins of the vitality of territorial-based systems of small and medium sized firms ultimately reside in the ability to develop dense networks of technical, economic, social and institutional relationships within and outside the region, capable of sustaining a continuous process of learning, innovation and change over the long run. We emphasise the need to overcome the localised approach of the 'industrial districts', focused on the concept of geographical concentration and sectoral specialisation, towards a 'territorial' approach, which aims at promoting a greater and better integration between the various production activities and the various actors, both within the single region and with the other regions in an interregional and international framework.

The chapter is organised as follows. In Section 2 we discuss some broad trends in the patterns of evolution of the prevailing forms of industrial organisation, emphasising the relevance of networks of large and small firms. In Section 3, the specific case of Lombardy is briefly presented. In Sections 4 and 5, we review various complementary conceptualisations of regionally embedded networks of small firms and on these bases we develop the concept of territorial networks. Section 6 introduces and discusses the implications for regional industrial policies, which originate from this conceptualisation.

2. THE EVOLUTION IN THE MODELS OF INDUSTRIAL ORGANISATION

The model of industry that emerges at the beginning of the 21st century is deeply different from the model of mass industrialisation, on which the traditional economic theory is based. In a modern industrial economy, the model of industrial organisation based on the concept of economies of scale has been replaced by a new organisational model based on an increasing integration, cooperation and competition between different firms that belong to the same ample sector of activity. The speed of adoption of product innovations and the flexibility of integration with other local and foreign firms or organisations are increasingly the crucial factors of the competitiveness of the firms, even more than the continuous expansion of the production capacities through the investments, or the containment of the production costs through the imposition of lower wage levels. The most dynamic regions are those where the negative impact on the employment levels determined by the inevitable closures and by the downsizing of the existing firms is compensated by the birth and the fast growth of many small and middle sized firms, often in new sectors of activity. Although the large and the small firms represent two alternative models of production organisation, they must face a common competitive challenge and they follow complementary organisation approaches. In fact, the process of search for more flexibility by the large firms that adopt a more decentralised structure, corresponds to the process of search by the small firms for an integration through networks, which may have a rather formalised and stable character.

Thus, the traditional paradigm of the large firm, which is usually adopted in modern business studies or in traditional neoclassical theory, differs in various aspects from the model of the 'networks of firms', as can be seen in Table 9.1. In fact, actors, who behave according to an entrepreneurial logic are becoming increasingly more important than actors who behave according to a managerial logic. Similarly, the flexibility of the complex relationships of financial partnership existing in a network of different firms becomes more important than the stable top-down relationships based on financial control, as is usual within a financial group. Within a network, the competitiveness is not assured by the decrease of labour costs and by the flexibility or the decrease of employees, as well as by the systematic decrease of prices paid to the suppliers and by the high flexibility of the contractual relationships with these latter. That flexibility contrasts with the relatively stable relationships, based on reciprocal trust and loyalty, with the workers, or at least with the most skilled workers, within each firm.

Table 9.1: Two Models of Industry

Classical Model	*Network Model*
Manager	Entrepreneur
Stable financial control relationships in subsidiaries	High variability of the financial participation both within and between different financial groups
Decrease of labour costs	Decrease of prices paid to subcontractors
Flexibility of labour and layoff of employees	Labour stability, loyalty and flexibility of subcontracting agreements
R&D investments in specific technological fields	Integration of different technologies and continuous investment in training
Incremental expansion of production capacity through investments in new production plants	Fast technological obsolescence and productivity increase through restructuring and downsizing
Maximisation of sales and share in the national market	Downsizing and focus on specific segments of the international market
Exploitation of 'scope economies' between different products	Focus on specific products and acquisition of complementary technologies
Increase of sales and firm size	'Spin-off' of new 'ventures' for the development of new products
Growth of sales through exports	Internationalisation of the firm and exchange of know-how
Greenfield investments in new countries and regions	Acquisition of and cooperation with local firms in new countries and regions

Technological progress is assured not only by incremental investments in R&D within a specific scientific field, but also by the integration of different technologies of the various firms belonging to the network and by a major investment in the continuous training of the workers. While individual firms seem to aim at an incremental expansion of production and at the increase of the productive capacities through the investments in new plants, the crucial objective within a network becomes to promote the speed of substitution of the existing production equipment, which is subject to an increasingly rapid technological obsolescence. This implies the objective of reducing the internal production capacity of the firms through downsizing and outsourcing processes. The firms of a network aim at increasing their own size not through the continuous growth of the market share held in their respective fields of traditional production, but through the spin-off of new productions into new firms, linked through financial links. Finally, while the individual firms aim to increase exports and to invest in the creation of new production plants in foreign countries, a network organisation leads to assign a greater importance to the process of internationalisation of the individual firm, the acquisitions of foreign firms and the various forms of cooperation with foreign firms, aiming at promoting the exchange of know-how.

Summing up, a thorough analysis of various mechanisms of crucial importance in the production organisation of modern industry demonstrates that these mechanisms are very different, when the perspective of analysis is enlarged from the case of the individual firm, which vertically integrates the various phases of a given production process, to the case of a system or a network of firms, which are relatively autonomous among themselves. Therefore, the increasing integration of the firms in sectoral or geographical clusters makes increasingly less adequate the methodologies of analysis, which aim at analysing mechanisms exclusively according to a traditional microeconomic or business approach. Rather, it indicates the need of new methods of analysis capable of considering the mechanisms that operate at the level of an overall system of firms or that have a 'meso-economic' or intersectoral character.

Moreover, the integration of the productions in a single large firm does not necessarily involve an organisation, more efficient in static terms and especially more robust, flexible and competitive in the medium and long term, with respect to a local production system or a sectoral cluster, which may be made by about 1000 small and intermediate firms and have an employment of 10 000 employees, working in the same sector or in various sectors, tightly integrated between themselves. In particular, it is clear that the tools of regional or national industrial policy, that have been elaborated in order to operate on individual firms, like the various tools of financial incentive, result in being absolutely inadequate in the case of the networks or of the groups of many large and small firms. Certainly, they appear rather partial, if they are not integrated with other policy tools, which aim at creating a system and operate on the mechanisms of relationship, that tie the different firms between themselves in a local production system, characterised by a strong internal integration.

Industrial policy should move from a 'distributive' logic, using financial incentives, to a logic of regulation or deregulation. This implies a shift from a 'prescriptive' policy, which in a dirigiste manner points out specific productions or technologies, to a 'transactive' policy (Cappellin 1997a), which acts on the transaction costs or on the relationships of integration between the individual firms and facilitates the technological and organisational changes in a given geographical or sectoral system of firms.

3. THE ECONOMIC CHARACTERISTICS OF LOCAL PRO-DUCTION SYSTEMS IN LOMBARDY

According to Becattini (1991), the district is the result of a combination of the specific socio-cultural characters of a community, of the historical-naturalistic characteristics of a geographical area and of the technical characteristics of the production process and it is the result of a process of dynamic integration (a virtuous circle) between the division of labour in the district and the widening of the market of its products. Although there is not a unique definition of 'industrial district', a wide consensus seems to exist on the following characteristics of an 'industrial district' (Garofoli 1991, Brusco and Paba 1997, Steiner 1998):

- high specialisation in a specific product,
- a population of small and medium sized firms,
- production processes decomposed in different phases with low optimal technical sizes,
- external economies for the individual firms, but internal in the local territory,
- subcontracting agreements and cooperative behaviours between the firms,
- high mobility from employee to self-employment status and high birth and death rates of the firms,
- a common production and organisational know-how embodied in the skills of the local labour force.

This traditional model of the 'industrial district' seems to correspond to the experience of specific local production systems of Lombardy during the 1960s, but it is absolutely inadequate to interpret the industrial structure of a developed regional economy. In fact, Lombardy is characterised by various 'local production systems', which are strongly rooted in their respective territory. However, these local production systems differ with respect to the traditional definition of the 'industrial district', based on a model of 'endogenous' development and strongly specialised in a specific sector, at least for the following characteristics:

- a great international openness not only in terms of exports, but also of international investments both in and from other countries and in terms of international commercial and technological agreements,
- a great and increasing sectoral diversification of productions and a tight integration of the various sectors and in particular of the manufacturing activities with the logistic and modern distribution sectors and with the technological and management consulting services,
- an enlargement of the local production know-how and a high diversity and complementarity of the technologies adopted by the individual firms within the same local production system.

These characteristics are the outcome of a continuous process of evolution of the form of the local production systems, that makes rapidly obsolete the traditional ideal representations of an 'industrial district', which may be found in the economic literature. In particular, during the 1990s, a process of intense restructuring of the industrial system has occurred in Lombardy and – albeit with a high degree of abstraction - two phases may be identified. After 1993, the industrial firms in Lombardy, favoured by the devaluation of the lira, have consolidated their direct presence in the developed countries, which were the traditional market of their export, through direct investments and the acquisitions of foreign firms. Instead, after 1998, the entry in the European Monetary Union and the increasing importance of cost competitiveness has forced firms to increase their efforts in the process of industrial restructuring. That has led to further investment in the adoption of process innovation within their production structures and also to increasing decentralisation of the most traditional productions to low labour cost countries. However, in the near future, the international competitiveness of Lombardy seems to require the capability to perform a 'technological shift' and to introduce important product innovation, both through R&D investments and through an original integration of various new technologies in the production of new products, even in the traditional industrial sectors of specialisation.

4. NEW CONCEPTS AND APPROACHES IN REGIONAL INDUSTRIAL POLICY

It is necessary to adapt the traditional model of the 'industrial districts', which may have been appropriate explaining the industrialisation process of the '1960s, to the actual specific characteristics of the 'local production systems' in a developed industrial region, such as Lombardy. The territorial production systems in many countries have evolved from the stage of the traditional mono-sectoral 'industrial district', that is analogous to a simple localised cluster of similar firms that work in the same productive sector, to the stage of 'territorial networks', made by many specialised and complementary firms. Moreover, various local production systems are increasingly linked in specific networks, which may extend within the same region and also among various regions and even at the international scale. That suggests the usefulness of various new theoretical concepts, which are tightly connected to the concept of 'industrial districts', such as: the local production systems, the territorial clusters, the local innovation systems, the territorial networks, which may provide useful insights into the recent evolution of the networks of firms and their embeddedness in their respective local environment.

4.1 The 'milieux innovateurs'

With respect to the concept of 'industrial districts' the concept of 'milieux innovateurs' is focused not only on the efficient and decentralised organisation of the local productions, but also on the role of the innovation processes that could take different forms, like the processes of imitation and development of specific technology or the ability to reallocate the local resources from the sectors in decline to new emergent sectors, when the local production system is hit by a crisis and by external shocks. Two typical elements of a 'milieu' are a 'logic of interaction', that it is revealed by the creation of 'innovation networks' and by an explicit cooperation between the different local, private, public and collective actors (Maillat 1995), and a 'dynamic of collective learning', that implies the ability by the local actors to gradually modify their behaviour according to the change in the external environment and to activate the internal resources of the 'milieu', in order to create solutions that are appropriate to a new situation.

4.2 The 'regional innovation systems' (RIS)

This approach emphasises the systemic dimension of the innovation process, which derives from the fact that a regional system of innovation is made by a plurality of actors, like large and small firms working in a production sector, where network relationships exist or could be economically foreseen, and institutes of research and of superior training, private laboratories of R&D, agencies of technological transfer, chambers of commerce, associations of enterprises, organisations of professional training, specific governmental agencies and various offices of the public administrations. This sense of belonging represents the base of an 'associative approach' or of an 'associative governance', that leads to the creation of clubs, fora, consortia and different institutional schemes of partnership (Cooke 1998, Cooke and Morgan 1998). A regional system of innovation could be defined as a system in which the firms and the other organisations are systematically engaged in an interactive learning process, through an institutional environment characterised by local embeddedness. The concept of regional innovation systems (RIS) appears broader than the traditional concept of 'industrial districts' and is able, like the concept of 'milieux innovateurs', to analyse different types of local production system. In this perspective a typology of RIS could be built (Cooke 1998). For instance a 'localist RIS', like Tuscany, is characterised by a few large firms, both of local and of external origin, and by a spectrum of activity of research or by a research reach, which is not very broad. On the other hand, an 'interactive RIS', like Catalunia and Baden Wuerttemberg, is characterised by a relative balance of large and small firms, both indigenous and external, while the spectrum of research activity includes diversified structures of regional research and the reliance on external innovations. Finally, a 'globalised RIS', like California or North Rhine Westphalia or Midi Pyrénées, is characterised by the domination of global firms, often supported by a localised supply chain made by SMEs, which are rather dependent on the large companies.

4.3 The approach of the 'proximity dynamics'

This approach introduces the notion of territorial proximity, given by the intersection or overlap of three different dimensions of proximity, which may be classified respectively under the name of 'geographical proximity', of 'organisational proximity' and of 'institutional proximity' (Rallet and Torre 1998, Bellet et al 1993). While the organisational proximity deals with the links in terms of production organisation, the geographical proximity deals with the links in terms of distance. The organisational proximity is based upon the logic of organisational membership and of intrinsic similarity of the actors. Instead, the geographical proximity refers to the natural and physical limits and it includes the effect of the transport infrastructures. An industrial district combines in its definition these two components, since the firms that constitute an industrial district are tied up among themselves in terms of relationships of similarity or of membership and they are also located at a short functional distance. Finally, the institutional proximity refers to agents belonging to a territory with common representations, models and rules of thought and of action. It is based on relationships of intentional nature, like the relationships of cooperation, trust, exchange of technological information, partnership, that determine the strategy of the actors. It implies forms of collective action and the creation of institutions both formal and informal, that perform an often fundamental role in the mechanisms of operation of the economic actors.

The geographical proximity allows the development of knowledge interactions, when this is accompanied by an appropriate organisational and institutional context. However, the experience accumulated in the international transfers of technology has demonstrated that the geographical distance is less important as an obstacle to the international cooperation than the organisational and technological distance. In fact, cooperation is greater between firms with similar technology, even when they are localised in different regions, than between organisations of the same region which do not share the same problems and objectives.

4.4 The 'learning regions'

According to this approach, 'knowledge represents the fundamental resource in the contemporary economy and the process of learning represents the most important process' (Lundvall 1992, Lundvall and Johnson 1994). That leads to a strategy which is based on the belief that the development opportunities and the exogenous risk factors, which have an objective character, do not determine automatic results, but they may be enhanced or opposed through the development of the local technical, organisational and entrepreneurial abilities, which have a subjective character and must be built through a process of learning. The objective of a 'learning region' refers to the integration of the tacit or implicit traditional knowledge, which is bound to the local context, with the codified knowledge available at the world level, in order to stimulate the regional endogenous potential. The creation of new knowledge implies an intense process of interaction (Nonaka and Konno 1998), which is characterised by transfers both of tacit knowledge and of explicit knowledge and which requires face to face contacts and a physical proximity, like contacts through the information and communication technology (ICT) on long distance. The knowledge networks are based both on vertical customer–supplier relationships, which stimulate the development of incremental product innovations, and also on horizontal relationships, that could promote the innovation process through the supply of information on new technological opportunities and through the process of imitation and adaptation of successful innovations adopted by other firms and organisations (Maillat and Kebir 1999).

4.5 The 'institutional thickness'

This approach is based on the idea that the economic development process is not the result of completely endogenous dynamics of the economy, but rises from the interaction between the economic and the social system, to be considered in their different and also institutional aspects (Rullani 1998). The 'institutions', according to the approach of the 'neo-institutional contractualism', represent the framework that the social and political action creates in order to coordinate the individual behaviour of the economic operators in more or less organised and coherent forms. Therefore, the institutions are not confined in the public sphere, but they emerge in the complex interaction between the individual local actors. The 'institutional thickness' has a definite evolutionary character, since the institutional fabric is the result of a long and gradual process of learning or of 'institutional learning'. This constant evolution and creation of the different organisations and institutions that integrate and guide a local production system, corresponds to the dynamism of the organisational forms in the system of the private firms.

Typical examples of 'institutions' that offer a new decisional infrastructure to the post-fordist economy, are the 'collective actors' that perform a fundamental role in the implementation of the principle of self-organisation of local production systems. In fact, in the post-fordist stage, public regulation must be, at least partly, transformed in self-government of the (individual and collective) actors, by adopting on a wide scale what, in the institutionalist debate, is called the principle of subsidiarity (Rullani 1998, Cappellin 1997a).

5. THE APPROACH OF TERRITORIAL NETWORKS

The model of 'territorial networks' is tightly linked with the previous approaches to the analysis of a local production system. However, territorial networks imply a greater formalisation of those relationships between the firms, which were mainly informal and based on reciprocal personal knowledge and trust in the traditional 'industrial districts' (Cappellin 1998). In particular, this model implies a greater sectoral diversification of the local economy and a tight integration among the various sectors. A modern local production system is characterised by the specialisation and the complementarity of the various firms and it produces forms of vertical integration, like the 'filières', which allow the combination of the continuous evolution of the know-how, that insures a time sustained competitive advantage, with an increasing tight access to the final market, where the value added is created.

The model of 'territorial networks' highlights the tight complementarity between the organisation of the economic relationships among the firms and the physical organisation of the regional territory. This is characterised by an intense network of industrial settlements, such as the 'industrial districts', and of small and medium sized urban centres and by the complex relationships of these latter with the largest metropolitan areas, where the modern producer services are concentrated (Cappellin 1988 and 1997b). The types of the relationships between the firms and in particular relationships of subcontracting and financial integration continually evolve and they stretch both at the intersectoral level and on a wider geographical scale (Cappellin and Cersosimo 1998). The concept of 'territorial networks' indicates that the characteristic of the territorial embeddedness does not contradict an increasing external opening on an interregional and international scale. On the contrary it indicates that a tight integration exists between 'endogenous' capabilities and external openness.

This concept differs from the traditional concept of 'industrial districts' or of production 'cluster' as it indicates a shift from an approach of relative 'selective closure', based on the territorial homogeneity, to an approach based on the concept of territorial integration. That leads to the consideration of networks, which may have a variable geometry and include both various local actors and various external regions and foreign countries (Cappellin and Batey 1997). Thus, according to the 'territorial network' approach a 'local production system' seems to be characterised by the following different types of integration linkages:

- *technological integration*, characterised by the development of the local production know-how, the sharing of knowledge and values promoted by on-the-job learning processes, the continuous education of the workers, the vocational education of young workers, the joint investments in R&D by local firms and the technological cooperation with external firms,
- cooperation between the workers and the firms and *integration of the local labour market*, related to the mobility of the workers between the firms of the same sector and also to the capability of attracting qualified workers from other regions and from other sectors,
- *production integration* between the firms, through subcontracting relationships between the firms, which play a crucial role in promoting the diversification of local productions,
- *intersectoral integration* between the service sectors and the manufacturing firms, related to the development of modern commercial distribution services, transport and logistic services and also qualified services in

the certification of product quality and in the diffusion of modern technologies,

- *financial integration* of the firms, as indicated by the creation of financial groups made by several firms belonging to the same entrepreneurial family and by pro-active bank–industry relationships, which promote the creation of spin-off and the capability of attracting external investments and also the investments of local firms in other countries and regions,
- *territorial integration* at the local level, which requires an improvement in the infrastructure endowment and promotes effective physical planning regulations, aiming to defend the quality of the territory,
- *social and cultural integration*, determining the existence of a local identity and the creation of consensus on a shared developed strategy within a wide spectrum of the local community,
- relationships of *institutional integration*, related to the development of local administrative capabilities and the capability of local institutions to interact with regional and national institutions in the implementation of strategic development projects,
- territorial *integration at the interregional and international level*, leading to a greater openness in an interregional perspective, to the development of a local 'foreign policy' or of a 'territorial marketing policy', which are crucial in attracting external investments and in promoting the internationalisation of local firms.

6. THE LIMITATIONS OF ACTUAL POLICY APPROACHES

The developments of industrial organisation discussed so far have implied a gradual but deep reconsideration of the strategies and the tools of regional industrial and labour market policy. At the cost of oversimplification, it can be suggested that in the 1980s a new conceptualisation of industrial policies has been emerging, which significantly departs from the previous experiences. In the 1960s and in the 1970s, the dominant style of industrial policies in many European countries (and regions) was largely inspired by what might be termed the 'French Model'. This was essentially a centralised and vertical approach, aimed at specific industrial sectors (and in many cases specific large firms) and largely based on the distribution of financial or fiscal subsidies (Bianchi 1995). Since the following decade, the notion has been gradually diffused that policy interventions ought to be articulated in a horizontal fashion, mainly through the supply of those production factors that are necessary to sustain growth. In particular, a growing role started to be attributed to policies aiming at sustaining innovation and technological change, which were increasingly recognised to be the main engines of growth. Finally, it was also recognised that industrial policies ought to be characterised by a decentralised, regional dimension, in order to be more flexible regarding the specific needs of particular local areas. In this respect, the dominant mode of industrial policies shifted somewhat towards the 'German Model' (Bianchi 1995).

These developments were largely based on the recognition of the role played by small firms – and specifically by geographical agglomerations of SMEs, as in the industrial districts of local productive systems – and, thus, of the territorial and specifically local character of economic growth. In particular, the notion of industrial districts was actually formalised in Italy by a national law in the early 1990s. This bill identified districts as specific objects of regional industrial policies. Districts were defined by each region according to a predetermined set of parameters and they could then propose programmes and initiatives to the regional authorities. As a consequence, an impressive variety of interventions were devised and implemented in these years aiming above all at the supply of so-called 'real services' to companies, the creation of centres for the supply of business services and technology transfer being prominent examples. This kind of interventions had a mixed and highly differentiated record, across geographical areas and over time. With specific reference to the case of Lombardy, the observation of some intrinsic limitations of this type of policy stance, jointly with the transformations that were taking place in the local productive structures, have progressively suggested some further developments in the approach to policy-making.

The actual policy experiences are extremely diversified and the results are often considered as not completely satisfactory. Thus, a further step is required, which explicitly considers the most recent advances in our understanding of the processes of local development, the processes of technological, organisational and institutional innovation as well as networking. First, the previous experiences in regional industrial policies in Lombardy showed that an essential pre-condition for the success of the initiatives consisted in the actual existence of capabilities (and willingness) within firms to use and exploit the services and the other production factors supplied through policy interventions. Similarly, the capabilities of local institutions to identify and implement strategic projects are equally important. In the absence of these capabilities, the impact of purely 'horizontal' policy interventions becomes too often very limited or even irrelevant: the increased supply does not meet with an effective demand for them.

Secondly, policies aiming at establishing linkages among agents are also likely to fail if the nodes of the network have little to transfer and/or have strategies and organisational structures excessively inward-oriented. This is typically the case regarding the programmes for technology transfer, often implemented through the establishment of intermediate institutions, which in principle should build a bridge between firms and the producers of knowledge (e.g. universities, research centres, etc.). As a consequence, an adverse selection problem emerges: the transfer agencies are unable to link with both the small, 'low tech' firms and with the relatively more 'high-tech'- oriented companies. If anything, the establishment of an intermediate agent, who is unable to communicate with universities and with the firms, might paradoxically increase, rather than decrease, the distance between the agents that are supposed to be linked (Orsenigo and Cancogni 1999). Thus, more generally, a policy aiming at developing networks cannot simply focus on establishing the edges of the network, without considering at the same time the specific characteristics of the nodes, their position within the network, and the overall structure of the emerging network itself.

Thirdly, it is increasingly recognised that the main objective of industrial policies must consist essentially in the competitiveness and therefore in the growth of firms, industries and specific geographical areas. However, the notion of competitiveness has been increasingly recognised to be influenced by the interaction of different and heterogeneous factors. Competitiveness has to be understood as the outcome of an integrated set of infrastructures, resources, capabilities and competencies, and in particular of the endogenous capability to generate technological, organisational and institutional innovation. Innovation, in turn, is the result of systematic and persistent learning processes, the creation of integrated sets of complementary activities and appropriate organisational and institutional arrangements (Breschi et al. 2000; Cefis and Orsenigo 1998). In particular, an increasing role is being attributed not only to technological innovation as such, but also to organisational capabilities and organisational innovation at the level of individual firms, groups of firms, geographical areas and institutions (Andreasen et al. 1995, Coriat 1997, Orsenigo 1999). In fact, a crucial aspect of the processes of innovation-diffusion appears to be linked to the ability to identify and exploit the complementarities among differentiated fragments of knowledge through specific organisational devices, i.e. what might be loosely defined as 'organisational capabilities' (Nelson 1991, Chandler 1992, Orsenigo 1999).

Fourthly, the evolution of the local production systems discussed previously suggests that the processes of knowledge creation, dissemination and exploitation are intrinsically more complex and variegated, than it was usually assumed in the traditional conceptualisation inspired by the notion of 'industrial districts'. While 'soft' institutions like trust, norms, codes of communication, conventions remain crucially important, the more recent literature tends to attribute a higher role – as compared to the past – to the processes leading to higher degrees of formalisation of relationships, to codification of knowledge, to the construction of 'hard' organisational devices to coordinate knowledge flows (e.g. including markets for technology and know-how, formal training programmes facilitating the transmission of knowledge; Breschi and Lissoni 1999). This requires deep involvement and collaboration in the research and production process, and resources have to be invested not simply to search for new knowledge, but to build the competencies to absorb the knowledge developed by others and to understand the highly context-specific 'codes' into which knowledge is translated (Cohen and Levinthal 1989, Breschi and Lissoni 1999). Thus, knowledge does not simply spill over, but people (teams) embodying knowledge move (locally) across organisations in order to exploit the value of their knowledge. Similarly, local sources of knowledge are key in determining success in the development of new products and processes only in areas with a large accumulation of knowledge. On the other hand, innovations in firms located in areas with a relatively small accumulation of knowledge depend on the relationships with sources of knowledge (e.g. universities, other high-technology firms, suppliers and customers) located elsewhere, especially in urban centres.

Fifthly, the notion is gradually diffusing that a narrow and static definition of 'industrial districts', largely based on strong productive specialisation and – as discussed previously – on 'selective closure' and territorial homogeneity, is no longer adequate to reflect the evolving structure and needs of local production systems. In particular, excessive specialisation and closure are likely to become factors hindering rather than favouring innovation, economic growth and employment.

Sixthly, policy design and implementation were characterised by a deep ambiguity. On the one hand, 'bottom-up' initiatives from local authorities and districts had often an excessively local character, with little strategic vision and poor implementation capabilities. On the other hand, regional initiatives often maintained an excessive 'top-down' and centralist nature, resulting in an insufficient appreciation and understanding of the specific local needs.

Summarising drastically, it would appear that the dynamic competitive strength of a local productive system may be the outcome of different factors, but mainly of:

- a strong critical mass of *technical and productive knowledge* in absolute terms. Without this, firms (incumbents and/or prospective entrepreneurs) might look for other locations for tapping the relevant knowledge. Moreover, diversity is also important. Insofar as innovation rests on the integration of different fragments of knowledge, the presence of a diversified technical and productive base becomes a key issue.

- a *strong and diversified industrial base* with accumulated capabilities and organisational structures enabling them to actually participate in the network of cognitive and social relationships that are necessary to get access to, absorb, integrate the new knowledge and, on these bases, to engage in successful innovative activities.
- *specific and often formal organisational devices* (including markets for know-how) that allow flows of knowledge to take place.

7. TOWARDS A NEW APPROACH IN REGIONAL INDUS-TRIAL AND LABOUR MARKET POLICY

The recent approach of the 'territorial network' suggests the need of adopting a systemic approach at the regional level, as the overall development of a region is not the simple summation of the development of single local production systems, but also the result of their integration and synergy on a general regional scale. Therefore, a modern local production system seems to be characterised by a strong interaction between three different dimensions of a local economic development process:

Figure 9.1: Three factors in the development of a regional production system

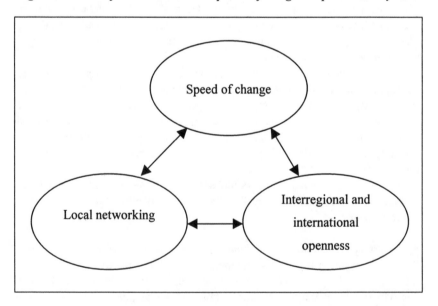

First, the challenge represented by the *speed of change* stimulating the local actors to cooperate. Conversely, the cooperation between the local actors facilitates the processes of change.

Secondly, the speed of change of the local and regional economy determines the ability of the local production system to sustain the increasing international competition induced by a greater *interregional and international openness* of the local economy. On the other hand, the openness of the local economy and the possibility of promoting arrangements of cooperation at interregional and international scale facilitate the speed of change.

Finally, *cooperation at the local level* represents an important prerequisite for common actions at the interregional level. While the challenge represented by the international competition leads the local actors to forms of cooperation.

In very general terms, the previous discussion suggests three broad areas as main objectives of a regional industrial and labour market policy:

- the development of the learning processes at the territorial level, as indicated by the theories of the 'milieux innovateurs', by the 'regional systems of innovation' approach and by that of the 'learning regions',
- the development of relationships of territorial embeddedness of the production activities, as pointed out by all the above-mentioned theories, from the traditional 'industrial districts' theory to that of the 'territorial networks',
- the development of 'intermediate' institutions and organisational tools of cooperation, which may be formalised but also informal, between different local firms and between these and the local and regional public administrations. This has been underlined especially by the approach of the 'institutional thickness', but it is also implicit in all other approaches.

In turn, each of these objectives requires policies which focus much more – as compared to the previous experiences – on favouring the integration, the openness and the formalisation of competencies and relationships at each level and among all the three levels. More specifically, at the level of 'learning processes', policies should emphasise less specialisation than the promotion of processes of (related) diversification, with an aim to increasing the productivity of industry through a technological upgrading of regional productions, both within 'traditional' sectors and through the diversification towards more technologically advanced productions. Moreover, policies should favour processes of organisational change and 'organisational thickening', at the level of individual firms and institutions and at the level of the relationships among them.

This type of policy would also immediately and directly favour processes of increasing 'territorial embeddedness', by constructing specific and distinctive technological and organisational competencies, which are difficult to imitate and replicate. At the same time, however, and on these grounds, policies should also foster interregional relations, productive diversification and 'international openness' in order to avoid closure and to promote instead openness, the development of interregional networks and the integration of individual districts or local production systems into a 'regional system of innovation'.

At the level of 'institutional thickness', policies should primarily aim at improving local strategic capabilities and policy design. In other words, regional industrial policies in Lombardy should go beyond the tension between excessive centralism and the 'do it yourself' approach of individual firms and local districts previously referred to. Rather, the promotion of joint programmes among firms and local production systems aiming at strategic objectives relevant at the regional level should become the fundamental methodology of regional policy-making. In this context, the regional administration should be primarily responsible for defining priorities, general strategic programmes and guidelines, resulting in few leading projects based on public–private partnerships. On the other hand, single 'districts' or 'local production systems' elaborate specific innovative projects, which must go beyond narrow sectoral or local interests in order to become eligible for the regional support. Moreover, the definition of districts should not be pre-determined through the application of fixed and static statistical parameters. Rather, 'districts' or 'local production systems' ought to be able to define and identify themselves, by demonstrating the actual existence of a well-defined set of common interests, strategic vision and implementation capabilities. Thus the definition of a 'district' may (and perhaps should) very well be different as a function of the nature of specific programmes.

8. CONCLUSIONS

The network approach justifies the shift from a regional and labour market policy approach based on the enhancement of the economies of specialisation and of the territorial concentration of the various sectors, like the traditional *'industrial districts'* approach. This new approach should lead to the promotion of the sectoral and territorial integration of regional economies and the development of networks at the local, at the interregional and at the international level. Thus the regional industrial policy should not necessarily focus the interventions on specific traditional *'industrial districts'*, but rather adopt a territorial approach based on the enhancement of the territorial embeddedness. That requires the definition of flexible and overlapping territorial sub-divisions of the regional territory, which may allow the organisation of the various regional policies aiming at the accumulation of the human capital, the development of the technological innovation, the process of international integration, the adoption of modern logistic systems, the territorial and environmental quality and the improvement of the infrastructure networks.

NOTES

1. This contribution has been elaborated in the framework of the project: 'Local production systems, technological and organisational change and implications for the labour market', coordinated by the Formaper – Chamber of Commerce of Milan within the ADAPT II (1997-1999) programme of the Lombardy Region.

REFERENCES

Andreasen, L.A., B. Coriat, F. den Hartog and R. Kaplinsky (eds. 1995) , *Europe's Next Step. Organisational Innovation, Competition and Employment*, London: Frank Cass.

Balloni V., M. Cucculelli and D. Iacobucci (1998), 'Le politiche del governo locale nel modello NEC', *Economia Marche*, (2), 9-118.

Becattini, G. (1991), 'Il distretto industriale marshalliano come concetto socio-economico', in F. Pycke, G. Becattini and E Sengenberger (eds.), *Distretti industriali e cooperazione tra imprese in Italia*, Firenze : Banca Toscana, Studi e Informazioni, 51-65.

Bianchi, P. (1995), *Le politiche industriali dell'Unione Europea*, Bologna: Il Mulino.

Bellet, M., Colletis, G. and Y. Lung (1993), 'Economie de proximités', Numero Spécial, *Revue d'Economie Régionale et Urbaine*, (3).

Breschi, S. and F. Lissoni (1999), *Geographical boundaries of sectoral systems*, Milano: CESPRI, Bocconi University, mimeo.

Breschi, S., F. Malerba and L. Orsenigo (2000), 'Technological Regimes and Schumpeterian patterns of innovation', *The Economic Journal*, forthcoming.

Brusco, S. and S. Paba (1997), 'Per una storia dei distretti produttivi italiani dal secondo dopoguerra agli anni novanta', in F. Barca (ed.), *Storia del capitalismo italiano dal dopoguerra a oggi*, Roma : Donzelli Editore, 263-333.

Cappellin, R. (1988), 'Transaction costs and urban agglomeration', *Revue d'Economie Regionale et Urbaine*, (2).

Cappellin, R. (1997a), 'Federalism and the network paradigm: guidelines for a new approach in national regional policy', in M. Danson (ed.), *Regional Governance and Economic Development*, London: Pion.

Cappellin, R. (1997b), 'The economy of small and medium-size towns in non metropolitan regions', in OECD (ed.), *Programme of Dialogue and Cooperation with China*, Paris: OECD.

Cappellin, R. (1998), 'The transformation of local production systems: interregional networking and territorial competitiveness', in M. Steiner (ed.), *Clusters and Re-*

gional Specialisation: On Geography, Technology, and Networks, London: Pion Editor, European Research in Regional Science.

Cappellin, R. and P. Batey (1997; eds), *Regional Networks, Border Regions and European Integration*, London: Pion.

Cappellin, R. and D. Cersosimo (1998), 'Sud chiama Nord: le reti interregionali di piccole e medie imprese' in AAV.V. (ed.), *Le vie del Mezzogiorno. Storia e scenari*. Lamezia Terme: Meridiana Libri.

Cefis, E. and L. Orsenigo (1998), *The Persistence of Innovative Activities. A Cross-Countries and Cross-Sectors Comparative Analysis*, Trento: Discussion Paper n. 4, Department of Economics, University of Trento.

Chandler, A.D. (1992), 'Organisational capabilities and the Economic History of the Industrial Enterprise', *Journal of Economic Perspectives*, 6 (3), 79-100.

Cohen, W. and D. Levinthal (1989), 'Innovation and Learning: The Two Faces of R&D', *Economic Journal*, 99, 569-96.

Cooke, P. (1998), 'Introduction: origins of the concept', in H.J. Braczyk, P. Cooke and M. Heidenreich (eds), *Regional innovation systems. The role of governances in a globalized world*, London: UCL Press, 2-27.

Cooke P. and K. Morgan (1998), *The associational economy. Firms, Regions and Innovation*, Oxford: Oxford University Press.

Coriat, B. (1997), *The New Dimensions of Competitiveness*, The IPTS Report, Seville, n. 15, June.

Garofoli, G.(1991), *Modelli locali di sviluppo*, Milano : Franco Angeli.

Hassink, R. (1999), *Towards regionally embedded innovation support systems in South Korea*, relazione presentata al 16th Pacific Regional Science Conference, Seoul.

Lundvall B.A. (1992; ed.), *National systems of innovations: towards a theory of innovation and interactive learning*, London: Pinters Publishers.

Lundvall B.A. and B. Johnson (1994), 'The learning economy', *Journal of Industrial Studies*, 1 (2), 23-42.

Lyons, D. (1995), 'Agglomeration economies among high technology firms in advanced production areas: the case of Denver/Boulder', *Regional Studies*, 29 (3), 265-78.

Maillat, D. (1995), 'Territorial dynamic, innovative milieus and regional policy', *Entrepreneurship & Regional Development*, 7, 157-165.

Maillat, D. and L. Kebir (1999), 'Learning region et systèmes territoriaux de production', *Revue d'Economie Regionale et Urbaine*, (3), 430-448.

Morgan, K. (1997), 'The learning region: institutions, innovation and regional renewal', *Regional Studies*, 31 (5), 491-504.

Nelson, R. (1991), 'Why Do Firms Differ and How Does It Matter?', *Strategic Management Journal*, 12, 61-74.

Nonaka, I. and N. Konno (1998), 'The concept of 'Ba': building a foundation for knowledge creation', *California Management Review*, 40 (3), 40-54.

Orsenigo, L. (1999), 'Organizational Innovation and Organization of Innovative Activities in a Global Economy: the impact on competitiveness and growth', in K. Rubenson and H. Schuetze (eds)., *Transition to the knowledge society*, University of British Columbia Press.

Orsenigo, L. and E. Cancogni (1999), 'Le relazioni università-industria in Italia', in C. Antonelli (ed.), *Conoscenza tecnologica. Nuovi paradigmi dell'innovazione e specificità italiana*, Torino: Edizioni Fondazione Agnelli.

Rallet, A. and A. Torre (1998), 'On geography and technology: proximity relations in localised innovation networks', in M. Steiner (ed.), *Clusters and Regional Spe-*

cialisation: On Geography, Technology, and Networks, London: Pion Editor, European Research in Regional Science.

Rullani, E. (1998), 'Riforma delle istituzioni e sviluppo locale', *Sviluppo Locale*, (8), 5-46.

Steiner, M. (1998), 'The discrete charm of clusters: An introduction', in M. Steiner (ed.), *Clusters and Regional Specialisation: On Geography, Technology, and Networks*, London: Pion Editor, European Research in Regional Science.

PART THREE

Perspectives with regard to European learning processes

10. From regional policy towards preventive labour market policy? – A multi-level governance perspective on the case of Denmark

Henrik Halkier[1]

Since the beginning of the 1990s, the aims and methods of Danish regional policy have changed dramatically. In the 1960s central government began to operate financial incentives programmes designed to redistribute economic activity within the country by making it more attractive to invest in designated 'problem regions' with high levels of unemployment and a limited degree of industrialisation. But as of January 1991 all central government incentive schemes were terminated, and since then the main components of spatial economic policy have been a host of regional and local initiatives supplemented by European Structural Funds. Policies tend to focus strongly on improving the competitiveness of firms within the region, and as sub-national initiatives in economic development can be found everywhere, the preferential treatment traditionally accorded to 'problem regions' has been eroded. In many ways it could be argued that Denmark is an extreme example of more general trends in European regional policy,[2] namely a declining role of national policy programmes of reactive and redistributive policies in favour of 'problem regions' towards a new paradigm in which regional policy involves many tiers of government in proactive intervention. This intervention is aimed at preventing labour market problems such as high levels of unemployment by making indigenous firms better equipped to operate in an increasingly competitive economic environment.

Impressions may, however, be deceptive in public policy, and while 'competitiveness' and 'indigenous development' clearly did become expressions that no statement of regional development strategy could be without in the 1990s, the extent to which this was translated into qualitatively different policies may have been more limited. The aim of this chapter is to examine the transformation of regional policy in Denmark from the perspective of the evolving strategies and positions of the public actors involved, and because many tiers of government have played a role, a multi-level governance perspective will be adopted.

The text is divided into three parts. The following section provides a brief outline of the analytical framework, based primarily on contributions from traditions within policy analysis, network theory and the new institutionalism. The main body of the text examines the changing face of spatial economic policy in Denmark, dealing in turn with the development of policies and initiatives emanating from the national, European and regional levels respectively. Finally, the interaction of the three levels of spatial economic policy is assessed within a multi-level governance framework in order to establish the overall degree of strategic change and the new patterns of resource dependency between the various tiers of government.

1. THE ANALYTICAL APPROACH

The literature on regional policy has traditionally been concerned mainly with the economic impact of development initiatives, and in order to be able to undertake an in-depth analysis of changing strategies and institutional relations it can therefore be helpful to draw inspiration from approaches developed in connection with studies of other areas of public policy, especially writings adopting an inter-organisational perspective on policy analysis and the emerging literature on multi-level governance.[3]

A general analytical framework has been developed around the proposition that regional policy is essentially about attempting to change patterns of behaviour amongst private actors in pursuance of public priorities with regard to spatial development. This suggests that three types of actors and their interaction are central:

- As a form of public policy, regional policy will have *political sponsors* from whom the political authority to institute options and incentives for private firms is derived.
- The *implementing organisation* may or may not be identical to the administrative arm of the political sponsors and interacts directly with firms and other private actors by instituting the options and incentives entailed in a particular form of regional policy.
- The *targeted private actors* are crucial in the sense that spatial economic objectives are to be achieved by making individual firms and other private actors behave in ways they would not otherwise have done, and while policy instruments entailing options and incentives are employed by the implementing organisation in order to bring about the changes

desired, the outcome still depends on a response from private actors that may or may not be forthcoming.

It follows from this that two types of inter-organisational relations are at the centre of any form of regional policy: the relationship between the political sponsors and the implementing organisation on the one hand, and the relationship between the implementing organisation and the private actors targeted by policy measures on the other. But these actors and their interaction are set within the context of broader inter-organisational relations and institutional features, and the economic and political environments which influence the positions and strategies of the three central sets of actors should therefore also be taken into account, especially in a situation where several forms of regional policy sponsored by different tiers of government coexist. While each of these individual policies can be studied as a set of inter-organisational relations as summarised in Figure 10.1, the entire field of regional development must be seen as a number of more or less parallel policies interacting because sponsorships overlap, implementing organisations are involved in more than one policy programme and the same firms are targeted by several public initiatives.

Figure 10.1: Actors, inter-organisational relations and environments of regional policy

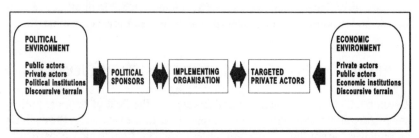

This general approach can be translated into a very detailed conceptual framework for in-depth studies of particular organisations or policies,[4] but as this chapter focuses on a more limited range of issues a simplified version has been adopted which treats each tier of government as a single entity and focuses on their key organisational features and relations. For each tier of government three dimensions are seen as crucial, namely the resources at its disposal, the assumptions on which it operates, and the strategies pursued in relation to its environment.[5] *Resources* are the means by which organisations maintain themselves and influence their surroundings, either by employing them as policy instruments vis-à-vis private actors or as means of linking up with other organisations to achieve specific goals, and the text distinguishes between four basic resources: authority, information, finance and organisation.[6] The way particular phenomena are interpreted and the basic values espoused may have important bearings on the strategies adopted, and from the perspective of regional policy key *assumptions* will relate to the nature of 'the regional problem', namely the interregional inequalities perceived to be significant, and the underlying values that transform interregional inequalities into a social problem warranting public intervention. Finally the *strategies* are an obvious object of study, both as positioning strategies vis-à-vis other organisations and operational strategies which entail particular goals and policy instruments in relation to the private firms targeted.

Table 10.1: Implementing organisations in regional policy: Analytical dimensions

Dimensions	Subdimensions
Resources	Authority, information, finance, organisation
Assumptions	Interregional disparities, underlying values
Strategies	Operational positioning

Source: Halkier 2000

All three dimensions clearly have implications for inter-organisational relations and the development of policies: resource dependencies between organisations will make some courses of action more feasible or attractive than others, and assumptions and strategies may be more or less compatible.

2. REGIONAL POLICY AND THE DANISH REGIONS

Given the high level of inter-tier collaboration in the field of regional policy, the picture drawn is bound to be a complex one. In the following, the analysis is organised according to the tier of government from which a particular programme originates, and for each of the three levels - the national, European and regional - the analysis begins by an outline of the development of policies from the 1970s to the late 1990s, followed by an assessment of the changing strategies and resource dependencies with regard to this particular set of programmes and initiatives.

2.1 National Policies

In Denmark overall responsibility for regional policy rests with national authorities and is subject to national legislation, and from the late 1950s to the early 1980s the proclaimed objective of regional policy was to promote

equality between different parts of the country with regard to economic welfare, especially between the urban centres and the rural peripheries. From the
mid-1980s the assumptions underpinning national regional policy did, however, change when the case was primarily put in economic terms, i.e. mobilisation of indigenous regional resources in support of the general attempt to
improve the international competitiveness of Danish firms.[7] Direct subsidies
to individual firms were the mainstay of central government regional policy
from 1958 to 1990, and the administration of the grant schemes was firmly
centralised and did not involve input from the regional level. The first decade
saw a gradual introduction of an array of schemes primarily targeting individual firms (soft loans, investment grants) but also local authorities (soft
loans for construction of industrial property). From 1967 support was restricted to designated problem areas, and since the beginning of the 1980s
spatial coverage has been gradually reduced, partly because of pressure from
the European Commission, and currently designated areas comprise only
around 17% of the total population.[8] National-level regional subsidy schemes
were supported by both subnational and European means, but still the dominant trend in central government expenditure on regional policy would appear to have been one of decline at least since the late 1970s. Until the mid-
1980s accounting conventions did, however, artificially inflate the figures,[9]
and thus in expenditure terms the turning point must be located much later,
i.e. around the year 1988.

The circumstances leading to the termination of all regional subsidy
schemes operated from the national level by the end of 1990 is in need of
further inquiry,[10] but it is already clear that in addition to short-term factors
like party-political manoeuvring in connection with the yearly budget negotiations in late 1989, underlying long-term causes must also have been present. These include generally waning support for financial subsidies to individual firms as a policy instrument, a significant decrease in the economic
differences between the Danish regions on a range of key indicators, and
perhaps also the availability of alternative - European - sources of funding for
regional development. The outcome was, however, that from 1991 onwards
the role of central government in regional development was very different
from what it used to be. A Danish map of Assisted Areas did continue to be
produced by the Danish Agency for Trade and Industry (DATI), and its approval by the European Commission allowed central government to give
financial support to individual firms in problem regions when providing
matching funding in connection with Structural Fund programmes.[11] However, the most important generic task of central government has been to continue to ensure access to business and technological services also in disadvantaged regions.[12] The existing network of regionally based Technology
Information Centres (TICs), sponsored by central government but co-funded

by subnational actors, has sometimes been heralded as a new form of national-level regional policy,[13] but as there is no preferential treatment built into the TIC network,[14] this is essentially a deconcentrated delivery of national business services. Furthermore, a flexible system of 'fire-fighting' has gradually been put in place, and since 1996 the so-called Notification Pool has provided funding for new targeted regional initiatives in e.g. temporary advisory services in localities threatened by major industrial closures.[15]

Table 10.2: National policies for regional development in Denmark: Resources and levels of government

Input	Authority	Finance	Information	Organisation
European	Increasing influence on designated areas and grant levels	Some co-funding from mid-1980s till early 1990s		
National	Redistribution latent since 1991, consensus changing	Self-financing, from 1991 mainly potential	Statistical surveys maintained	DATI maintained, deconcentrated TIC network becomes central
Regional		Limited co-funding	Notification Pool project design	

On the basis of the above analysis it is clear that the nature and role of national-level regional programmes changed profoundly from the 1970s to the 1990s. *First*, the *raison d'être* of regional policy changed from addressing inter-regional inequalities to boosting the contribution of every region to national economic competitiveness. *Secondly*, national-level strategies shifted away from redistributive programmes of financial incentives to a deconcentrated form of industrial policy. And *thirdly*, the pattern of resource dependencies also changed, albeit in a perhaps less dramatic fashion. As illustrated by Table 10.2 summing up the changing input of resources from the three levels of government implicated in national programmes, it is of course evident that the abolishing of traditional grant schemes in the early 1990s affected the situation profoundly. In the original set-up national policies were a largely self-contained entity, financed and administered by central government, and given the generally relatively low level of expenditure on national-level regional programmes compared to other European countries,[16] it would be reasonable to assume that the continuation of national programmes cannot have been contingent on co-funding from other tiers of government. With the introduction of a new approach central government abandoned its role as redistributor of private economic activity between the regions and, apart from a minor fire-fighting role in connection with major industrial closures, adopted a position in which its direct role with regard to regional development was limited to ensuring that national business development programmes were made available in every region, weak as well as strong ones. As the limited sub-national co-funding for the TICs is probably political commitment rather than a financial prerequisite, an independent role of nationally sponsored organisations in regional development was maintained in the new policy regime. The main difference was that central government did not enjoy a monopoly on implementing the new type of economic development initiatives, as will become evident in the following.

2.2 European Policies

Regional policy acquired a new dimension with the establishment of the European Regional Development Fund (ERDF), and although it is clear that the operation of the Structural Funds differs between the member states of the EU,[17] the basic features of the development of its operation in Denmark do of course reflect the general direction in which these European programmes have moved, with the changes introduced by the 1988 reforms constituting a major watershed.[18]

From 1975 until 1988 regional policy at the European level was essentially a mechanism for redistribution between the member states, operating through a system of national quotas employed either as an outright reimbursement of expenditure on national policy programmes or as co-funding of major improvements of the regional and local infrastructure. In Denmark the Structural Funds did, however, only come to play a significant role from the mid-1980s, because until Greenland left the EU in 1985 most of the European funds had been spent on the Arctic dependency.[19] The Danish expenditure pattern was in line with that in other relatively prosperous member states in that more innovative types of projects only began to emerge gradually, e.g. more advanced forms of infrastructure such as sector-based industrial parks or comprehensive regionally-based development programmes such as Nord-Tek in North Jutland.[20] Central government played an important role in the administration of the Structural Funds prior to the 1988 reform, and although regional authorities were given the opportunity to indicate their preferences with regard to applications from their own area, the final decision was taken on the national level.[21]

The 1988 reform of the Structural Funds introduced a multi-year programme-based approach to regional policy on the basis of partnership between the Commission, national government and subnational actors. Under the new rules Denmark was allocated two Objective 2 programmes, targeting areas of industrial decline in North Jutland and Storstrøm respectively, and one Objective 5b programme covering rural areas on a number of small and medium-sized islands. In the second round of programming, starting in 1994, the designated areas were expanded significantly and came to cover 15.3% of the Danish population while the budget allocation of European monies nearly doubled,[22] and eventually the level of expenditure on European regional programmes in Denmark ended up surpassing that of the then abandoned national programmes by a significant margin. Also the profile of Structural Funds projects changed: in the programming periods starting in 1994 support for so-called 'knowledge projects' - supporting capacity-building in firms with regard to e.g. research or marketing - was planned at 41%, while infrastructure projects and investment subsidies account for only 31% and 26% respectively of budgeted public expenditure, a trend that continued in subsequent European programmes in Denmark.[23]

The introduction of the partnership principle has often been heralded as a measure that advanced the role of regional actors in the policy process,[24] but as the role of a particular tier of government may well differ in the various phases of the policy process,[25] a more detailed analysis capable of distinguishing between planning and implementation is needed.[26] In the planning stages of Structural Funds programmes the role of central government is primarily concerned with negotiating area designations and the proposed development strategies with the Commission ensuring that strategic priorities are in accordance with basic principles of national policy, especially the current preference for framework measures. The partnership principle is also evident in the way in which ERDF programmes are funded, with sizeable contributions from both central government and subnational public bodies. Although the structure of co-funding varies between different types of projects, making national and/or regional/local co-funding a precondition for approval of Structural Funds programmes deliberately creates a mutual resource dependency between the three tiers of government involved. The lead in the actual programme formulation is to be found at the subnational level with regional government organising a process of consultation with local government and private sector 'social partners', developing new policy initiatives and producing the draft version of the development programme for the region. Also in the implementation phase the role of central government has gradually become a limited one: although DATI provides matching funding for subsidies to individual firms and undertakes a formal appraisal of applications especially with regard to issues of legality, the crucial early and substantive stages of project evaluation in which the economic, technical and organisational prospects of an application are assessed are now firmly situated at the regional level.

Table 10.3: European policies for regional development in Denmark: Resources and levels of government

Input	Authority	Finance	Information	Organisation
European	Establish ground rules; increasing influence on objectives and strategies	Part-financing	European statistics	DG XVI
National	National procedures; negotiate with Commission; define strategic principles; decreasing role in approval of individual projects	Co-funding of subsidies to firms from 1988	National statistics	DATI
Regional	Increasingly since 1988: strategic planning, processing of applications, recommendation of projects	Co-funding of infrastructure and framework measures	Regional statistics; knowledge of firms	Regional programme administrations

On the basis of the above analysis it can be concluded that the Structural Funds programmes in Denmark represent an interesting combination of different regional policy strategies within a new organisational framework. In terms of assumptions and strategies the European programmes clearly maintain the notion that some disadvantaged regions should be given preferential treatment at the expense of more well-off localities, but at the same time the operational strategies have come to focus more and more on improving the competitiveness of indigenous firms rather than merely redistributing economic activity to problem regions by means of investment subsidies. With regard to resource dependencies, the 1988 reforms of the Structural Funds which introduced the new partnership-based approach certainly made a major difference in the case of Denmark, as illustrated by Table 10.3. While the European Commission and the nation state still establish the basic spatial and financial delimitation of Structural Funds activities, substantive issues are primarily dealt with by subnational institutions, although central government maintains a general role with regard to process management, legality and basic policy principles. Two conclusions can be drawn on the basis of this. *First*, that the European measures never constituted a self-contained programme of spatial economic policy, and that, even in its present form, depends crucially upon national and regional levels of government for access to a wide range of resources. *Secondly*, the internal division of labour between the national and regional levels now places Denmark among the most decentralised countries in the EU with regard to Structural Funds programming.[27] All in all the Danish approach to administration of the Structural Funds can perhaps best be described as having evolved towards a state of 'controlled decentralisation' within a multi-level governance setting which in designated areas delivers policies that increasingly resemble a decentralised form of industrial policy.

2.3 Regionally-based policies

Also the field of subnational development policies must be analysed in terms of 'before' and 'after', although the boundary between the two is not as clear-cut as was the case with national and European regional policies. Bottom-up initiatives in economic development began with the setting up of public–private partnerships in the form of Development Committees in the 1930s and 1950s, aimed at attracting firms from outside to locate in the area by means of promotion and advice and, from the late 1950s, trying to attract support from the new national policy schemes. The importance of the Development Committees did, however, wane as local and regional government gradually became more active in economic development.[28] The political motivation for the recent economic activism at the subnational level seems to have been fuelled by practical experience with the decentralised administration of labour market policies in a period of high levels of unemployment in combination with the dominance of a liberal discourse of economic management on the national level in the 1980s[29] - plus, of course, in the 1990s the policy void created by the termination of central government schemes and the example set by the decentralised management of Structural Funds projects and programmes.

The net result was a conspicuous increase in the level of subnational initiatives, and from the early 1990s all regional and the majority of local governments were engaged in activities aiming to stimulate indigenous economic activity, promote employment within their area, and secure a higher level of taxable income. The new emphasis on indigenous growth in the 1980s also involved a notable shift with regard to policy instruments: more or less specialised advisory services came to dominate - supplying information on e.g. markets, technology and general management issues - supplemented by provision of various forms of technological and organisational infrastructure such as incubator units, test facilities and collective marketing efforts.[30] Reliable statistics have only been obtained from 1994 onwards, but the level of expenditure has been relative stable and a yearly average of 185 million DKK in the period 1994-97 certainly establishes the regional level as a major player in spatial economic policy.[31] The extent to which co-funding of Structural Funds projects is included in this grand total is unclear,[32] but the availability of funds from the European level has undoubtedly in many ways played a catalytic role by prompting sub-regional actors to engage in economic development activities.[33]

The role of central government as a regulator of regional and local development initiatives has evolved gradually. While it was always crystal clear what subnational government was *not* allowed to do, namely to grant financial subsidies to individual firms, what they actually *could* do remained unclear until 1992 when a new parliamentary act designated collective business services - i.e. measures targeting all or a group of firms within its area - as the field in which regional and local authorities could engage.[34] The other central plank in central government regulation has been attempts to bring about a higher degree of coordination amongst actors at the subnational level. In most of the regions bottom-up development activities have involved a large number of relatively small organisations since the beginning of the 1990s, including both regional and local government organisations, a host of quangos and a wide range of public–private partnerships.[35] This complex institutional pattern would seem to have been brought about by a number of factors - political preference for collective framework measures, the uncertain legal position, a need to maintain a business-like image and a high public profile - and has given rise to concerns about duplication and waste of public resources. The attempts by central government to promote coordination have, however, relied exclusively on voluntary organisational measures backed by limited financial incentives, and the impact of these schemes in terms of improved cooperation between implementation of policies remains to be seen.[36]

Table 10.4: Regionally-based policies for regional development:Resources and levels of government

Input	Authority	Finance	Information	Organi-sation
European		Co-funding of some initiatives		
National	Regulation of policy instru-ments; Since early 1990s en-couragement of cooperation	Limited co-funding for coopera-tion		DATI
Regional	Since late 1980s: Institution building and strategic priori-ties	Since late 1980s a large aggre-gate divided between many actors	Increasing knowledge of firms	Since late 1980s: Many small actors and regional-local Quangos Partner-ships

On the basis of the above analysis it is clear that although the underlying assumption has remained the same - public intervention is needed to promote economic development in particular localities - strategies have gradually come to focus primarily on attempts to improve the competitiveness of indigenous firms. Also in terms of input of resources from the three levels of government implicated in regionally-based programmes for economic development it is noticeable that the situation has changed profoundly since the end of the 1980s. From playing at best a marginal role through place promotion, bottom-up development has become a growth industry in its own right with a large number of actors involved and important links to actors on the national and European level, as illustrated by Table 10.4. On the one hand central government regulation has established the legal framework for regional development initiatives, thereby preventing the introduction of financial or other subsidies to individual firms as policy instruments, and it is therefore hardly surprising that subnational activities have been dominated by in particular advisory services and various forms of organisational infrastructure. On the other hand funding from the European Structural Funds has undoubtedly acted as a catalyst for the development of a burgeoning bottom-up economic development scene by enlarging the financial scope for regional and local action. The degree of dependency created by this would, however, seem to be moderate because the Danish Structural Funds programmes rely on the generation and development of projects by subnational actors, and - with the possible exception of small units of local government - European co-funding could in most cases be substituted by e.g. regionally generated tax revenues if regional or local government decided to give priority to this area of public policy.

2.4 Conclusions and Perspectives

The preceding pages have demonstrated that the regional development policies pursued by each of the three tiers of government have changed beyond recognition since the late 1980s. What remains to be discussed are the consequences of these developments for the overall strategic direction of spatial economic policy and the resource dependencies between the public actors involved in what has increasingly become a complex multi-level activity.

As illustrated by Table 10.5, summing up the key features of the policy regimes before and after the changes taking place around 1990, there can be little doubt that both strategies and resource dependencies have been recast dramatically. In the traditional policy regime the underlying assumptions and strategies were unambiguous in the sense that interregional disparities in economic development were seen as a legitimate reason for public intervention, and strategies centred on redistributing economic activity from prosperous regions to designated 'problem areas'. Central government enjoyed a de facto monopoly on policy implementation, managing the only major economic policy programme entailing systematic spatial discrimination and effectively controlling the necessary resources: political authority based on cross-party consensus and the means of implementation in terms of finance, information and organisation. In this phase both European and subnational actors played very minor roles, either as co-funders or by pursuing policies like infrastructure development that supported the redistributive strategies of central government.

*Table 10.5: Levels of government and the changing regimes of regional pol-
     icy in Denmark*

Level / Dimensions		*Traditional (till the late 1980s)*	*New (from the early 1990s)*
Euro-pean	Strategy	Interregional redistribution	Interregional redistribution; Regional competitiveness
	Re-sources	Co-fund national programmes; regulate national subsidies	Spatial discrimination; significant source of finance
National	Strategy	Interregional redistribution	Regional competitiveness
	Re-sources	Spatial discrimination; control key policy resources	Control own programme resources; regulate EU/regional programmes; Co-fund European programmes
Regional	Strategy	Attract investment to locality	Regional competitiveness
	Re-sources	Control own programme resources	Co-fund European programmes; crucial informational and organisational resources

After the transition to the new policy regime the strategic emphasis has
generally shifted from redistribution of growth between regions to attempts to
improve the competitiveness of indigenous firms within the regions. Only the
European programmes maintain preferential treatment of 'problem regions',
while both national and subnational initiatives have essentially become de-
central(ised) forms of industrial policy operating throughout the country. In
fact the Structural Funds programmes also have predominantly adopted a
'preventive' approach within their designated areas aimed at improving the
competitiveness of local firms. Although subnational policies originate in
what is perceived as regional problems, their spatial effects on the aggregate
national level may well cancel each other out, even if weaker regions spend
more on economic development than stronger regions in order to make up for
the advantages of the latter, and thus 'these ... activities probably no longer

contribute to the evening out of regional discrepancies, but rather to contribute to *national* economic development'.[37]

In terms of resource dependencies the traditionally self-contained nature of
regional policy as a central-government activity has been substituted by much
more complex patterns in the new policy regime. Although the national level
still maintains a role in policy implementation through the TIC network, the
new set-up clearly involves a separation of the roles formerly concentrated at
the national level: the authority to instigate spatial discrimination is now
exercised via the European level, regional and local actors dominate the sharp
end of the implementation process on the basis of their informational and
organisational resources, and the critical contribution of central government
would appear to be to promote and regulate initiatives emanating from the
two other levels.

Taken together these changes have produced a new dominant paradigm in
spatial economic intervention which emphasises indigenous development
through industrial-policy type measures in a multi-level governance setting
with asymmetrical resource dependencies. From a regional perspective a
conspicuous feature of this new institutional set-up is the increased capacity
of regional actors to influence strategic decisions with regard to economic
development initiatives: under the traditional regime they had been excluded
from the policy process altogether, now they are capable of designing programmes, setting up institutions and shaping individual projects. Of course
bottom-up activities still depend on external resources, primarily central
government regulation and to some extent funding from European programmes, but given the relatively broad nature of both the former and the
latter, targeting the needs of the individual locality should certainly be possible. What this means in terms of the spatial distribution of economic development would, however, be good to know. Contrary to traditional central
government policies that involved highly visible financial transfers from
prosperous to less prosperous regions, the spread of economic development
activities to relatively well-off regions will also intensify interregional competition, and the fate of weaker localities will therefore depend on much less
tangible qualities such as the will and capacity to mobilise resources in order
to create an environment conducive to innovation and growth.

All in all this would seem to suggest that the medium-term outlook for
spatial economic policy in Denmark is stable, at least compared with the
turbulence of the preceding decade. As in Europe at large, the organisational
and informational resources with which subnational actors are associated are
likely to be particularly critical in a period where not just the quantity but
also the quality of investment is seen as crucial to regional development, and
the enhanced position of subnational actors would seem to be more than a
fickle whim of political fashion. Moreover, in terms of politics, central gov-

ernment has played an important role in furthering decentralisation in the domain of spatial economic policy, and the framework-oriented approach to industrial policy continues to enjoy broad political support. The endurance of the new policy paradigm will certainly be tested in the coming years when the enlargement of the EU towards the east results in a major reform of the Structural Funds in which continuation of the current levels of support in the relatively prosperous North Western member states is highly unlikely, and this could of course lead to the resurrection of traditional forms of central government regional policy. In Denmark, however, with limited regional disparities and increasing international competition, the political will to target resources to address geographical imbalances at the expense of competitiveness must be in doubt, and the consensual preference for framework-types of policy instruments rather than financial subsidies would probably suggest that - apart from doing nothing - continuation of a programme-based national programmes along the lines of the Structural Funds could be the least unlikely option. Such an approach could be presented as a regional form of industrial policy, and by leaving the coordination within the regions to regional-based actors and merely providing some measure of additional funding, central government would avoid becoming too heavily entangled in territorial politics and inter-organisational strategies at the subnational level. For the time being, at least, the new and decentralised approach to spatial economic policy is unlikely to be abandoned.

NOTES

1. This text is partly based on work undertaken as part of a comparative research project conducted in conjunction with the European Policies Research Centre, University of Strathclyde, Glasgow. Earlier versions of the paper have benefited from suggestions from workshop participants in Helsinki, Frankfurt/Oder, Aalborg and Grenaa, and from the lucid and sceptical comments of Staffan Zetterholm and Charlotte Damborg of Aalborg University's European Research Unit, and Susana Borrás of Roskilde University. Full responsibility for the final version of the text rests, as ever, with the author.
2. See e.g. Stöhr 1989, Albrechts and Swyngedouw 1989, Martin and Townroe 1992, Bachtler 1993 and 1997, and Keating 1997.
3. See Halkier 2000.
4. See Halkier 2000.
5. This approach is primarily inspired by an institutionalist reading of inter-organisational contributions to the literature on policy analysis such as Rhodes 1988, van Waarden 1992, and Heinelt and Smith 1996.
6. See Hood 1983 and Windhoff-Héritier 1987, cf the discussion in Halkier 2000.
7. Bogason 1982, Gaardmand 1988, Bogason and Jensen 1991, Erhvervsministeriet 1995.
8. Direktoratet for Egnsudvikling 1980-87, Industri- og Handelsstyrelsen 1988-91, Erhvervsfremmestyrelsen 1992-96. Overviews are provided by Bogason 1982, Gaardmand 1988 and Industriministeriet 1990.
9. See Yuill et al. 1992, Table 5.3.
10. For a preliminary analysis, see Halkier 1998, pp. 24ff.
11. Yuill et al. 1998; cf. Erhvervsfremmestyrelsen 1996.

12. Erhvervsministeriet 1995.
13. E.g. Erhvervsministeriet 1995.
14. See Bogason and Jensen 1991, Jensen 1994.
15. Arbejdsministeriet 1997, cf Susanne Johansen, personal interview 19.6.97.
16. See Yuill et al. 1996, table 5.6.
17. Cf Conzelmann 1995, Heinelt 1996, Bachtler and Taylor 1997.
18. See Staeck 1996 and Wishlade 1996.
19. Erhvervsministeriet 1995, pp. 19ff.
20. See Direktoratet for Egnsudvikling 1980-87.
21. Direktoratet for Egnsudvikling 1984, p. 12.
22. Yuill et al. 1992, p. 64; 1996, p. 78.
23. Erhvervsministeriet 1995, table 3.3, Halkier 1997, Damborg et al. 1999.
24. See e.g. Hooghe and Keating 1994, Bullmann 1996 and Keating and Loughlin 1997.
25. Heinelt 1996, Marks 1996.
26. Halkier 1997, Damborg 1998.
27. For a comparative perspective, see Heinelt 1996 and Bachtler and Taylor 1997.
28. See Bogason 1982, Industriministeriet 1987 and Erhvervsministeriet 1995.
29. Industriministeriet 1987, Jørgensen and Lind 1987.
30. See Damborg and Halkier 1998, Erhvervsministeriet 1995 and Industriministeriet 1987.
31. Calculated on the basis of the aggregate regional government accounts. Thanks are due to Janet Samuel of the Association of County Councils in Denmark for providing access to the figures.
32. It is interesting to observe that the three regions which have the highest per-capita expenditure on economic development by regional government – Bornholm, NorthJutland and Storstrøm – are traditional peripheral areas with a major involvement in European programmes.
33. Halkier and Damborg 2000.
34. Lov, 383, 20.5.92.
35. Damborg and Halkier 1998, Halkier and Damborg 2000.
36. Industriministeriet 1987 and 1992, Erhvervsministeriet 1995, cf. SusanneJohansen, personal interview 16.6.98.
37. Oscarsson 1989, p. 50.

REFERENCES

Albrechts, L. and E. Swyngedouw (1989), 'The Challenges for Regional Policy under a Flexible Regime of Accumulation', in L. Albrechts et al. (eds), *Regional Policy at the Crossroads - European Perspectives*, London: Jessica Kingsley, 67-89.

Arbejdsministeriet (1997), *Bekendtgørelse om en varslingspulje*, 72, 28.1.97.

Bachtler, J. (1993), 'Regional Policy in the 1990s - The European Perspective', in R. T. Harrison and M. Hart (eds), *Spatial Policy in a Divided Nation*, London: JKP, 254-69.

Bachtler, J. (1997), 'New Dimensions of Regional Policy in Western Europe', in M. Keating and J. Loughlin (eds), *The Political Economy of Regionalism*, London: Frank Cass, 77-89.

Bachtler, J. and S. Taylor (1997), 'EU Regional Development Strategies: Comparisons and Contrasts Among Objective 2 Programmes', in J. Bachtler and I. Turok (eds), *The Coherence of EU Regional Policy. Contrasting Perspectives on the Structural Funds*, London: Jessica Kingsley, 219-45.

Bogason, P. (1982), 'Denmark: The Regional Development Council', in D. Yuill (ed.), *Regional Development Agencies in Europe*, Farnborough: Gower, 107-28.

Bogason, P. and L. Jensen (1991), 'Statens ansvar for regional udvikling i Danmark', *NordREFO* (3), 51-82.

Bullmann, U. (1996), 'The Politics of the Third Level', *Regional and Federal Studies*, 6 (2), 3-19.

Conzelmann, T. (1995), 'Networking and the Politics of EU Regional Policy: Lessons from North Rhine-Westphalia, Nord-Pas de Calais and North West England', *Regional and Federal Studies*, 5 (2), 134-72.

Damborg, C. (1998), *The North Jutland Objective 2 Programme: Coordination and Evaluation*, IQ-NET Occasional Paper 2.

Damborg, C. and H. Halkier (1998), 'RDAs in Denmark - Towards a Danish Approach to Bottom-up Regional Policy?', in H. Halkier et al. (eds), *Regional Development Agencies in Europe*, London: Jessica Kingsley, 80-99.

Damborg, C., D. Østergaard Nielsen and H. Halkier (1999), *The North Jutland Objective 2 Programme: The Final Cut?*, IQ-NET Occasional Paper 3.

Direktoratet for Egnsudvikling (1980-87), *Orientering og årsberetninger, 1980-87*, Silkeborg: Direktoratet for Egnsudvikling.

Erhvervsfremmestyrelsen (1992-96), *Årsberetning, 1992-96*, København: Erhvervsfremmestyrelsen.

Erhvervsfremmestyrelsen (1996), *Rapport om afgrænsning af støtteberettigede områder*, Silkeborg: Erhvervsfremmestyrelsen.

Erhvervsministeriet (1995), *Regionalpolitisk Redegørelse 1995*, København: Erhvervsministeriet.

Finansministeriet (1988-96), *Statsregnskabet*, København: Finansministeriet.

Gaardmand, A. (1988), 'Jobbet til manden eller manden til jobbet? Om dansk regionalpolitik 1945-85', in NordREFO (ed.): *Om regionalpolitikken som politikområde*, Helsinki: NordREFO, 67-108.

Halkier, H. (1997), *The North Jutland Objective 2 Programme: Institutions and Implementation*, IQ-NET Occasional Paper 1.

Halkier, H. (1998), *Danish Regions and the Europeanisation of Regional Policy*, European Studies Series of Occasional Papers, European Research Unit, Aalborg University 27.

Halkier, H. (2000), 'The Regionalisation of Danish Regional Policy - Governance and Resource Dependencies in Transition', in M. Danson, H. Halkier and G. Cameron (eds), *Governance, Institutional Change and Regional Development*, Aldershot: Ashgate.

Halkier, H. and C. Damborg (2000), 'Development Bodies, Networking and Business Promotion - The case of North Jutland, Denmark', in M. Danson, H. Halkier and G. Cameron (eds), *Governance, Institutional Change and Regional Development*, Aldershot: Ashgate.

Heinelt, H. (1996), 'Conclusions', in H. Heinelt and R. Smith (eds): *Policy Networks and European Structural Funds*, Aldershot: Avebury, 294-321.

Heinelt, H. and R. Smith (1996), 'Introduction', in H. Heinelt and R. Smith (eds), *Policy Networks and European Structural Funds*, Aldershot: Avebury, 1-8.

Hood, C. (1983), *The Tools of Government*, London: Macmillan.

Hooghe, L. (1996), 'Building a Europe with the Regions: The Changing Role of the European Commission', in L. Hooghe (ed.): *Cohesion Policy and European Integration. Building Multi-level Governance*, Oxford: Oxford UP, 89-126.

Hooghe, L. and M. Keating (1994), 'The Politics of European Union Regional Policy', *Journal of European Public Policy*, 1 (3), 369-92.

Industri- og Handelsstyrelsen (1988-91), *Årsberetninger 1988-91*, København: Industri- og Handelsstyrelsen.

Industriministeriet (1987), *Lokal erhvervspolitik - debatoplæg om forholdet mellem statslige og lokale initiativer*, Arbejdsnotat 7.

Industriministeriet (1990), *Regional erhvervspolitik i Danmark - Rapport afgivet af arbejdsgruppen vedrørende regionalpolitik*, København: Industriministeriet.

Industriministeriet (1992), *Pejlemærker for fremtidens erhvervspolitik*, København: Industriministeriet.

Jensen, L. (1994) 'Ændringer i dansk opfattelse af statens ansvar i 80erne og 90erne', *NordREFO*, (3), 89-112.

Jørgensen, H. and J. Lind (1987), 'Decentralised Welfare Capitalism: The Case of Employment and Industrial Policies', *Acta Sociologica*, 30 (3-4), 313-37.

Keating, M. (1997), 'The Political Economy of Regionalism', in M. Keating and J. Loughlin (eds), *The Political Economy of Regionalism*, London: Frank Cass, 17-40.

Keating, M. and J. Loughlin (1997), 'Introduction', in M. Keating and J. Loughlin (eds), *The Political Economy of Regionalism*, London: Frank Cass, 1-13.

Lov om kommuners og amtskommuners deltagelse i erhvervsudviklingsaktiviteter, (383), 20.5.92.

Marks, G. (1996), 'Exploring and Explaining Variation in EU Cohesion Policy', in L. Hooghe (ed.), *Cohesion Policy and European Integration. Building Multi-level Governance*, Oxford: Oxford UP, 388-422.

Martin, R. and P. Townroe (1992), 'Changing Trends and Pressures in Regional Development', in P. Townroe and R. Martin (eds), *Regional Development in the 1990s - The British Isles in Transition*, London: Jessica Kingsley, 13-24.

Oscarsson, G. (1989), 'Regional Policies in the Nordic Countries - Origin, Development and Future', in NordREFO/OECD (eds.): *The Long-term Future of Regional Policy - A Nordic View*, Copenhagen: NordREFO, 41-58.

Rhodes, R. A. W. (1988), *Beyond Westminster and Whitehall - The Sub-central Governments of Britain*, London: Unwin Hyman.

Staeck, N. (1996), 'The European Structural Funds - Their History and Impact', in H. Heinelt and R. Smith (eds), *Policy Networks and European Structural Funds*, Aldershot: Avebury, 46-73.

Stöhr, W. (1989), 'Regional Policy at the Crossroads: An Overview', in L. Albrechts et al. (eds), *Regional Policy at the Crossroads - European Perspectives*, London: Jessica Kingsley, 191-97.

Waarden, F. v. (1992), 'Dimensions and Types of Policy Networks', *European Journal of Political Research*, 21 (1-2), 29-52.

Windhoff-Héritier, A. (1987) *Policy-Analyse - Eine Einführung*, Frankfurt: Campus.

Wishlade, F. (1996), 'EU Cohesion Policy: Facts, Figures and Issues', in L. Hooghe (ed.), *Cohesion Policy and European Integration. Building Multi-level Governance*, Oxford: Oxford UP, 27-58.

Yuill, D. et al. (1992), *European Regional Incentives 1992-93, 12th edn*, London: Bowker Saur.

Yuill, D. et al. (1996), *European Regional Incentives 1996-97, 16th edn*, London: Bowker Saur.

Yuill, D. et al. (1998), *European Regional Incentives, 17th edn*, London: Bowker Saur.

Personal interviews
Susanne Johansen, senior civil servant, DATI, Silkeborg, 19.6.97 and 16.6.98.

11. European labour market policy and national regimes of implementation

Josef Schmid and Christian Roth

---

1. FRAMING THE PROBLEM AND ITS CONTEXT: COPING WITH COMPLEXITY

European employment and labour market policy can be conceived as a *dynamic multi-level phenomenon* (cf. Jachtenfuchs and Kohler-Koch 1996). It is exposed to a tense relationship between supra-nationality, on one side of the continuum and national sovereignty on the other. On the one hand, European employment and labour market policy operates at the nation-state level. On the other hand, it is increasingly practised at the European level. At the same time, both levels are characterised by a significant degree of dissimilarity and differentiation. Simultaneously, increasing interdependence of the employment and labour market policy on the different levels leads to increased intertwining of sovereignty. To put it into more concrete terms: nation-states continue to control national labour markets, while the European Union's capacity to solve unemployment problems is limited to distributive instruments and co-ordination. In addition, political obstacles restrict the European Union's ability to act.

These phenomena lead to *increased complexity* (cf. Luhmann 1978 and Simon 1962) and result in policy formulation and implementation structures which are difficult to analyse. Three factors are particularly problematic:

- First, the lack of political *consensus* among the actors at the European level and the level of the member states. This becomes obvious when considering the heterogeneity of concrete problems, interests (regarding further integration), sovereignty reservations and resources. Progress in labour market and employment policy is only made at a snail's pace (Keller 1999).
- Second, significant barriers to implementation remain even if treaties and summit decisions provide the EU with more competence and enable it to undertake concrete measures. Implementation remains the responsibility of member-states and is often quite problematic. The

degree of this problem varies and is, in our opinion, primarily dependent upon the established regimes of implementation at the national
level.
- Third, significant differences exist between the just mentioned regime
  of implementations of member states (in the horizontal perspective)
  and the specific problems and restrictions of *national labour markets*,
  thus complicating governance even further.

Figure 11.1: Framing the problem – vertical and horizontal dimension

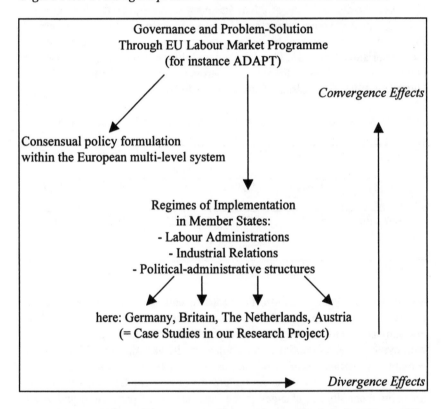

In a new research project, we use the term *'regime of implementation'* in
order to draw upon comparative politics research. These studies view the
labour market as a system which mediates between the economic system, on
the one hand, and the social security system and state intervention (welfare
state) on the other hand (G. Schmid 1994, Esping-Andersen 1990, Schmid
1996). Accordingly, our study goes beyond the narrow conception of the
labour market's regime of implementation. It considers some important
structural characteristics of the political-administrative and industrial rela-

tions system. This broadening of the analytical perspective is necessary for methodological reasons. Significant variation in political and economic conditions can result when studying several states.[1]

2. TWO FACES OF LABOUR MARKET POLICY: DIVERGENCE OR CONVERGENCE?

Currently, all European countries are facing the challenge of unemployment. However, the degree of the problem, its specific causes, and the strategies for fighting unemployment differ significantly. Examining the unemployment figures in Western Europe shows a surprising range: Successful cases such as the Netherlands, Denmark, Great Britain and Portugal contrast with 'problem children' such as Spain, France and Germany (cf. for example Bosco and Hutsebaut 1996; Europäische Kommission 1997a).

Table 11.1: Unemployment figures in selected EU member states, 1998

Country	Germany	Denmark	Nether-lands	Great Britain	Spain
Unemploy-ment rate	8.6%	5.1%	4.3%	6.2%	18.8%
Labour force participant rate	64.1%	75.3%	69.8%	71.2%	51.2%

Source: OECD

Significant differences can also be identified among the EU regions; unemployment ranges from around 3% in Luxembourg to 30% in Andalusia. Several indicators such as long-term and youth unemployment, part-time work, employment rate, productivity etc. display similar variation. In addition to the economic situation a number of long-term developments influence European labour markets. Among these are the growth of new capital- and knowledge-intensive technologies, changes in the organisation of production and work, continuing globalisation, and changes in the international division of labour. At the same time the fact that different political measures are undertaken seems to indicate that *no perfect solution* for battling unemployment exists (Bogai 1998, Jochem 1999, Rehm and Schmid 1999). For instance, some states are deregulating, while others are successfully using innovative forms of regulation.

Because of this diversity, it is difficult to formulate a homogenous, supranational, European policy. In addition, the EU cannot directly influence

macro-political governance of the European labour market due to reservations about national sovereignty. In its annual report 'Employment in
Europe', published in 1997, the Commission has emphasised again that
Europe is lagging behind. The failure to boost employment is a consequence
of failing to pursue an active labour market and employment policy. In addition to *different views* concerning the importance and function of European
labour market and employment policy, (rational) differences in the assessment of employment programmes exist. These are not just consequences of
specific economic problems, but also of different political structures, preferences, and resources (Janoski 1996, Schmid 1998). Furthermore, structural
limits to state interventions in the economy exist. These have been systematically identified and analysed in the debate concerning different forms of
capitalism (cf. for instance Albert's *'rheinischen'* and the 'anglo-saxon'
model, Albert 1993; cf. also Crouch and Streeck 1997). The challenges resulting from differences in national conditions are a characteristic of European politics. They require new 'soft' forms of governance, which can be
referred to with such terms as *contextualisation, proceduralisation,* and *regionalisation* (Willke 1992; Tömmel 1998; Voelzkow 1999).

3. SOFT GOVERNANCE OF EU LABOUR MARKET POL-
ICY – SQUARING OF THE CIRCLE?

One can identify a number of characteristics and trends in the EU's labour
market and employment policy, which indicate its problematic nature. Three
aspects deserve to be emphasised here: (1) differentiation of the issue-area;
(2) centralised decision-making structure and allocation of resources; (3) last
but not least new forms and instruments of governance.

3.1 Differentiation of the issue area

In the debate about the EU's political dimension, labour market and employment policy plays an increasingly important role. The development of the
issue area as 'constitutional politics' and its long term repercussions on the
labour markets of member states have demonstrated that European labour
market and employment policy has developed into an independent EU issue
area. The development has been influenced by the extent of the unemployment crisis in Europe, as well as changes of government in important member states in the 1990s. Previously, European labour market and employment
policy has been conceived as a component of European social policy. However, the issue area has reached a new quality with the inclusion of an em-

ployment title in the Treaty of Amsterdam (1997) which will result in further differentiation of policies (cf. Roth 1998).

However, one cannot regard EU labour market and employment policy as a clearly defined concept. Rather, it is a number of measures which seek to increase the supply of jobs and encourage the active promotion of employment-creating measures. Three forms of employment policy can be distinguished (cf. Deppe 1996: 14):

1. *Efficiency-oriented regulatory policy*: for instance, promoting increased flexibility of labour markets
2. *Objective-oriented promotion of employment sectors* (target groups and/or regions)
3. *Distributive policy*: includes the expansion of EU competences as well as mobilisation of financial resources for employment policy.

The '*acquis communautaire*' and the concrete objectives of European labour market and employment policy are for the most part based on norms contained in the Amsterdam and Maastricht treaties, the 'White Paper on Growth, Competitiveness, and Employment' published in December 1993, as well as the decisions of the EU's 'Employment Summit' held in Essen (1994).

The promotion of a high level of employment (Art. 2 TEU, Art. 2 EC-Treaty) is defined as a central task for the European Union. Furthermore, Art. 118 EC-Treaty enables member states to coordinate their employment policy. Since Amsterdam, the EC-Treaty includes a new employment title (title VII, Art. 125-130 EC-Treaty). Art. 123 EC-Treaty defines the European Social Fund as a financial instrument for improving the common market's employment opportunities.

The *White Paper* suggests some concrete measures: flexible working hours including part-time work; changing incentive structures (reduction of labour costs by redesigning tax and social security systems); special support for small and middle-sized businesses; public–private partnerships and/in labour-intensive sectors such as the health care and home services sectors; increased investment in education (Human Resource Management). The aim was to reduce unemployment by 50% by the year 2000.

Reacting to the European Commission's document, the heads of government and state adopted an '*Action Programme against Unemployment*' during their December 1993 meeting in Brussels. In December 1994, the European Summit in Essen adopted *core elements of a European employment strategy* as well as *coordinating measures*. Five priorities are formulated for guiding national employment policy:

1. Investment in vocational training
2. Increasing the labour-intensity of economic growth
3. Reducing labour costs
4. Increasing the efficiency of labour market policy
5. Special measures for long-term unemployed, unemployed youth, under qualified and older workers, and women

In addition, member states were called upon to include and implement these elements of a European strategy in their national multi-year programmes. These national programmes were observed and supervised by the Council and the Commission. During the Madrid summit in December 1995 both European bodies presented a report. Since then, this report had to be published annually.

The Treaty of Amsterdam's *Employment Title* contains a coordinating procedure for economic policy and is based on the decisions made in Essen. Five aspects are included:

- Member states are required to work towards the establishment of a coordinated employment strategy. Special emphasis is placed on the skills, education and flexibility of employees and to ensure that labour markets adapt to the requirements of economic change.
- Employment policy remains the principal responsibility of member states. However, they regard the promotion of employment as a matter of common concern and coordinate their actions in the Council. The European Union supports and promotes cooperation between member states and takes into account the objective of a high level of employment.
- The support of the Union consists of the adoption of employment policy guidelines by the Council which member states have to take into consideration. The guidelines are used to evaluate the employment policy of member states. As a result of the evaluation, the Council may issue recommendations to member states.
- To promote cooperation between member states the Council can adopt incentive measures (for instance pilot projects).
- To promote employment the Union will create an advisory committee on employment issues.

Materially, European labour market and employment policy is characterised by an emphasis on '*social inclusion*', '*employability*' and '*workfare*' (cf. Tidow 1999a: 77). According to Aust, promoting the skills, education and flexibility of employees as well as ensuring employees' adjustment to the requirements of economic change are the main concerns of the European

employment strategy. The objective of labour market and employment policy
is to increase employees' 'employability' by ensuring their skills and flexibility (cf. Aust 1997: 765). In contrast to Great Britain these are currently
only secondary aims of German labour market policy.

The European Union's concept of *'employability'* has two objectives:
First, to identify suitable networks, target groups and measures, which can
(preventatively) ensure the creation and maintenance of a mobile and flexible
workforce. The EU Commission emphasises the concept of *'lifelong learning'*. Secondly, active labour market policy seeks to ensure the employability
of target groups, such as the long term unemployed. The coordinated EU-
employment strategy considers the creation of 'employability' as one of its
central objectives (cf. Roth, Blancke and Schmid 2000). Of primary importance are those who often-times lack the basic skills necessary for 'lifelong
learning'.

European labour market and employment policy possesses a strong *eclectic character*. At the supranational level, it is characterised by a large degree
of *fragmentation*. At the national level *complementarity* of European and
national labour market policy can be observed. Community law envisioned
complementarity of the issue area with its national counterpart from the start.
It shaped the labour market's and employment policy's integration process.

European labour market and employment policy is influenced by economic as well as social- and wage policy. It is closely intertwined with the
various 'integrated' Community policies. It is therefore influenced directly
and indirectly by the developments in these issue areas. In particular, common market and foreign economic policy, monetary policy, the economic and
monetary union, the sectoral policies (for instance, coal and steel and agri-
culture) and the different coordinated or partially integrated (social-, research
and development, industrial, regional, and structural policy) fields have to be
considered (cf. Platzer 1997: 235). Not all of the Amsterdam Treaty's norms
possess the same legal quality. Different provisions require different decision-making procedures. This eclectic character is reinforced by the fact that
policies are directed at and formulated on different levels and operate with
different instruments.

A further characteristic of European labour market and employment policy
is a *'policy-mix'*. In addition to coordinated measures a number of specific
Community regulations exist. By and large these Community regulations do
not constrain national law (cf. Roth 1998: 91). During the evolution of the
issue area, supranational actors, specifically the Commission, have increased
their steering capabilities.

3.2. Central decision organisation and allocation of resources

During the development of the issue area attempts have been made to organise labour market and employment policy by following national patterns closely. The EU developed a number of (mostly *distributive*) financial instruments. One has to distinguish between subsidies in the coal and steel sector, the Structural Funds (especially the European Social Fund). The most important EU employment policy programmes have been the Community initiative 'Employment and Creation of Human Capital' with the initiatives NOW, HORIZON, INTEGRA, YOUTHSTART as well as the Community initiative ADAPT. The objective of these programmes has been to allow employees who are threatened by unemployment due to industrial change, to adapt to new working procedures and methods.

The objective of the Structural Funds and in particular the *European Social Fund* (ESF) is to support the following groups and programmes: unemployed people who are able to work; on-the-job and off-the-job training programmes; support for innovative training programmes. Approximately 80% of social fund resources allocated by the ESF were used to: combat long-term unemployment and the exclusion from the labour market; to provide skills and employment opportunities for every young person; to promote equality of opportunity; and, last but not least, to aid in achieving the 'adaptation of employees to economic changes' as part of objective 4. After the decision was made in 1993 to double fund resources by 1999, the importance of Structural Funds for regional- and labour market adjustment/equalisation significantly increased. Until 1999 the ESF's budget amounted to approximately 47 billion ECU, i.e. about 10% of the EU budget. These resources were distributed in the following manner: between 10% and 33% of resources for the analysis of labour market developments and for skill promotion; between 34% and 52% of resources for vocational training to prevent exclusion from the labour market; between 5% and 30% of resources to improve the training and education systems and structures; between 5% and 17% of resources for technical aid (Agence Europe 17.11.94:8). In addition, the Commission decided to fund 32 innovative projects in the 12 'old' member states with 18 million ECU from the ESF budget. The objective of these projects was to discover new ways for job creation and vocational training. In Objective-1-regions the ESF funded 75% of project costs. In other regions, the ESF contributed 50% of funds.

Summarising employment and labour market policy measures which have been supported with funds from the Structural Funds, and in particular the European Social Fund, a priority on the promotion of education and training can be observed. This development results out of the fact that labour market policy is the principal responsibility of member states. Different political-administrative conditions and socio-political traditions in each member state makes co-ordination of labour market measures extremely difficult. However, with the Structural Funds the Commission possesses a meaningful distributive instrument for controlling European labour market and employment policy. During the agenda-setting and policy formulation phases the Commission can use these instruments strategically. In fact, the Commission has indirect influence on labour market policy of member states since the financial volume of measures is substantial. Approval or non-approval can have considerable consequences for the employment situation in individual member states and regions. In addition, the Commission can influence national labour market policy by setting a particular objective for its programmes. During the implementation of programmes and projects by regional and local actors, the Commission's room for manoeuvre decreases, resulting in unintended consequences and restrictions for steering (cf. Roth 1999: 223f.; also cf. Lang, Naschold and Reissert 1998; Hannowsky 1998).

Today, European labour market and employment policy is based on three pillars.[2] The *'Luxembourg process'* established a procedure which allows for the coordination of national employment polices and aims at a better integration of the various measures and instruments (Bogai 1998). The Commission mentions four aims: Improving employability, developing entrepreneurship, promoting the adaptability of companies and employees, strengthening measures to ensure equality of opportunity. The *'Cardiff Process'* seeks to improve competitiveness in the service sector, the information society, and of small and medium-sized companies. The *'Cologne Process'* adds macroeconomic coordination to these two approaches. It aims to ensure a policy mix free of tension between monetary, fiscal and wage policy, which ensures economic growth (cf. Platzer 1999: 189).

Employment-promoting measures of member states are not bound by the Coordinated Employment Strategy. However, the procedure does oblige member states to grapple with promoting employment and to learn from each other through 'benchmarking' (cf. Meinhardt and Seidel 1998: 131). The future will have to show how this mechanism for coordination or 'politically-staged competition' will work. The mechanism combines the possibility for pilot projects with a procedure to support 'policy learning' and the diffusion of 'best practices' of the welfare states who created labour market policy (cf. Heinze, Schmid and Strünck 1999). It would have been necessary for the *'European Employment Pact'* first to combine macroeconomic, structural policies and labour market policy instruments and second, to set binding and verifiable targets for the years 2000 to 2006 – in line with the next EU budget.

Figure 11.2: Implementation of employment policy guidelines (The 'Luxembourg process')[2]

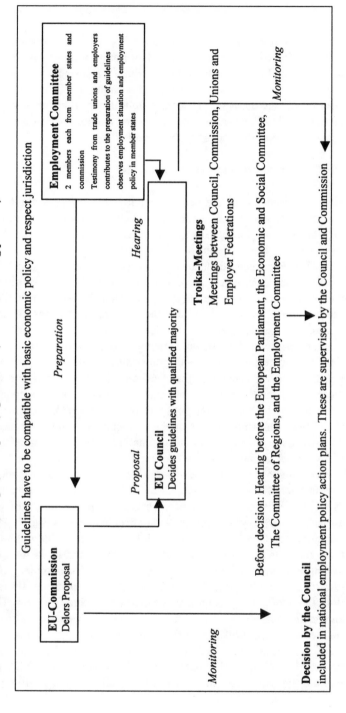

Guidelines have to be compatible with basic economic policy and respect jurisdiction

Employment Committee
2 members each from member states and commission

Testimony from trade unions and employers contributes to the preparation of guidelines observes employment situation and employment policy in member states

Monitoring

EU-Commission
Delors Proposal

Preparation

Proposal

Hearing

EU Council
Decides guidelines with qualified majority

Troika-Meetings
Meetings between Council, Commission, Unions and Employer Federations

Monitoring

Before decision: Hearing before the European Parliament, the Economic and Social Committee, The Committee of Regions, and the Employment Committee

Decision by the Council
included in national employment policy action plans. These are supervised by the Council and Commission

Monitoring

The Cologne Summit failed to fulfil these hopes. The 'European Employment Pact' adopted during the summit does not go further than the 'Coordinated European Employment Strategy'. Employment-policy objectives are only stated in general terms. The single new emphasis of the Cologne Paper is 'macroeconomic dialogue'. Delegates from the 15 governments, the Commission, the GTUC as well as employers and employees will gather to discuss innovative employment and labour market policy.

3.3. 'Soft' governance and new instruments

Making European labour market and employment policy a reality requires meaningful reforms for all actors to undertake. From a political science standpoint, the question is how can or must the state – here the European Union despite its limited problem solving capacities – contribute governance functions? In European labour market and employment policy the *Commission* plays a key role, since it is committed to the EU as a whole. It is required to mediate between the EU system's functional requirements, conflicts of interest among member states, and the needs of EU citizens. Although the Commission possesses little real political power it sets the course of European labour market and employment policy through its role as a mediator and its right to initiate policies. The Commission as 'pace-setter' of integration shaped the political agenda of European social policy during the intergovernmental conferences in Maastricht and Amsterdam. It was responsible for the inclusion of labour market policy in the Treaty of Amsterdam and the constitution of a new policy field on the supranational level.

By presenting guidelines for labour market policy the Commission successfully acted as agenda-setter during the 'Luxembourg Process'. The guidelines sought to increase the pressure for reforms of labour market policy by setting quantifiable targets (cf. Tidow 1999b: 9). Territorial employment pacts are also of special importance. Through its programmes the Commission was able – by bypassing the national level to a certain degree – to see its vision implemented at the local and regional level. In addition, the Commission advances its notion of an integrated approach and its vision of an employment-promoting transition of Europe's political economies (cf. Tidow 1999a: 76) and condenses it into a 'European Social- and Societal Model'.

With the 'Community-coordinated Employment Strategy' and 'Territorial Employment Pacts' a new conceptual approach has been established to react to the increasing consolidation of the issue area and to the already mentioned steering restrictions. The background: Since the completion of the Single European Market and the EU-enlargement (keyword 'Agenda 2000') seemed to indicate the exhaustion of the EU's distributive and regulative potential, new emphasis has been placed on new, soft – especially communicating and interactive – forms of governance.

The *coordinated employment strategy* can only be labelled a 'soft' coordinating instrument. Nonetheless, it does include a number of positive elements, which seek to ensure convergence of national labour market policy through context control. The treaty-provisions on monitoring procedures for employment promotion, and processes of 'benchmarking' are currently being developed.

The 'Coordinated Employment Strategy' seeks to increase the exchange of knowledge and experience among member states and offers the opportunity to analyse and compare projects which have proved successful in member states. Which measures work and which do not? The objective is to achieve common progress by learning from the successes and failures of others. To ensure common progress, other EU member states are to be enabled to successfully implement these concepts into national policy. The Common Report of Employment (cf. Europäische Kommission 1997b), adopted jointly by the European Commission and the Council includes eleven selected areas for 'best practices'. Regarding 'employability', for instance, Great Britain (cf. Finn 1999) and Denmark (cf. Fuhrmann 1999) are mentioned as 'best practices'. The Commission criticised the fact that the member states agreed on the necessity of active measures, but the specification of relevant measures to reach this EU-wide objective was insufficient and the willingness to make domestic changes varied (cf. Europäische Kommission 1998: 7f).

A further example for 'soft' governance within the EU is the *Territorial Employment Pacts*. Within these the above mentioned principles of contextualisation, proceduralisation, and regionalisation are of key importance. At the centre of Territorial Employment Pacts is the integrated strategy for regional or territorial employment promotion, as well as the promotion of local and regional initiatives which include social groups, economic groups and the public administration. Since the objective is to bring together local actors – state institutions and societal groups – it could be labelled a self-regulating strategy. The strategy does mostly without traditional governance instruments, i.e. money and law and sets only vague objectives (Tömmel 1998; also cf. Chapter 7 by Jørgensen in this volume). Instead, 'benchmarking' and 'policy learning' are used, thus trusting that the 'soft pressure' of the good example will be effective. However, no one can guarantee and control success (Tidow 1999b; Cox and Schmid 1999; Heinze, Schmid and Strünck 1999). The instrument of Territorial employment pacts can be characterised as follows:

- They seem to be a reaction of *economic policy* to de-regulation and flexibilisation of labour markets.

- A reaction of *labour market policy* to the erosion of standard employment patterns (full-time employment, fixed-term contracts). It seeks to make available new, formal (and informal) forms and opportunities of employment outside the primary labour market.
- An attempt of *social policy* to prevent the problem of social exclusion and to provide the European Union with more legitimacy.
- An answer of *integration policy* to the subsidiary principle and the enhancement of the status of regions during the last two reforms of the EU-Treaty.
- From the *governance strategy perspective*, the Commission enjoys new room for manoeuvre.

The German state *Bremen* is one of nine German model regions in which the EU supports territorial employment pacts. Bremen's regional labour market policy (cf. Mittelstädt 1999) aims at training of those employees who are affected and threatened by unemployment. On the other hand structural policy and programmes, which seek to assist the adaptation to economic and social changes, can be observed. The largest share of the labour market measures have been training measures with, on average, 6000 persons benefiting each year. These were distributed among almost 5100 persons receiving further vocational training, approximately 1200 who were retrained, and 250 who received on-the-job training. In the previous four years, the 'Qualifizierungsfond' (Bremen, Senator für Arbeit 1997: 37ff.) funded 119 projects and two state programmes with a total financial volume of about 120 million DM. ESF objectives 2, 3, and 4 and the Community initiative ADAPT supported the following measures: vocational orientation, pre-training, pre-qualification, refresher training, retraining and IQL initiative for the qualification of long-term unemployed welfare recipients, institutional support, identification of needed skills and transnational measures. On the one hand, the instrument of further training is an effective addition (to structural policies of) to BAP's 'Qualifizierungsfond'. At the same time, it ensures the skills required for the adaptation of the location factor.

In addition, priorities for action were determined and new innovative projects were supported. These relate to: new working time models; new jobs in the service sector; new approaches for supporting specific target groups; and increasing transparency of labour markets. To coordinate the 'regional labour pact of Bremen and Bremerhaven' a 'pact secretariat' was established in the employment ministry. The pact's participants are: trade unions, employers' associations, the labour administration in Bremen and Bremerhaven, the Bremerhaven council (and relevant ministries). The discussion among pact partners resulted in projects which sought to increase employment. Innovative employment promoting projects with companies, provisions of training measures, and employers were to be started and monitored.

Figure 11.3: Territorial employment pacts between state, market and the third sector

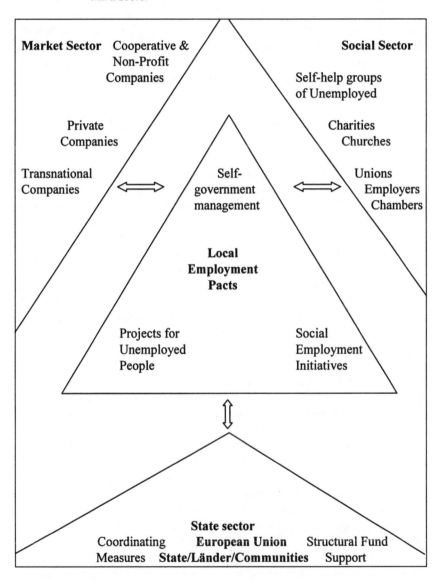

Here, too, the *complex* structure of the issue area and the heterogenous actor constellations are obvious. The Commission does not seek to change or to curtail the authority of existing national labour market institutions. Instead, it tries to improve the incentive structure for active labour market policy and create an optimal adaptation to the specific regional problems and endogenous potentials for development. Within the process, territorial employment pacts play a key role. Significant overlap exists with other issue areas as well as state, economic and informal bodies (cf. Figure 11.3). Here, too, conceptional reflections result in the enlargement of the network to include free and small groups in the so-called Third Sector (cf. Schmid 1999).

4. REGIMES OF IMPLEMENTATION – EMPIRICAL APPROACHES FOR EUROPEAN GOVERNANCE

Regimes of implementations are an important factor for the success of labour market and employment policy, especially considering soft forms of governance (Höcker 1998; Héritier 1993). The conception of the EU as a dynamic multi-level system is of special importance when it comes to the implementation of EU common market policies. The centre of gravity shifts from the supranational to the national level. In fact, regional and local levels play a key role. We are therefore interested in including member states and their reactions to challenges from the European Union. This emphasis promises to be rewarding in issue areas such as European labour market and employment policy, where the initiation of new political strategies and the indirect influence over labour markets in member states is at stake. The benefit of analysing regimes of implementations in the European Union is that lessons can be learned regarding organising governance more effectively and legitimately. For instance, effective policies can only be organised in a potentially successful manner if one is aware of the EU's difficulties when it attempts to achieve its objectives and implement its policy effectively. The scientific benefit of analysing regimes of implementation is the ability to add another element to the puzzle so as to be able to realistically assess the EU system. The effectiveness and efficiency of common market policies can only be assessed during the implementation phase. Only then, can statements about the EU's ability and potential (ability) to govern be made.

These considerations do not view *problems of political governance* as an 'exogenously-determined non-ability' of politics (and its administration). Instead, problems which affect political ability to govern are at stake. These are conceived as 'endogenous' – but not insurmountable – political obstacles to achieve the objectives that are desired, known, and (objectively) achievable (cf. Scharpf 1988: 64f.). A number of governance problems deserve to be mentioned (cf. Mayntz 1987: 96f): implementation: i.e. implementing policy in a manner that conforms to the original aims; i.e. the motives and willingness to adapt of addressees of policies; knowledge, i.e. knowledge about the policies' effect. These structures create political and organisational focal points. They can promote innovation or become a barrier to it. However, these mechanisms have not yet been thoroughly investigated and remain unclear at this time. In fact, considering the complexity of the EU's dynamic multi-level system in general and labour market and employment policy in particular, one has to take into account differences and dissimilarities. Table 11.2 illustrates a number of concurrent effects which can be observed in complicated, multi-level, multi-issue area networks.

Table 11.2: Effects of policy- and implementation-networks in dynamic multilevel systems

Perspective/ Effect	Negative	Positive
Top down	Blockade Misuse	Innovation Legitimisation
Bottom up	Disintegration	By-pass Imitation, Diffusion, Learning

The *top-down perspective* emphasises the central control of (decentralised) implementation and begins by analysing a policy decision. It then assesses whether the implementation is consistent with the policy decision, asks whether the policy's objective has been achieved, and seeks to identify the principal factors for the effect and output of programmes as well as the reformulation of policies (cf. Sabatier 1986). Negative effects of regimes of implementation can be blocked decision-making or the misuse of material resources/funds. Positive effects can be a higher degree of innovation and a greater willingness to innovate as well as an increase in the legitimacy of EU common market policies. The *bottom-up perspective* focuses on the actors implementing a policy decision, not those who make the original decision to establish a programme. Discretionary power is desirable since a programme needs to be 're-invented' during implementation to adapt to local needs (cf. Najam 1995: 13). On the one hand, these discretionary powers can have disintegrative effects and increase variation among implemented programmes in the member states. On the other hand, discretionary powers can cause learning processes in regimes of implementation.

The regimes of implementation in all member states consist of three key components: (1) the structure of labour market administrations; (2) the system of industrial relations; (3) general political-administrative structures.

4.1. Structure of Labour Market Administrations

The labour administrations in West European states are characterised by significant divergence. One can distinguish among

- a *centralised and integrated* organisation (especially in Germany and Austria)
- a *centralised and fragmented* organisation (in France, for instance), and
- a *decentralised* organisation (in the Netherlands, Great Britain, and Denmark)

Considering the current debate concerning 'best practices' and 'model states' (cf. Heinze et al. 1999), one is tempted to attribute great innovative capability and problem-solution capacity to the latter group. In any case, such a hypothesis possesses a certain plausibility.

4.2. System of Industrial Relations

In a similar manner industrial relations can be placed on a continuum between *corporatism and pluralism*. Our reflections start with the assumption that an intended relationship exists between preferred governance strategies and interest-mediation in member states. The assumption is based on the hypothesis that particular characteristics of a political system influence the preferred governance strategies (Peters et al. 1976). For instance, corporatist states tend to prefer regulative or distributive governance strategies due to the need for a high degree of cooperation and willingness to compromise. Pluralistic states, on the other hand, prefer re-distributive solutions.

Our hypothesis posits that the inclusion of societal actors, especially unions and industrial federations/federations of industry, as partners would improve the quality of decentralised governance (cf. Pekkarinen and Rowthorn 1992; for an overview, see also Höppner 1997).[3] At the very least some compatibility problems exist between the EU's governance strategy and national systems of industrial relations. This should become particularly obvious in the case of Britain. However, as we have said previously we are currently only generating hypotheses which require empirical testing.

4.3. General political-administrative System

In a first analytical step, the general political-administrative framework can be described as a dichotomy of *unitarism vs. federalism*. Our hypothesis postulates that federal systems are better suited to adapt to new governance strategies, since they are familiar with complicated negotiation and self-organisational processes. State and non-state institutions possess the corresponding organisational infrastructure. Some empirical evidence exists, that shows the German Länder's ability to bypass the nation-state and that they made use of it (Blancke and Schmid 1998; Heinze and Schmid 1994; Keating and Hooghe 1996).

During the Structural Funds' implementation phase, the Commission sought to use the expertise of regional actors. The setting up of planning committees on a regional and supraregional level is just one indicator. Moreover, the introduction of the partnership principle and the territorial employment pacts led to an institutionalised participation of interest groups and thereby to greater openness of the European policy-network. Thus, regions can influence the implementation of projects. To a somewhat lesser degree, they are able to influence policy formulation (cf. Marks 1996: 328). The higher the degree of autonomy the affected regions enjoy – for instance the institutional particularities of the federal state - the greater their influence. The increasing inclusion of regions in European policy processes seems to correspond with the objective of a subsidiary European labour market and employment policy. However, it conflicts with national constitutional norms and values.

4.4. Conclusion

For the cases which we analyse in our project analyses the following configuration results. It is obvious that no clear model exists, which could serve as a 'blueprint' for EU political strategies or which could delineate a common trend among national developments. Optimistically, one can postulate that the internal complexity and differentiation of regimes of implementation which have been sketched should be sufficient to manage the complexity of labour market and employment policy in a European dynamic multi-level system.[4] We have the opportunity to learn from the variety of national patterns of communication, feed-back mechanisms and benchmarking procedures (cf. Cox and Schmid 1999; also cf. Klemmer et al., Chapter 12 in this volume). But again, these are just hypotheses.

Figure 11.3: Regimes of implementation in selected EU states

Member state / Component of Regimes of Implementation	Germany	Great Britain	Austria	Netherlands
Political-Administrative System	Federalism	Unitarism	Federalism	Unitarism
Industrial Relations	Corporatism	Pluralism	Corporatism	Corporatism
Organisation of Labour Administration	Centralisation + Integration	Decentralisation	Centralisation + Integration	Decentralisation

NOTES

1. In our research project 'Governance of Complexity', funded by the DFG, we analyse the labour market and employment policy of Germany, Great Britain, Austria, and The Netherlands.
2. See Figure 11.2. Source: IG Metall (1997), p. 34.
3. In a further step, industrial relations could be complemented to take account of typical characteristics of a states economy such as (manner of the) production regime, importance of the service sector etc. Some new comparative political economy research takes these factors into account (Crouch and Streeck 1997; Rehm and Schmid 1999; also cf. Cappellin, Chapter 9 in this volume).
4. In addition to the reconstruction of implementation structures and the comparison of governance results understood as policy outputs regarding other states and the common European programme, we seek to analyse feedback and learning processes in our project, which result from the tension between integration and variation in this issue area. These could result in important consequences for governance in the EU's multi-level system and for the European labour market and employment policy regarding its problem-solution capability.

REFERENCES

Albert, M. (1993), *Capitalism against Capitalism*, London.

Aust, A. (1997), 'Der Amsterdamer Vertrag: 'Vertrag der sozialen Balance'? Sozial- und Beschäftigungspolitik in der Regierungskonferenz 1996/97', *Zeitschrift für Sozialreform,* **43** (10), 748-777.

Bogai, D. (1998), 'Arbeitsmarktpolitik in der Europäischen Union', *WSI Mitteilungen,* **51** (12), 845-854.

Blancke, S., C. Roth and J. Schmid (2000), *Employability als Herausforderung für den Arbeitsmarkt. Auf dem Weg zur flexiblen Erwerbsgesellschaft.* Stuttgart: Akademie für Technikfolgenabschätzung Baden-Württemberg.

Blancke, S. and J. Schmid (1998), *Die aktive Arbeitsmarktpolitik der Bundesländer im Vergleich. Programme, Konzepte, Strategien.* Tübingen, EZFF Occasional Papers No. 18.

Bosco and Hutsebaut (1996), *Sozialer Schutz in Europa. Veränderungen und Herausforderungen,* Marburg: Metropolis.

Bremen, Senator für Arbeit (1997), *Das Beschäftigungspolitische Aktionsprogramm. Aktive Arbeitsmarktpolitik für Bremen und Bremerhaven.*

Cox, R. H. and J. Schmid (1999), *Reformen in westeuropäischen Wohlfahrtsstaaten - Potentiale und Trends.* Tübingen, WIP-Occasional Paper No. 5.

Crouch, C. and W. Streeck (1997), *Political Economy of Modern Capitalism. Mapping Convergence and Diversity,* London.

Deppe, F. (1996), *Beschäftigungspolitik in der EU als neues Politikfeld im dynamischen Mehrebenensystem? Eine Studie zur europäischen Regulation der Arbeitsmarktkrise,* Marburg, mimeo.

Esping-Andersen, G. (1990), *The Three Worlds of Welfare Capitalism,* Cambridge.

Europäische Kommission (1997a), *Beschäftigung in Europa,* Luxemburg.

Europäische Kommission (1997b), *Der Beschäftigungsgipfel.* Forum-Spezial, Luxemburg.

Europäische Kommission (1998), *Mitteilung der Kommission. Von Leitlinien zu Massnahmen: Die nationalen Aktionspläne für Beschäftigung.* KOM (1998) 316.

Finn, D. (1999), *From Full Employment to Employability: New Labour and the Unemployed.* Paper for the European Forum Workshop 'The Modernisation of Social Protection and Employment'. European University Institute, Florence.

Fuhrmann, N. (1999), 'Emanzipation am Arbeitsmarkt: dänische Reformkonzepte', in *Frauen und Arbeitsmarkt.* Tübingen, WIP Occasional Paper No. 4, 2-13.

Hannowsky, D. (1998), 'Der europäische Sozialfonds: ein wirksames Instrument zur Bekämpfung der Arbeitslosigkeit?', *List Forum für Wirtschafts- und Finanzpolitik,* **24** (4), 425-442.

Heinze, R. G. and J. Schmid (1994), 'Mesokorporatistische Strategien im Vergleich: Industrieller Strukturwandel und die Kontingenz politischer Steuerung in drei Bundesländern', in W. Streeck (ed.), *Verbände und Staat.* PVS-Sonderheft 25, Opladen, Westdeutscher Verlag.

Heinze, R. G., J. Schmid and C. Strünck (1999), *Vom Wohlfahrtsstaat zum Wettbewerbsstaat. Arbeitsmarkt- und Sozialpolitik in den 90er Jahren,* Opladen: Leske + Budrich.

Héritier, A. (1993), 'Policy-Netzwerkanalyse als Untersuchungsinstrument im europäischen Kontext. Folgerungen aus einer empirischen Studie regulativer Politik', in Héritier, A. (ed.): *Policy-Analyse. Kritik und Neuorientierung,* PVS-Sonderheft 24, Opladen, Westdeutscher Verlag, 432-447.

Höcker, H. (1998), 'The Organisation of Labour Market Policy Delivery in the European Union', in P. Auer (ed.), *Employment Policies in Focus. Labour Markets and Labour Market Policy in Europe and Beyond – International Experiences,* Berlin, 191-214.

Höppner, M. (1997), *Politisch koordinierte Ökonomien 1973-1996,* Düsseldorf, WSI-Diskussionspapier No. 42.

IG Metall (1997), *Europäische Beschäftigungspolitik. Gipfel von Luxemburg 20./21. 11. 1997, Ergebnisse und Bewertung;* Frankfurt/M.: IG Metall.

Jachtenfuchs, M. and B. Kohler-Koch (1996), 'Regieren im dynamischen Mehrebenensystem', in Jachtenfuchs, M. and B. Kohler-Koch (eds), *Europäische Integration,* Opladen: Leske + Budrich, 15-44.

Janoski, T. (1996), 'Explaining state intervention to prevent unemployment', in G. Schmid et al (eds.), *International Handbook of Labour Market Policy*, Cheltenham: Edward Elgar, 697-723

Jochem, S. (1999), 'Vollbeschäftigungswunder im Vergleich', in G. Schmidt (ed.), *Europa ohne Arbeit*, Opladen: Leske + Budrich, 83-107.

Keating, M. and L. Hooghe (1996), 'By-passing the Nation State? Regions and the EU policy process', in J. Richardson (ed.), *European Union – Power and Policy Making*, London, 216-229.

Keller, B. (1999), 'Supranationale Regulierung von Arbeitsverhältnissen. Das Beispiel der EU. Oder: Der Fortschritt ist eine Schnecke und manchmal nicht einmal dies', in K. Busch et al. (ed), *Wege zum sozialen Frieden in Europa*, Osnabrück, 208-224.

Lang, J., F. Naschold and B. Reissert (1998), *Management der EU-Strukturpolitik. Steuerungsprobleme und Reformperspektiven*, Berlin.

Leibfried, S. (1994), 'Wohlfahrtsstaatliche Perspektiven der Europäischen Union. Auf dem Weg zu positiver Souveränitätsverflechtung?', *Kritische Justiz*, (3), 263-269.

Luhmann, N. (1978), 'Komplexität', in K. Türk (ed), *Handlungssysteme*, Opladen, Leske + Budrich, 12-37.

Marks, G. (1996), 'Politikmuster und Einflusslogik in der Strukturpolitik', in M. Jachtenfuchs and B. Kohler-Koch (eds), *Europäische Integration*, Opladen, Leske + Budrich, 313-343.

Mayntz, R. (1987), 'Politische Steuerung und gesellschaftliche Steuerungsprobleme – Anmerkungen zu einem theoretischen Paradigma', *Jahrbuch zur Staats- und Verwaltungswissenschaft*, (1), 89-110.

Meinhardt, V. and B. Seidel (1998), 'Beschäftigungs- und Sozialpolitik', in W. Weidenfeld and W. Wessels (eds.), *Jahrbuch der Europäischen Integration 1996/97*, Bonn, 147-152.

Mittelstädt, A. (1999), 'Die aktive Arbeitsmarktpolitik der Bremer Landesregierung', in J. Schmid and S. Blancke (eds), *Die aktive Arbeitsmarktpolitik der Bundesländer*, Tübingen. WIP Occasional Paper No. 6, 6-12.

Najam, A. (1995), *Learning from the Literature on Policy Implementation: A Synthesis Perspective*, Laxenburg, IIASA Working Paper 95-61.

Pekkarinen, J. P. and B. Rowthorn (eds; 1992), *Social Corporatism. A superior Economic System?*, Oxford: Clarendon.

Peters, G.B., J.C. Doughtie and K.M. McCulloch (1976), 'Types of Democratic Systems and Types of Public Policy. An Empirical Examination', *Comparative Politics*, 9 (1), 327-355.

Piehl, E. (1999): 'Europäisches Gesellschaftsmodell fördern. 'Beschäftigungspolitische Leitlinien' und 'Europäischer Beschäftigungs-Pakt'', *Das Parlament*, 05.02.99, 13.

Platzer, H.-W. (1997), 'Beschäftigungspolitik als Herausforderung und Aufgabe der EU. Perspektiven der Regierungskonferenz', in R. Hrbek (eds): *Die Reformen der Europäischen Union. Positionen und Perspektiven anlässlich der Regierungskonferenz*, Baden-Baden: Nomos.

Platzer, H.-W. (1999), 'Die EU-Sozial- und Beschäftigungspolitik nach Amsterdam: Koordinierte und verhandelte Europäisierung? ', *Integration*, (3).

Rehm, P. and J. Schmid (1999), *Vier Welten der Beschäftigungsförderung – eine Längsschnittanalyse arbeitsmarktpolitischer Performanz*, Tübingen, WIP-Occasional Paper No. 11.

Roth, C. (1998), 'Beschäftigung', in J. Bergmann and C. Lenz (eds), *Der Amsterdamer Vertrag. Eine Kommentierung der Neuerungen des EU- und EG-Vertrages*, Köln, 73-91.

Roth, C. (1999), 'Perspektiven einer europäischen Arbeitsmarkt- und Beschäftigungspolitik zwischen Koordination und Redistribution', in A. Heise (ed), *Makropolitik zwischen Nationalstaat und Europäischer Union*, Marburg: Metropolis, 209-232.

Roth, C., S. Blancke and J. Schmid (2000), *Das Konzept der Beschäftigungsfähigkeit in der Europäischen Union*, Tübingen, WIP-Occasional Paper No. 13.

Sabatier, P.A. (1986), 'Top-down and Bottom-up Approaches to Implementation Research: A Critical Analysis and a Suggested Synthesis', *Journal of Public Policy*, **6** (1), 21-48.

Scharpf, F.W. (1988), 'Verhandlungssysteme, Verteilungskonflikte und Pathologien der politischen Steuerung', in M.G. Schmidt (ed.), *Staatstätigkeit, International und historisch vergleichende Analysen*, PVS-Sonderheft 19, Opladen: Leske + Budrich, 61-87.

Schmid, G. (1994), *Reorganisation der Arbeitsmarktpolitik. Märkte, Politische Steuerung und Netzwerke der Weiterbildung für Arbeitslose in der Europäischen Union*, Berlin, WZB.

Schmid, J. (1996), *Wohlfahrtsstaaten im Vergleich. Soziale Sicherungssysteme in Europa: Organisation, Finanzierung, Leistungen und Probleme*, Opladen, Leske + Budrich.

Schmid, J. (1998), 'Arbeitsmarktpolitik im Vergleich. Stellenwert, Strukturen und Wandel eines Politikfeldes im Wohlfahrtsstaat', in J. Schmid and R. Niketta (ed), *Wohlfahrtsstaat. Krise und Reform im Vergleich*, Marburg: Metropolis, 139-169.

Schmid, J. (1999) 'Europäische Integration und die Zukunft der kirchlichen Wohlfahrtsverbände in Deutschland', in K. Gabriel (ed), *Herausforderungen kirchlicher Wohlfahrtsverbände. Perspektiven im Spannungsfeld von Wertbindung, Ökonomie und Politik*, Berlin: Edition Sigma.

Simon, H.A. (1962), 'The Architecture of Complexity', *Proceedings of the American Philosophical Society*, **106**, 467-482.

Tidow, S. (1999a): 'Aktive Politik oder 'Passive Revolution'? Beschäftigungspolitik als neues Politikfeld in der EU', *Zeitschrift für Sozialreform*, **45**, (1), 64-81.

Tidow, S. (1999b), 'Benchmarking als Leitidee. Zum Verlust des Politischen in der europäischen Perspektive', *Blätter für deutsche und internationale Politik*, (März), 301-309.

Tömmel, I. (1998), *Jenseits von regulative und distributive: Policy-Making der EU und die Transformation von Staatlichkeit*, Osnabrück, mimeo.

Voelzkow, H. (1999), 'Europäische Regionalpolitik zwischen Brüssel, Bonn und den Bundesländern', in H.-U. Derlien and A. Murswieck (ed), *Der Politikzyklus zwischen Bonn und Brüssel*, Opladen: Leske + Budrich, 105-120.

Willke, H. (1992), *Ironie des Staates: Grundlinien einer Staatstheorie polyzentrischer Gesellschaft*, Frankfurt a.M., Campus.

12. Institutional learning of preventive labour market policy – an evolutionary approach

Paul Klemmer, Kerstin Baumgart,
Dorothee Becker-Soest and Rüdiger Wink

1. TRANSNATIONAL LEARNING PROCESSES – POLICYMAKING ALONG THE LINES OF MULTINATIONAL CORPORATIONS?

Never before in the history of employment policy[1] have countries in Europe had such a mass of information about the policy strategies deployed by other countries. Structural adjustment pressures of similar intensity operating on all national labour markets, and differing experience with instruments of employment policy in the separate countries are creating incentives to draw inspiration for one's own national employment policies from reports on the success factors of labour market policy in other countries (cf. e.g. Schmid 1999; Cox 1999 and Klemmer et al. 2000). A plethora of summary analyses by research institutions and international organisations, not forgetting the reporting commitments under the 'Joint Employment Policy' of the European Union, provide the basis for international ranking and benchmarking systems to identify examples of good employment policies (cf. Schütz et al. 1998; Heinze et al. 1999; Höcker 1998; Bertelsmann Stiftung 1998; Walwei 1999/2000). However, all that is addressed thereby is the technical availability of experiential, policymaking know-how. Before this experiential knowledge can be translated across national boundaries into actual political reforms, information must be gathered and interpreted, adapted to the specific action context in the 'recipient' country and implemented as action by political and private actors. What is needed, in other words, is active management of information, a process of 'learning' to transfer experience to other situative conditions. From the academic vantage point, one can centre analysis on the impulses exerted by *institutional structures*, in the EU for example, on political learning processes in the member states (cf. Schmid and Roth, Chapter 11 in this volume). On the other hand, and this is the aim of this chapter, one can adopt a *learning-centred (procedural) perspective* in order to examine how different institutional arrangements and political decision-making instances contribute towards the 'learning' of new employment policy instruments and programmes.

An insight into the meaning of learning processes for the application and implementation of new knowledge is still a relatively new field of economic analysis. Emergent concepts for identifying learning processes are based on market observations and are aimed at explaining the differing competitive strengths of competing companies (cf. for overviews Argote 1999; Rycroft and Kash 1999). Accordingly, the objects of analysis were productivities and market success achieved by companies in the same or similar sectors of the economy. In most cases, after the introduction of new production methods and products, only relatively minor cost savings were observed in the short term, although these tended to grow along a 'learning curve' as the production volumes and experience increased (Dasgupta and Stiglitz 1988; Adler and Clark 1991; Cimoli and Dosi 1995). Successful companies are distinguished by their capacities to translate new knowledge relatively quickly and continuously into cost savings by means of routines, and also to detach such cost savings from the activities of specific individuals and their 'implicit' ('tacit') knowledge (cf. Senker 1995). With intensifying internationalisation of corporate structures, improvements in information and communication infrastructure and competition between multinational enterprises, a growing importance of organisational incentives to increase both the generation of new knowledge and for rapid transboundary transfer and implementation of new ideas can be observed. Modern-day corporations are therefore characterised by a particularly strong ability to develop and absorb new ideas and competencies in the global diffusion of new ideas for products and processes. The problems faced by multinational corporations thus resemble the challenges confronting politicians, academics and citizens in identifying, from the pool of experience in Europe and the world over with strategic employment policies, those strategies that are conducive to overcome specific adjustment problems.

In the following, generalised knowledge from case studies about learning processes in multinational companies, combined with a theoretical approach to explain the evolutionary process of creating and using knowledge about institutional solutions, form the starting point for analysing the institutional prerequisites to initiate institutional learning processes. This analysis proceeds in three steps. In the first, causes for the growing importance of transboundary institutional learning and the high probability of its success, particularly in the field of preventive labour market policy, will be presented. In the second step, some general determinants of transboundary learning of institutional solutions are derived to discuss their importance for preventive labour market policy in Europe. The third step outlines the prospects for specific reform approaches and the research needs, in terms of both content and methodologies, that remain for the analysis of transnational institutional learning processes.

2. PREVENTIVE LABOUR MARKET POLICY – AN IDEAL EXAMPLE FOR THE POTENTIAL OF TRANS-NATIONAL LEARNING?

2.1 Preventive labour market policy in a new 'learning atmosphere'

Learning processes within enterprises relate to their capacities for generating or borrowing new ideas from existing experience, competencies and routines, to translate these ideas into production methods and products, and to engage in continuous improvement (cf. Malerba 1992; Kim 1993; Yeung et al. 1998; Dixon 1999). Many decentralised self-management mechanisms have been developed within companies in the course of these developments. With the globalisation of sales and procurement markets, as well as the internationalisation of production, the challenges involved in organising learning are intensifying. Multinational corporations must be able to adopt ideas from different countries with specific sociocultural frameworks and to adapt their own ideas to different country-specific contexts, to develop and network decentralised in-company organisational structures and competencies in order to put such a diversity of ideas into practice, and to form transboundary development teams with the aim of achieving the creative enhancement of their methods and products. Established systems of organisation in and between companies are confronted with insurmountable problems in the face of these changing tasks. Experience with new institutional methods for developing and flexibly implementing new ideas in countries with highly divergent conditions for investment and sales are just as necessary as the rapid exploitation and transboundary transfer of such methods between corporate entities.

Preventive labour market policy faces similar challenges. The situation, as will be described in the following, features

- new and increasingly transboundary responsibilities,
- new relations between actors and
- new transmission channels.

The notion of preventive labour market policy embraces all those labour market measures that have the common aim of improving the competitive situation of people threatened or affected by unemployment (cf. Knuth, Chapter 5 in this volume). These measures are extensive in their variety, ranging from initial and further training to the promotion of start-ups. Structural changes in the labour markets lend increasing importance to such early adjustment of competencies and options for deploying human resources, before all contact is lost with corporate reorganisation processes and new skill profiles. However, these trends also impact on the setting for corrective action and influence the requirements that measures in the field of preventive labour market policy must meet.

2.2 New and transboundary challenges

In most industrialised countries, the conditions in which workers are deployed have undergone substantial change in recent years. Simple, standardised work is being superseded more and more by machinery, or relocated to countries with lower wage levels. Skilling requirements are not limited to formal qualifications and competencies in the specific field of work. What companies are now looking for are the ability to combine specialist knowhow with social competencies and a focus on the service ideal, even within industrial enterprises, and to adapt knowledge continuously and flexibly to new knowledge and production conditions (cf. Falk and Seim 1999; Wink 1997; Welfens 1999). As a consequence, the points at which preventive labour market policy must take hold are also changing. Whereas efforts to prevent unemployment previously centred on conveying standardised knowhow and on promoting the acquisition of occupational qualifications by means of retraining schemes, what is now necessary is

- to develop specialist knowledge while also training social competencies,
- to link skilling with in-house restructuring so that the new competencies are adapted to operational requirements and can be translated directly into practical impacts,
- to modularise the range of skills, qualification and counselling provided in order to address the specific needs of specific companies and groups of people, and
- to embed preventive measures within a process of personal and corporate development, within which competencies can be continuously extended and refreshed.

The impulses for this change in the conditional framework for preventive labour market policy derive from structural trends that are modifying labour markets throughout Europe. Whereas the need for reform related previously to occupational skills for particular sectors, or in some countries to educational qualifications, the systems for preventive labour market policy in all EU countries are now challenged by similar and fundamental changes (Klemmer et al. 2000a). As a consequence, the locational decisions made by international companies also integrate knowledge about the response mechanisms of preventive labour market policy in alternative countries. Thus, in all countries, incentives are generated for the acquisition of new experiential knowledge and for monitoring the experience that others are acquiring with institutional rules in the field of preventive labour market policy. This is all the more pertinent given that changing responsibilities are also linked to the need for integrating new groups of actors in preventive labour market measures.

2.3 New relations between actors

The focus on conveying standardised skills and promoting vocational qualifications was accompanied by a concentration of preventive labour market policy on relations between labour administrations and certain providers of public training and employment schemes. However, the broader range of tasks to be performed means that it is now necessary to integrate other groups of actors in the design and implementation of preventive labour market policy (cf. Becker-Soest and Wink, Chapter 4 in this volume). These groups include

- companies in which skilling processes run parallel to the reorganisation of production processes,
- start-ups functioning as an alternative for people threatened by unemployment and which also lead to the creation of new employment structures,
- business development institutions whose activities must be combined with measures to increase the competitiveness of workers, and
- business consultancies, whose services relate not only to guiding corporate adjustments, but also and increasingly to personnel development and hence to increasing the competitiveness of workers.

Integrating these groups puts pressure on established actors to adapt accordingly. Existing measures in the field of preventive labour market policy were characterised by labour administrations farming out activities to specified providers of training and consultancy services. For established organisers of training and employment schemes, the increase in potential competitors, combined with restrictions on government support for established programmes has necessitated their adapting their range of services and the general thrust of their operations to structural changes in order to establish arrangements with private-sector enterprises and to counteract the competition emanating from business consultancies. Labour administrations and political decision-makers in the field of preventive labour market policy consider it imperative to change the procedures and criteria for support in order to en-hance the attractiveness of programmes conducted by companies or their multipliers. Even if the starting point for integrating new groups of actors into preventive labour market policy differs from one EU country to another, there are many common aspects when defining the objectives of changes being made. The objectives being pursued in many programmes to support small and medium sized enterprises (SMEs), and the linkage observed in many countries between overt programmes for initial and continuing training, on the one hand, and corporate reorganisation processes, on the other, are examples of these common features. In examples of good practice in inte-grating new groups of actors from other countries, many ideas for reforming one's own institutional regulations can thus be found. Finding such examples is facilitated by the emergence of new transmission channels, which are ex-amined in the next section of this chapter.

2.4 New transmission channels

The term 'transmission channels' has two dimensions, one technical, one institutional. *First*, there is a *technical dimension* that is attributable to inno-vations in respect of information and communications infrastructure. The Internet is facilitating access to new information about other countries' expe-rience with institutional solutions, as well as transboundary communication between actors, and hence the exchange of knowledge that is not fixed in writing and partly implicit (cf. Klodt et al. 1997). For example, instruments of preventive labour market policy such as new curricula can be used in this way across national boundaries, and assessments of the employment policy instruments can be published beyond national confines.

Secondly, one can observe an *institutional dimension* to transmission channels. Recent years have seen employment policy mutating more and more from an exclusively national preserve to become an integral part of the European integration process (cf. Schmid and Roth, Chapter 11 in this vol-ume). In addition to the various measures adopted by the European Structural Funds in recent decades, there are now obligations to report on and coordi-nate employment policy strategies. Cooperation within an institutional, multi-level system produces three driving forces for national development of pre-ventive labour market policy. First, the obligations in respect of reporting and consultation provide information on the employment policy experience in the various countries, in addition to existing studies. Since most studies concen-trate on certain countries and individual countries understand their reports as a 'marketing instrument' aimed at their own electorate or foreign investors, experience with less well-known approaches can also be discussed among a broader public as a result of these obligations. Secondly, supranational coordination enables the generation of experiential knowledge to be managed. By jointly defining objectives and strategies, the search for institutional solutions can be standardised, thus compelling each member state to adapt to predefined structures. Thirdly, an improved atmosphere for transnational processing of experience is engendered, beyond the diffusion of 'hard facts'. Routines are established for the cognition and exchange of experience; personal networks between politicians and staff in the relevant authorities are produced as a result of joint consultations, and facilitate an understanding for the content and preconditions of employment strategies.

The member states differ in the extent to which and the way in which they exploit these transmission channels. Adaptation to supranational integration depends above all on the importance and stability of preventive labour market policy at national level, and on the compatibility with the 'soft' governance mechanisms in the EU (cf. Lang et al. 1998). However, since preventive labour market policy in most countries was not pursued until the onset of severe, structurally rooted employment crises, there is much openness towards new approaches, and flexibility in the implementation of other employment policy measures.

2.5 Conclusions regarding the potential for transnational learning

The structural developments in preventive labour market policy open up radically improved opportunities for transboundary collaboration in the exchange of experience and for implementing new approaches for the specific design of consultancy and training measures. Consequently, increasing integration within the 'Joint Employment Policy' activities of the EU can be observed not only at the policymaking level. Transboundary cooperation is also being extended to include the providers of training and consultancy services, and international value-creation systems operate to transmit experience with personnel development and restructuring programmes among SMEs. This institutional concentration forms an analogy to private-sector market processes. Companies are prompted by the elimination of geographical boundaries to internationalise the way they promote and use the generation and transfer of knowledge, to expand on their ability to exchange experience between separate, decentralised entities within the corporation, and to translate these developments into productive action in different socioeconomic and legal contexts. But which factors have a bearing on the success of transnational learning within private companies and can they be translated to the policymaking level? Answers to these questions will be developed in the following.

3. POLICY LEARNING AS AN EVOLUTIONARY PROCESS

3.1 The general idea of evolutionary processes

For decades, economic models use technical progress and the handling of knowledge as an exogenous factor that cannot be influenced in any direct sense. At the same time, it was assumed that the availability of knowledge and information automatically led to a growth in productivity. It was not until recently that an evolutionary analysis of the generation, diffusion and exploitation of knowledge became established (Hodgson 1993; Dosi and Nelson 1994; Wegner 1997; Tomlinson 1999). Learning new skills and knowledge is understood as being a process, the separate phases of which are networked through the action of feedback loops. Learning processes are not necessarily controlled in a deliberate manner for specific ends, but in many cases occur intuitively and lead to implicit knowledge that is difficult to communicate to others in any adequate form. How an individual is able to learn depends also on the experience and routines that he or she already possesses. One speaks in economics of *path dependencies* when investment is made to access certain sources of information, in making certain learning techniques available or in specialising in specific realms of knowledge (Kiwit 1996; Ruttan 1997; Witt 1997). What and how individuals learn can be managed in such cases to a limited extent only.

This entails a wide range of problems for any learning within organisations – and hence in the political domain as well. *Organisational learning arises as a product of individual learning and the exchange of knowledge between learners*. Organisations therefore have to create institutional capacities and incentives in order to foster individual learning processes and to network these to others in the best possible way. Another aspect within the European context refers to the different horizons of sociocultural experience, different legal options available and growing complexity due to the plurality of different entities that have to be coordinated. From exemplary cases in multinational corporations and from various models in economic and political science, one can distinguish between three phases in which, through institutional incentives, it is possible to facilitate not only individual learning but also networked learning in transboundary collectives (cf. Klemmer et al. 2000). In the following, these three phases are referred to as

1. the *awareness and motivation*, when a certain problem and a need to look for institutional solutions is realised generally which leads to a(n) (implicit) definition of learning objectives;
2. the *interpretation and evaluation*, when experiences with institutional solutions (labour market instruments) strictly directed towards the problem realised before, are observed, integrated into the cognitive and normative background of the affected person (e.g. politician, entrepreneur, unemployed person or training service provider) and filtered out according to the situative determinants of political decisions, and
3. the *transfer and adaptation*, when starting from existing experiences and their interpretation, new labour market instruments are introduced and the experiences during this process of introduction are used to evaluate one's own decisions and to give input into institutional learning processes of others.

3.2 Awareness and motivation

The starting point for any learning process that is based on one's own experience or on the transfer of others' knowledge is the general willingness to absorb new knowledge and act upon it, and to pass on one's own experience. In many cases, people do not realise what can be gained through learning from or with others. Companies are often compelled to disband groups charged with specific development tasks because the members mutually block each other (cf. Argote 1999). Individual sites of multinational corporations are prompted to conceal deliberately their own experience or to dispense with any cooperation with other sites when they are anxious that exchanging experience will lead to them being exploited by others.

In politics, too, the benefit of using the experience of others is assessed rather ambivalently. Problems arise, for example, when political or cultural taboos are infringed, or when one has to admit that others have institutional arrangements that are more successful. In Germany, experience with preventive labour market policy in countries with a stronger market focus, such as Great Britain, is often rejected with the argument that transferring such institutional options would undermine the social consensus regarding social security for disadvantaged groups in the labour market (Klodt 1998). Additions to the dual training system in German (school-based instruction plus in-company training) in the form of modularisation and links with later further training options are rejected with the sweeping remark that they jeopardise the successful German system. For politicians, focusing on examples in other countries or regions engenders the risk that voters are being shown the weaknesses of existing systems. Unless a crisis is raising its head, weaknesses are not normally analysed (Siegenthaler 1993; Wegner 1998).

How can the willingness to learn from experience with institutional arrangements of preventive labour market policy be fostered? Three channels seem particularly relevant here:

- *First,* a *strategy of centralisation* can be pursued, i.e. it can be laid down by the central management in multinational corporations, or in the EU by more intensive political integration (cf. Kern 1999 with empirical evidence of the influence of central government on institutional diffusion processes in the USA). The agreement on common targets and priorities of employment policy in the EU exemplifies such centralisation strategies. The actors in separate countries are occasioned to 'learn' specific strategic foci, and through the specific focus on best practices, the transfer of experience is included by definition. Problems arise due to the limits to control at the central level. The extent to which certain forms of experience are actually translated into activity in all entities is decided in a context of specific action frameworks. Preventive labour market policy in Europe will therefore be characterised by diversity, even in this age of 'Joint Employment Policy'. The efforts at control by the EU will not go beyond 'soft governance'. However, this form of governance also harbours the opportunity to place certain issues on the agenda that have not been discussed at national level, for example the consequences of demographic changes for labour markets, and increasing problems in integrating older unemployed people into working life.
- *Secondly,* there is a chance of transboundary learning processes being *instrumentalised* in the form of policy borrowing (Cox 1999). The success of certain ideas – institutional arrangements – in a corporate entity (a country) can be used to place one's own ideas for reform on the political agenda, reforms that were already planned in the first place. Visionary campaigns, in particular, such as the 'knowledge society' offensive announced with considerable public impact in Great Britain, or in Denmark the model of a corporatist and interrregionally networked labour market policy, are suitable for adoption elsewhere because they counter opponents of reform with strong imagery and proven acceptance in other countries (cf. Heinze et al. 1999; Klemmer et al. 2000a; Kröger and Suntum 1999). This way of proceeding is all the more likely, the greater the similarity of political convictions and institutional traditions on the part of decision-makers and countries. However, the precondition is that there is already a willingness to make institutional changes. Established governments find it more difficult to concede the need for change in this way.
- *Thirdly,* learning can be stimulated by *competition.* The more transparent the options for comparing single corporate entities or companies by

means of benchmarking, the greater the pressure to focus on best practices and to generate best practices of one's own (cf. Hafner 1999; Wegner 1998). In private-sector enterprises, benchmarking techniques have thus been developed for a wide variety of corporate functions. These techniques give companies a chance to focus on successful examples and at the same time to enhance their attractiveness for customers and capital investors by means of their own positive ranking. In political processes, too, 'benchmarking' is playing an increasingly significant role (cf. Tidow 1999). On the one hand, international comparisons of labour market performance and alternative institutional arrangements serve successful governments as a means of gaining votes. In recent years, small countries like Denmark and the Netherlands have seen growing levels of satisfaction among the population with the direction being taken by the economy and the labour market, and this has been partially reflected in electoral results. On the other hand, labour market indicators are among the key factors on which international investors base their locational decisions (cf. Scheuer and Raines, chapters 2 and 6 in this volume). These indicators refer, *inter alia*, to the quality and quantity of available human capital, the functional efficiency of the labour markets, and the intensity of labour market regulation. Given the growing importance of international investment decisions and the mobility of skilled workers, nations are being pressurised to adopt successful practices and to disseminate their own success stories. There is therefore an increasing focus, in the European and global context, on experience with alternative labour market strategies.

   Which of these transmission channels is more or less important than others will depend on the specific conditions in the particular states. The big picture, however, is that nurturing motivation to participate in international learning processes is a learning process in itself, one in which companies, capital investors, politicians, civil servants and the general population are all engaged.

3.3 Interpretation and evaluation

Intermediate between the willingness to absorb the experience of others and the will to act on it, on the one hand, and the concrete application of acquired knowledge, on the other, is the need to understand and sort experience (cf. Slembeck 1997). Although international companies usually have efficient reporting systems and are informed by business consultants about 'best practices', the factor that is ultimately decisive in many cases for the enlargement of competencies is the implicit knowledge that the carrier of knowledge does not reflect upon, or applies in an intuitive manner only (cf. Argote 1999; Senker 1995). The point, therefore, is ultimately to understand the process of knowledge expansion and the application of new experience gained by others, and to examine this process for its transferability to one's own context, before any transfer to one's own sphere of activity can be effected.

This is particularly the case in the field of preventive labour market policy. Employment strategies are often linked in the various countries with certain slogans and instruments, e.g. in Denmark the instrument of 'job rotation' for linking continuing training and support for target groups of labour market policy (cf. Jørgensen, Chapter 7 in this volume), or in the Netherlands the cooperation between the state and the social partners in consensual 'alliances for jobs' (cf. Hartog 1998 and Penz, Chapter 8 in this volume). Merely transferring particular elements of a strategy to other countries risks failing to achieve the desired impact, and this for two reasons. First, it may be overlooked that certain key factors are preconditions that are not met in the transferee countries. In Germany, for example, it is important to realise when implementing job rotation schemes that the incentives for further training are totally different to those in Denmark (Klemmer et al. 2000a). There is a basic lack of modularised continuing training schemes, and given the protracted conflicts between the social partners on financing further training, the level of acceptance in society is not very high. Secondly, the impact of a single instrument may have been overestimated. In Denmark, job rotation is a much respected instrument, but one that has only modest impacts on the labour market (cf. Jørgensen, Chapter 7 in this volume and Madsen 1998). More radical measures in other countries, including greater wage restraint, the acceptance of socially insured low-wage sectors, or support for non-standard employment, are all practices that are politically less acceptable or even taboo in transferee countries like Germany (Kröger and Suntum 1999). There is thus an intuitive evaluation of such measures that suggests a concentration on other instruments, due to the fundamental rejection – on a normative basis or by particular interest groups – of an instrument's thrust, even if the instruments in question have symbolic force more than anything else.

The important aspect in this phase is therefore to perceive strategies and measures of preventive labour market policy in their overall context and to evaluate them with regard to the preconditions for their transferral. Two approaches are of paramount importance here:

- First, one can force the establishment of a *technical and organisational infrastructure* for gathering and distributing experiential knowledge. In multinational companies, this is done by pushing the documentation of experiential knowledge in an intranet, for example, and by using external information brokerages in order to feed in and distribute experiential knowledge (cf. Dixon 1999). Examples at the policymaking level include agreements on national monitoring of labour market policy experience, also with precise information on the institutional conditions for particular impacts and the concentration of strategic knowledge in joint plans of action. In view of the differences between the initial conditions and interests at national level, this coordination of policymaking is usually limited to rather general objectives, concrete achievement of which again depends on the conditions for action at regional level.

* Secondly, the problem of perceiving and evaluating implicit and intuitive knowledge must be responded to by intensifying *personal mobility* (cf. Yeung et al. 1998). Multinational companies recruit experience, on the one hand by headhunting knowledge-bearers from other companies, on the other by intensifying the exchange of experience through transboundary rotation of employees among the various corporate locations. In this way, employees are integrated into routines in which certain experience must be acted upon, and compelled to analyse the preconditions on which these routines are based. By changing the workforce structure, those involved are prompted to examine implicit knowledge and communicate it (cf. Argote 1999). At the policymaking level, such processes can be triggered in parallel by exchanging members of policymaking bodies and staff in government authorities. Given the specific local contexts of labour market policy, it is essential here to involve the regional level in such exchanges (cf. Cappellin 1993). By transferring decision-making competencies to the regional level, individual regions can be encouraged, with the help of partnerships with regions in other countries, on the one hand, to develop their own ideas for new employment policy instruments at the regional level, and, on the other, to facilitate transboundary contacts and exchange of experience between training and consultancy providers and SMEs in the regions.

These development processes result in routines for the cognition and evaluation of international experience with institutional arrangements. Whereas a transboundary transfer of strategies and instruments has been limited until now to one-off cases, increasing experience with transboundary learning processes can be expected to generate a greater focus on the complexity of institutional cause–effect relationships. By experimenting with different combinations of the strategic elements of preventive labour market policy, e.g. a pared-down dual training system combined with modularised further training and support for ongoing changes of occupational areas and employers by means of market-based forms of job placement and 'non-standard employment', the diversity of European labour market systems will then feature different 'patchworks' of policy elements.

3.4 Transfer and adaptation

So far in this chapter, learning processes have been considered up to the point where decisions are made on integrating the experience of others in one's own future activities (i.e. employment policy instruments). However, the implementation phase usually contains a number of other surprises for administrations and policymakers, regardless of how meticulous the preparatory work has been, since the relevant conditions on the ground can be anticipated to an inadequate extent only (cf. e.g. Wegner 1997). In multinational companies, this is clearly evidenced by the number of successive and sometimes contradictory reorganisations at the individual company sites. Successful models are supposed to be adopted from other companies and corporate entities without anyone knowing the extent to which routines, competencies and motivations lead to resistance to change or to unexpected outcomes. In economics, these barriers to change are explained in terms of irreversible investments in adaptation to corporate processes, which for their part are network assets (cf. Kiwit and Voigt 1995; Stahl 1998; Becker-Soest and Wink 2000). Irreversible investments refer to expenditures for specific purposes that are totally or partially devalued when the specific purposes in question are no longer relevant. These include specific skills pertaining to a particular activity or to the use of particular machines, as well as routines and social networks between companies along a value-creation chain. The structure of in-house routines in which one person can rely on the other behaving in a certain way, thus saving costs, as well as social relationships have characteristics of network assets, the benefits of which rise with increases in the number of actors involved. At the same time, these network characteristics mean that one individual alone is not sufficient to achieve cost savings. For companies with multinational operations, there is therefore a need to compensate for potential devaluations of irreversible investments and to generate trust in the establishment of in-house network assets.

Similar challenges are manifest at the policymaking level. Changes in the institutional environment of preventive labour market policy pressurise groups of actors to adapt. Organisations that have provided government-supported training and consultancy services over many years see their economic existence being jeopardised when their relevant 'market' is opened up to business consultants and new support providers for training and consultancy. The transboundary transfer of employment policy instruments can equally lead to new fields of application in the labour administration or even to certain fields of activity being eliminated. The consequence is mounting resistance to reforms. On the one hand, influence is exerted by organised groups on political decision-making processes in order to secure the livelihoods of established providers in such fields, and to cushion the social hardships entailed in more flexible employment. On the other hand, established networks between policymaking bodies, government authorities and established organisers of public-sector employment programmes are used to influence reforms in the way they are actually implemented. As a result, unintended impacts of employment policy reforms are generated, impacts that have little in common with the versions operating in the countries of origin.

Attention should be focused on two ways of overcoming these barriers to implementation:

- *First,* there is the option of creating *direct incentives for testing new fields of activity and organisational forms,* in order to mitigate the risk of irreversible investments being made. In multinational enterprises, these include personnel development programmes that promote the in-company mobility of employees, and targeted support for sites that experiment with new ways of organising the production process and their business relations with other companies. At the political level, too, such direct support can be given by supranational or national bodies. Programmes like the Community Inititiatives 'ADAPT' and 'Employment' at EU level help to support new project ideas and innovative forms of regional cooperation (cf. Lang and Reissert 1999; Klemmer et al. 2000a). This financial 'bait' is aimed at making it easier for training and consultancy providers, employees and entrepreneurs, as well as regional decision-makers in the political sphere to enter into a process of change and to establish the basis for their own, transboundary merging of experience.
- *Secondly,* a *decentralisation* of decision-making competence and responsibility serves to dismantle barriers to greater flexibility. In multinational enterprises, single sites or departments (profit centres) are assigned responsibility for their own results, in order to generate incentives for self-willed review of necessary and possible changes. The separate corporate entities then arrive at different incentives for overcoming the barriers to flexibility among employees, whereby these incentives are adapted to the respective conditions for action. At the political level, shifting decision-making competencies is bound up with increased opportunities for regionally independent reforms. Comparatively unitarist states, such as Great Britain and Denmark, have switched over in recent years to a system in which the formulation of objectives and the implementation of labour market programmes is being transferred increasingly to the regional level (cf. OECD 1999). Besides the opportunity of developing regionally specific ways for overcoming resistance to reforms among the organisers of public-sector training and consultancy programmes and among public administration bodies, regional exercising of competencies also provides

the option of integrating, into preventive labour market policy measures, regionally specific, transboundary partnerships between said providers and production companies cf. Becker-Soest and Wink, Chapter 4 in this volume). This requires that foreign providers be allowed to tender for government supported programmes under preventive labour market policy, and that market elements play a greater role in programmes, so that private-sector enterprises are shown the persistent benefits of such measures.

Creating the basis for the transboundary transfer of employment strategies and instruments does not put a stop to unintended effects of new measures of preventive labour market policy. This element of surprise is by no means alien to market processes, however, and to arrive at new ideas and experience is essential in any field that, like preventive labour market policy, is undergoing structural change. In contrast, the conditions mentioned serve primarily to overcome anti-reform incentives and to involve those actors in strategies for change who are mainly anxious, due to the structural pressures to change and their own lack of experience with change, about integrating foreign experience and extending the competition for support programmes to international providers.

4. LEARNING TO PREVENT UNEMPLOYMENT IN A EUROPEAN CONTEXT – THE INTERPLAY BETWEEN MARKET AND POLICY

The large number of international comparisons of labour market programmes and their impacts, as well as the intensification of transboundary cooperation under the 'Joint Employment Policy', convey the impression that a 'great new hope' has been discovered, in the form of transnational exchange of experience and shared learning, in the search for escape routes from structural unemployment. The comments made in the foregoing show that there are, indeed, chances for extending transboundary learning processes, and that valuable ideas are provided in this context by experience within multinational enterprises, or with international cooperation in value-creation chains. However, it has also become clear that learning does not signify an automatic progression from the availability of new information to modified action. Instead, these are complex processes with outcomes that cannot be foretold and which diverge from each other due to the different conditional frameworks operating in each case. This chapter ends up with the following theses, which form the starting point for a more detailed discussion on political implementation and research analysis:

1. In a context of globalised markets and production, *transboundary learning* will inevitably gain in significance. Preventive labour market policies, often regionally confined in their horizons, as well as private-sector service providers of training and consultancy for SMEs, will inevitably be affected by the international dimension.
2. The consequences for labour markets will be regionally different throughout Europe, since there are variations in both the socioeconomic and institutional contexts. That said, *transboundary providers* of training and consultancy services, and cooperation in value-creation chains, will exert a stronger influence on the development of employee competencies.
3. Policymaking bodies can *learn from multinational enterprises*, especially in creating incentives for documenting experience, for institutionalising forums for the exchange of experience, for boosting the geographical and occupational mobility of employees, and for independent exercise of decision-making responsibilities in decentralised entities.
4. This learning on the part of private-sector enterprises generates hopes that there will be less convergence in future to a specific coordination system in Europe (centralised-decentralised, pluralist-corporatist, unitary-federal) induced by centralised control. Instead, the common community in Europe consists of an *institutional 'patchwork'*, overlapping coordination processes involving regional, central government, supranational, private-sector and public-sector bodies.
5. In addition to 'soft governance' by the EU, private-sector companies and the information they disseminate over *markets* will be a key driving force in transboundary communication of experience with employment policy instruments and measures.
6. The *content of transboundary learning processes* will pertain less to specific individual instruments, and more to strategies for activating new actors in improving the competitiveness of workers threatened by unemployment, and to networking private-sector and local initiatives aimed at effective and sustained development of locational factors at regional level.

The changes in economic conditions that have occurred are thus directly reflected in forms of political organisation. The experience of private organisations and their international network links are therefore relevant to the design of institutional arrangements by policymakers. At the same time, the influence of market trends on policymaking scope and the compulsion to adjust political strategies are on the increase. How policymakers respond to the challenges this involves and to new opportunities, and which new coordination methods emerge, will be crucial issues in the future. Preventive labour market policy, with its responsibility for supporting adjustment to structural change and due to its interaction with politics and labour markets, will be among those policymaking fields in which these changes in political organisation will be apparent at an early stage. For economic and political science, this policy field will be a particularly fertile object of research in the years ahead.

NOTES

1. In the following, the terms 'employment policy' and 'labour market policy' are used synonymously for the sake of linguistic simplification.

REFERENCES

Adler, P.S. and K.B. Clark (1991): 'Behind the Learning Curve. A Sketch of the Learning Process', *Management Science*, **37**, 267-281.

Argote, L. (1999), *Organizational Learning. Creating, Retaining, and Transferring Knowledge*, Boston et al.; Kluwer.

Becker-Soest, D. and R. Wink (2000), 'Kooperative Beschäftigungspolitik – Voraussetzung des dänischen 'Arbeitsmarktwunders'?' in S. Frick, R. Penz and J. Weiß (eds), *Kooperative Politikverfahren*, Marburg; Metropolis, forthcoming.

Bertelsmann-Stiftung (ed, 1998), *Internationales Beschäftigungs-Ranking*, Gütersloh; Bertelsmann.

Cappellin, R. (1993), 'Interregional Cooperation and the Origin of a Regional Foreign Policy', in R. Cappellin and P.W.J. Batey (eds): *Regional Networks, Border Regions, and European Integration*, London; Pion, 70-88.

Cimoli, M. and G. Dosi (1995), 'Technological Paradigms, Patterns of Learning and Development: an Introductory Roadmap', *Journal of Evolutionary Economics*, **5**, 243-268.

Cox, R.H. (1999), 'Policy Borrowing and Welfare Reform', in R.H. Cox and J. Schmid (eds.), *Reformen in westdeutschen Wohlfahrtsstaaten – Potentiale und Trends*, Tübingen; WIP Occasional Paper, 11-25.

Dasgupta, P. and G. Stiglitz (1988), 'Learning by Doing, Market Structure and Industrial and Trade Policies', *Oxford Economic Papers*, **40**, 246-268.

Dixon, N.M. (1999), *The Organizational Learning Cycle. How we can learn collectively*, Aldershot; Gower.

Dosi, G. and R.R. Nelson (1994), 'Introduction to Evolutionary Theories in Economics', *Journal of Evolutionary Economics*, **4**, 153-172.

Falk, M. and K. Seim (1999), 'Workers' Skill Level and Information Technology: Evidence from German Service Firms', in L. Bellmann and V. Steiner (eds), *Panelanalysen zu Lohnstruktur, Qualifikation und Beschäftigungsdynamik*, Nürnberg; IAB.

Hafner, C. (1999), *Systemwettbewerb versus Harmonisierung in Europa am Beispiel des Arbeitsmarktes*, Frankfurt/Main; Peter Lang.

Hartog, J. (1998), *So, what's so special about the Dutch Model? Or: The Resurrection of a Lame Dutch*, Amsterdam; mimeo.

Heinze, R. G., J. Schmid and C. Strünck (1999), *Vom Wohlfahrtsstaat zum Wettbewerbsstaat. Arbeitsmarkt- und Sozialpolitik in den 90er Jahren*, Opladen; Leske + Budrich.

Höcker, H. (1998), 'The Organisation of Labour Market Policy Delivery in the European Union', in P. Auer (ed.), *Employment Policies in Focus. Labour Markets and Labour Market Policy in Europe and Beyond – International Experiences*, Berlin; Edition Sigma, 191-214.

Hodgson, G.M. (1993), *Economics and Evolution. Bringing the Life Back into Economics*, Cambridge; Polity Press.

Kern, K. (1999), *Die Diffusion von Politikinnovationen. Umweltpolitische Innovationen im Mehrebenensystem der USA*, Opladen; Leske + Budrich.

Kim, D.H. (1993), 'The Link between Individual and Organizational Learning', *Sloan Management Review*, 35, 37-50.

Kiwit, D. (1996), 'Path-dependence in Technological and Institutional Change - Some Criticisms and Suggestions', *Journal des Etudes Humaines*, 7, 69-93.

Kiwit, D. and S. Voigt (1995), 'Überlegungen zum institutionellen Wandel unter Berücksichtigung des Verhältnisses interner und externer Institutionen,' *Ordo. Jahrbuch für die Ordnung in Wirtschaft und Gesellschaft*, 46, 117-148.

Klemmer, P., D. Becker-Soest and R. Wink (2000), 'The European Union as a virtual learning forum for national labour market policy? – Comments on a 'late vocation' field of European governance', *German Policy Studies*, 1, forthcoming.

Klemmer, P., K. Baumgart, D. Becker-Soest and R. Wink (2000a), *Innovative Beschäftigungsinstrumente in Europa. Analyse der institutionellen Voraussetzungen ihrer transnationalen Implementation*, Bochum; mimeo.

Klodt, H. (1998), 'Großbritannien: Die marktwirtschaftliche Strategie', *Mitteilungen aus der Arbeitsmarkt- und Berufsforschung*, 31, 277-293.

Klodt, H., R. Maurer and A. Schimmelpfennig (1997), *Tertiarisierung in der deutschen Wirtschaft*, Tübingen: Mohr.

Kröger, K. and U. v. Suntum (1999), *Mit aktiver Arbeitsmarktpolitik aus der Beschäftigungsmisere? Ansätze und Erfahrungen in Großbritannien, Dänemark, Schweden und Deutschland*, Gütersloh; Bertelsmann.

Lang, J., F. Naschold and B. Reissert (1998), *Management der EU-Strukturpolitik. Steuerungsprobleme und Reformperspektiven*, Berlin; Edition Sigma.

Lang, J. and B. Reissert (1999), 'Reform des Implementationssystems der Strukturfonds – Die neuen Verordnungen vor dem Hintergrund der Leistungsfähigkeit des bisherigen Systems', *WSI Mitteilungen*, 52, 380-389.

Madsen, P.K. (1998), 'Arbeitszeitpolitik und Vereinbarungen über bezahlte Freistellungen. Die dänischen Erfahrungen in den 90er Jahren', *WSI Mitteilungen*, 50, 614-624.

Malerba, F. (1992), 'Learning by Firms and Incremental Technical Change', *The Economic Journal*, 102, 845-859.

OECD – Organisation for Economic Co-operation and Development (ed, 1999), *Decentralising Employment Policy. New Trends and Challenges. The Venice Conference*, Paris; OECD.

Ruttan, V.W. (1997), 'Induced Innovation, Evolutionary Theory and Path Dependence: Sources of Technological Change', *The Economic Journal*, 107, 1520-1529.

Rycroft, R.W. and D.E. Kash (1999), *The Complexity Challenge. Technological Innovation for the 21st Century*. London; Pinter.

Schmid, J. (1999),'Von den Nachbarn lernen. Reflexionen über eine Grauzone zwischen Bildungsreisen und komparativen Analysen', in J. Schmid and R.H. Cox (eds), *Reformen in westeuropäischen Wohlfahrtsstaaten. Potentiale und Trends.* Tübingen; WIP Occasional Papers, 2-10.

Schütz, H.; S. Speckesser and G. Schmid (1998), *Benchmarking Labour Market Performance and Labour Market Policies. Theoretical Foundations and Applications,* Berlin: WZB.

Senker, J. (1995), 'Tacit Knowledge and Models of Innovation', *Industrial and Corporate Change,* **4**, 425-447.

Siegenthaler, H. (1993), *Regelvertrauen, Prosperität und Krisen,* Tübingen; Mohr.

Slembeck, T. (1997), 'The Formation of Economic Policy. A Cognitive-Evolutionary Approach to Policy-Making,' *Constitutional Political Economy,* **8**, 225-254.

Stahl, S.R. (1998), *Persistence and Change of Economic Institutions − A Social-Cognitive Approach,* Jena; MPI Papers on Economics and Evolution.

Tidow, S. (1999), 'Benchmarking als Leitidee. Zum Verlust des Politischen in der europäischen Perspektive,' *Blätter für deutsche und internationale Politik,* 301-309.

Tomlinson, M. (1999), 'The Learning Economy and Embodied Knowledge Flows in Great Britain', *Journal of Evolutionary Economics,* **9**, 431-451.

Walwei, U. (1999/2000): 'Arbeitsmarkt- und Beschäftigungsprobleme in der Europäischen Union. Nationale Erfolgsstories als Wegweiser?', in H.-W. Platzer (ed), *Arbeitsmarkt- und Beschäftigungspolitik in der EU. Nationale und europäische Perspektiven,* Baden-Baden; Nomos, 13-33.

Wegner, G. (1997), 'Economic Policy From an Evolutionary Perspective: A New Approach', *Journal of Institutional and Theoretical Economics,* **153**, 485-509.

Wegner, G. (1998), 'Systemwettbewerb als politisches Kommunikations- und Wahlhandlungsproblem,' *Jahrbuch für Neue Politische Ökonomie,* **17**, 281-308.

Welfens, P.J.J. (1999), *Globalization of the Economy, Unemployment and Innovation. Structural Change, Schumpetrian Adjustment, and New Policy Challenges,* Berlin: Springer.

Wink, R. (1997), *Mehr Beschäftigung in einer innovationsorientierten NRW-Wirtschaft?,* Bochum; mimeo.

Witt, U. (1997), *'Lock-In' vs. 'Critical Masses' - Industrial Change under Network Externalities,* Jena; MPI Papers on Economics and Evolution.

Yeung, A.K. et al. (1998), *Organizational Learning Capabilities,* New York: Oxford University Press.

Index